THE MISSING WIRE

THE UTILITY COMPANIES' DIRTY LITTLE SECRET AND MY FIGHT TO EXPOSE THEM

RUSSELL ALLEN

SUNGRAZER

This book is dedicated to everyone who has been adversely affected by their utility company's poorly designed electrical distribution system, which whether you know it or not, may include you and your loved ones.

PROLOGUE

D eath often came to our Wisconsin dairy farm early in the morning, in the guise of a crusty old man. From out of the Rendering Plant, or Mink Ranch as my brother Bob called it with his gallows humor, would come the executioner: white-haired, sixtyish, impassive, wearing a battered Green Bay Packers cap, a half-chewed cigar clenched between his teeth. The man sent chills down my spine. I always wondered but never asked what he thought about his vocation: destroying animals with a bullet to the brain.

Our sick cows were my last thought at night and first in the morning. During the worst of it, we had cows dying every day. The Rendering Plant refused to take live animals even though they were about to die from their exposure to electric current in the ground; cows had to be *rendered* stone-cold dead before the carcasses would be winched into the truck with a cable hooked around their necks, stacked on the lift gate, hoisted into the bed and hauled off. During peak electric usage, when our animals were violently ill, the Rendering Plant, which charged twenty bucks per execution—with designs for the corpse—had more work than it could handle. Hence, the need for itinerant executioners, men like the judges of old who rode a circuit on horse-back, dispensing justice at the end of a rope.

It wounded my heart to watch emaciated, downed cows retch and twitch, kicking impotently in a vain struggle to rise, and be unable to help them, try as we might. Our veterinarian just shook his head and sighed. Their immune systems were completely shot, and there was nothing left for him to do. The animals had grown so weak from mastitis and other bacterial infections that my brothers and I were forced to push them onto pallets and ferry them to the birthing area with the forklift. The look in their eyes was uncanny as they watched us; they seemed to understand what was about to happen.

The cruel irony of populating the birthing barn with dying creatures was not lost on me. Normally a site of happiness, of wet, milky smells, where pregnant Holsteins delivered beautiful black-and-white, wobbly-legged little calves, the area had become a charnel house. I could never bring myself to watch the killing, turning away at the last instant. But I could smell the sickly-sweet odor of fresh blood, taste the acrid burn of cordite, and hear the animal's low grunt, its death rattle. And the short sharp crack of the executioner's .22. That round to a cow's head reverberated in my mind for hours afterward. It didn't matter how many times I'd heard it before; each gunshot tore away a chunk of my heart. The feeling of irreparable loss was always the same as the very first time.

My cows' health and behavioral problems worsened over time regardless of treatment. They suffered sore hooves and diminished appetites, refused to drink because of shocks at the trough, became panicked and unruly upon nearing the metal milking parlor, kicked off milking devices, and delivered sickly newborn calves which often died after several days. Had these things happened all at once, we might've been able to pinpoint the cause —electric current—which is well-conducted by the moisture and metal that form large parts of a cow's environment.

But that's the nature of the absorption of current by living things. Like AIDS, it kills without fanfare by destroying natural immunity. If a calf is born where AC current is flowing, her lifetime production capacity is greatly impaired. Should she develop pneumonia after birth—common after electrical poisoning—she is scarred for life.

And it isn't just farms being poisoned. My farm is a ten-minute drive from Lambeau Field, home of the Green Bay Packers. It would be interesting to have an independent investigator—say, a Martin Graham, inventor of the guidance system for the Patriot Missile—go there and measure for earth currents. I'll wager Lambeau is shot through with electrical pollution. And if so, those currents may well be harming Packer players who practice as well as play there. But more on that later.

The tragedy is that we didn't discover the cause of our misfortunes much sooner. But who'd have thought it? Who could've imagined a science fiction disaster, a war of the worlds, on our own property? It was a classic catch-22: we couldn't maintain the farm without electrical power but uncontrolled current flowing over the earth rendered death to our cows and our livelihood. That old man with the .22-long rifle was, in a real sense, a hitman for the utility.

Though I'd been born on the Allen family farm and worked it alongside my parents and ten siblings since I was five, I never thought of dairy farming as a job. It was a way of life. Our lives were simple and uncomplicated, sometimes hard, but always happy. We loved the wide, flat expanse of farmland, the cows and the cats, the fields and crops, corn and alfalfa, the green earth, the tall silver silos stretching away to the horizon, the infinite blue roof of Wisconsin sky, and one another.

The herd, which we all fed, milked, and tended, was more to us than a commodity or property. Our cows were part of the family. To lose them and our dairy business, which my father Alvin and mother Alice built over painstaking years of labor; to watch family members turn viciously against one another; to lose two beloved sisters to suicide and one brother to a heart attack before his time—and all for no better reason than corporate venality, were blows I couldn't tolerate without fighting back.

My story is quite painful to recall, but I must shout it from the rooftops so that the desperate plight of small farmers, ordinary men, and women without wealth or power or voice, may be made known, and the sinister methods of the utility companies, that newest breed of Robber Baron, held up for the world to see, because sunlight, that great disinfectant, may prove to be the most effective weapon of all.

Chapter 1

Evolution of Electricity in the United States

I n order to better understand what happened to me, and what I'm about to propose can happen to you, it's important that I briefly delve into the history of it all. You see, electricity isn't the enemy here. In fact, its integration into modern society marks one of the most significant technological revolutions in human history. But it didn't happen without a fight.

The battle for the electrical standard, famously known as the "War of Currents," was a defining period in the history of electricity. This intense struggle not only determined the technical standards for the distribution of electrical power but also set the stage for modern electric utility industries. At the heart of this conflict, were Thomas Edison and his direct current (DC) system, and Nikola Tesla's alternating current (AC) system.

Edison's advocacy for DC was driven by his massive investment in the technology, as well as his belief in its safety and reliability. However, DC had a significant limitation, as it could not be efficiently transmitted over long distances because power losses in the transmission lines were too high. This meant that power plants had to be located within a mile or so of the consumers, which was not practical for widespread and rural distribution.

Enter George Westinghouse, an industrialist and engineer who championed Tesla's alternating current (AC) system because it had a crucial advantage that made AC more suitable for a national-scale power grid. It could be transmitted over much longer distances with significantly reduced power losses, thanks to the ability to step up the voltage using transformers for transmission, and then step it back down for consumer use.

The struggle for supremacy between these two currents unfolded both in the public domain and through various forms of corporate sabotage and misinformation. Edison, determined to discredit AC, embarked on a campaign to portray it as dangerous, going so far as to publicly electrocute animals with AC to prove his point. This negative campaigning culminated in Edison's indirect involvement in the development of the electric chair by the way, which used AC in an attempt to associate the technology with death.

But the battle reached a pivotal moment at the 1893 World's Columbian Exposition in Chicago, where Westinghouse and Tesla showcased the safety and versatility of AC by lighting the entire fair with thousands of AC-powered incandescent lamps. This display of brilliance captivated the public and won the support of the industrial and scientific communities.

The implications of this battle were vast. The victory of AC as the standard for electric power fundamentally shaped the development of the electric utility industry. It enabled the creation of a centralized power generation system, with plants located far from population centers, transmitting high-voltage power across long distances. The scalability of AC systems allowed for the rapid electrification of cities and towns across the United States and the world.

But the implications of the War of Currents were not limited to the technical aspects of power transmission. They also had significant economic and social consequences. The AC system's ability to transmit power over long distances meant that electricity could be generated at the most efficient locations, whether that was near coal mines, at large hydroelectric projects like Niagara Falls, or at other natural resource sites. This led to economies of scale and the consolidation of power companies into larger utilities, which had profound effects on how these companies were regulated and how electricity was priced and sold.

As the electrical industry grew, the federal government began to take a more active role in regulation to protect consumers and ensure fair competition. The Federal Energy Regulatory Commission (FERC), established in 1977, was tasked with overseeing the interstate transmission of electricity, natural gas, and oil.

But the establishment of standards and regulatory bodies inadvertently contributed to the monopolization of the electrical industry. As standards became more widespread and enforced, the industry saw a decrease in the number of competitors. Large corporations, such as General Electric and Westinghouse, who had the resources to comply with and often influence regulatory standards, began to dominate the market. The high costs associated with setting up electrical infrastructure further limited competition, as new entrants found it difficult to compete with established firms that already had a significant presence in the market.

The government's role in granting exclusive franchises to certain companies to supply electricity to specific geographic areas contributed to the creation of monopolies. These companies who were regulated in terms of pricing and service standards, faced little to no competition, allowing them to control vast swaths of the electricity market.

The consolidation of these utility companies into larger entities significantly went on to impact their ability to self-regulate, a phenomenon that became increasingly apparent in the early to mid-20th century. This consolidation was driven by several factors, including economies of scale, the capital-intensive nature of the industry, and regulatory environments that inadvertently encouraged the growth of large monopolies. As these companies grew, they gained not only market power but also a greater ability to influence the policies and regulations that governed them.

Large consolidated electric companies possessed extensive technical and economic expertise, which they leveraged to shape regulatory standards and policies. Their in-depth understanding of the complexities involved in generating, transmitting, and distributing electricity allowed them to play a significant role in setting industry standards. Regulatory bodies often relied on the expertise of these companies to develop safe and efficient standards, giving the companies a direct hand in the rule-making process.

Over the years, with considerable resources at their disposal, large electric companies engaged in lobbying efforts to influence legislation and regulatory policies to their advantage. By contributing to political campaigns and employing lobbyists, these companies sought to sway public policy and regulation in ways that favored their interests. This political influence was a significant factor in the industry's ability to self-regulate, as it helped shape the regulatory landscape in which they operated.

A phenomenon known as "regulatory capture" occurred when the regulatory agencies tasked with overseeing the electric companies came to be dominated by the companies themselves. This came to happen through various means, such as the revolving door between the private sector and government, where individuals moved between roles in industry and regulatory agencies, potentially carrying with them biases and interests from the private sector. As a result, regulators often prioritize the interests of the industries they are supposed to regulate over the public interest, leading to regulations that favor the companies' business models, at the detriment of those they serve.

This lack of real oversight is what allowed utility companies like Wisconsin Public Service to install a faulty electrical distribution system under our family's ranch, and all across America.

This same system was responsible for the slow and painful death of my cattle, and quite possibly, for the death of an untold number of American citizens every day.

CHAPTER 2

MIDWESTERN IDYLL

The little town of De Pere, where our farm is located, a
suburb of the city of Green Bay, must have appeared as a
pristine land of milk and honey to the first Europeans who set
eyes upon it. Oddly enough, before Wisconsin became a dairy
state in the mid-nineteenth century, it was best known for its lead
mining and the creation of wild boomtowns like Mineral Point,
Platteville, Shullsberg and New Diggings. Prospectors, carpetbag-
gers and soldiers of fortune arrived from every part of the country
to mine the "gray gold," as lead was often called. Because many
miners did not build homes but chose instead to live inside their
mines (perhaps to discourage claim jumpers), they unwittingly
supplied the state with its nickname: "The Badger State."

The rise of dairy farming roughly coincided with the tapping-
out and decline of lead mining in the immediate pre-and post-
Civil War period. For one thing, our climate is extremely favorable
to dairying. Summers are relatively cool and rainfall adequate;
eighty percent of rain falls in the April–October period and
covers the growing season. There is much less tendency toward
droughts than in nearby farm states like Iowa and Illinois, and
conditions here favor grasses, hay and grain crops, which nourish

our herds. Cattle, originally imported by drovers from Illinois and Indiana, thrived immediately in the excellent pasture lands of the state.

In De Pere, life and society are dominated by two all-encompassing factors: dairy farming and the Green Bay Packers. Back when I grew up in the '50s and '60s, Wisconsin was insulated from the march of history. That is until the Vietnam War intruded. Folks here were concerned with local issues, like the pollution of the Fox River by firms like NCR, Appleton Paper, Georgia Pacific, Sonoco, Kimberly Clark and Riverside Paper. I take pride in the fact that we stood up to big business the way we did.

Less praiseworthy was the shameful racial discrimination against blacks and native Americans in those days. Surprisingly, Milwaukee was one of the most segregated cities in the nation. Its schools didn't even pretend to integrate after the 1954 *Brown v. the Board of Education of Topeka* Supreme Court Decision ordering desegregation.

By 1976, the courts had enough of Milwaukee's foot-dragging and ruled that the city's schools were in violation of federal law. But not until 1979—a quarter century after *Brown*—did the school board finally get around to implementing a desegregation plan.

The situation was surprising, given Wisconsin's political past, its liberal, progressive spirit—it was the first state to ratify female suffrage. This spirit was personified in the career of former Wisconsin governor, senator, and national leader Robert M. La Follette, whose life's work was protecting ordinary people from abuses by powerful special interests.

I point these things out because I realize that my attitudes have been shaped and molded by the social climate I was born in. I've absorbed the mental atmosphere of this place. It couldn't be otherwise. Raised to be suspicious of power, the damage inflicted by the Utility on my animals and business—on my way of life—

has only confirmed my worst fears about corporate greed and misconduct.

You might say that I'm *of* the farm, that dairying is in my genes. Both my parents were born on farms in Green Bay, Dad in 1917 and Mom in 1921.

Alvin and Alice Allen

One of eleven children, my father, who had three brothers and seven sisters, was uneducated in the formal sense, having been schooled only through the eighth grade, like my mother. But he was a smart, industrious farmer as well as a shrewd businessman and bold entrepreneur.

Both my parents were knowledgeable about the dairy

business. They bought an old farm consisting of one hundred sixty acres, an old farmhouse, and a weather-beaten old barn.

This is the first farm my mom and dad purchased in 1937.

Dad added a new milkhouse onto the barn, which he then extended, increased his herd to 32 cows, and cleared dozens of acres of woodland. By the time of their sixth child in 1948, they'd built a brand-new, five-bedroom brick house. Dad built it with his own hands, with help from my grandfather, his father-in-law. Restless and energetic as ever, thinking always of new ways to grow the business, in 1954 Dad rented another farm and added twenty-seven more milking cows. Business was brisk and our income was good.

In 1962, with all of the Allen kids having arrived, we built our first new barn, 100 stalls. These days I think frequently about my family and those times, partly because I'm remembering them as they were, but also because of the untimely losses, the pain of which never subsides.

Mom, Dad, and their 11 kids; Larry, Les, Jim, Cletus, Bonnie, Bob, Kevin, Russell, Josie, Yvonne, Geri Lynn

Mom and Dad were old and are now gone. She died in 2003 and he passed in 1993. As much as I miss them, they were elderly and that's the natural order. But not my siblings. They died before their time, while their parents remained alive. The pain and sorrow my father and mother felt at losing their children was indescribable. Those deaths were unnatural and unforgivable, ghoulish in the case of my sisters. My brother Les, second oldest, who died of a massive coronary, would be sixty-five today. My younger sisters, Josephine, who would be fifty now, and Geri Lynn, four years her junior, both committed suicide.

I know that back in my parents' time, and their parents' time, large families were the norm. Unlike today, when families are much smaller and longevity much greater, the medical reality back then was that childhood disease claimed many infants and young children, so you needed to have ten kids if you wanted six or seven to survive. Coupled with the need for labor and parental support, and with the fact that birth control was shunned by Catholics, well, conceiving lots of children is understandable enough.

Alvin Allen circa 1976.

I learned dairy farming early on, as my father had. By age four I was working alongside the rest of the family. We put in lots of hours, starting around 5 a.m., regardless of whether we were in school or home for the summer. Kevin and I would milk cows before school started and then again when we got home in the afternoon. We'd change their straw bedding every day, and we particularly enjoyed birthing newborn calves, sometimes helping to pull a baby out if the delivery was difficult. We watched them grow, spent a lot of time with them, and that's why it hurt us deeply when the animals became so sick, and we were unable to aid them. We felt about them just as my father did.

Every day when Dad would market our milk, he'd take a couple of kids along and toss us nickels or dimes so we could go into the store and buy some candy. He was always making affectionate little gestures like that. At the end of haying, he'd allow us to stand atop a wagon loaded full of hay bales and grasp the hanging hooks so we could swing madly from one side of the barn to the other. It was important to him to that we had fun and were happy.

As I got older, I came to realize how well-respected and well-liked Alvin Allen was by the whole community. And why not? He had excellent manners and great courtesy, both because of how he was raised and because it was his nature. He was a man of honesty, integrity, and humility. He taught us to be polite, even to those we disliked, and to keep silent rather than say something nasty about another person. The daily example of his own manly, forthright conduct was the best lesson of all.

Devout Catholics that my parents were, Sundays were always very important in our home. We had to be finished with breakfast by 7 a.m., or we could not eat until after church at St. Mary's because we fasted in preparation for Communion—one hour without water and three without food was the rule.

Every week found us in the same pew in the same order: Mom first, then kids, then Dad on the aisle where he could stretch out his legs. Inevitably, my father's head would begin to droop during the sermon until his chin rested against his clavicle, eyes shut, solidly asleep. Mom would always lace into him about it afterward, in the car on the way to Zellner's grocery store, where she would buy our Sunday dessert, a half-gallon of ice cream which we got after dinner, provided we behaved. I used to wonder if my father confessed his little Sunday morning naps to the priest when he made his weekly confession on Saturday nights. Mom sure made it sound like those catnaps were mortal sins, one of the seven deadly.

On Sunday afternoons neighboring kids would come over or

we'd go spend time at their places. At the risk of sounding like an old billy goat, I'll admit that we didn't do the things kids normally do nowadays. Possessing much less in the way of toys and other gizmos, we were more active physically, and very creative. We made rafts and floated down the creek that ran through the nearby woods where we had field trips in the first and second grade, and the same woods where a good friend and I picked flowers for our mothers in the springtime. We constructed tree houses and slept in them. We built go-carts and raced them. Every year on our farm we boarded horses for the winter. Magnificent animals, we loved them, cared for them, and rode them to our hearts' content, hitching them to sleds and toboggans for rides in the snow.

Christmas was always my favorite time of year though—still is, in fact. I recall that early in December, just after Thanksgiving, Mom and her friends would go out into the woods and start gathering evergreen branches to make wreaths, and sometimes we would get to go with her. The women would make gorgeous wreaths for their homes, for friends, and for the church, wreaths decorated with bright candy canes and pine cones and tiny silver bells and red velvet ribbons. Those wreaths signaled the holiday to us, that Christmas was just around the corner.

Above our fireplace was a big mirror on which we glued snow and window frost and fastened a miniature Santa, sleigh, and reindeer. We frosted over most of the windows of the house and wrote different Christmas messages and holiday greetings on each. The spirit of the season was a strong presence in the Allen household, and our anticipation of the 25th seemed to build and build as the December days passed.

On the 24th Dad would select and bring home the Christmas tree. He would sweep through the door in a grand entrance, with the pride of an arborist with his prized seedling. Each year the tree had to be absolutely perfect in height, shape, and fullness, fit to appear on a Christmas card. He would place the tree on the stand, switch it into various positions and study it with his expert's eye, making certain there were no bare spots. If he detected even a hint of one, he would drill tiny holes in the trunk and insert branches to thicken the area.

On Christmas Eve we had to be in bed by seven while Mom and Dad "attended Midnight Mass". They would then rouse us at about 2 a.m., with the movie camera ready to roll. I always marveled at how Santa could decorate the tree, place the gifts, set up the train and tracks, and repeat that magic in houses throughout the world, all in one night.

We'd play with our toys, which weren't very many by today's standards—a few colored pencils, notepads, and some miniature cars or dolls—till about 6 a.m. and then we fed and milked the cows. After that it was off to church at St. Mary's.

As the years passed, Christmas grew larger in our imaginations and even more meaningful. Just like in most families, it went from Mom and Dad buying gifts for everyone to everyone buying gifts for them. When we were older and business was better, Dad would give us money, a couple of hundred or so each, depending on how good a year he was having.

The bucolic life I've described and the sprawling, happy family I grew up in were things I loved and never rebelled against, as many children do. And so, I followed in my father's footsteps, determined to earn a living as he had, and his father before him. It seemed as good a vocation as any and better than some. Perhaps my feelings about the farm and about my parents, about my father's teachings and about our way of life, may sound hokey to modern ears, and maybe they are. But that does not make them less true. My parents were rustics, products of a vanished time, a simpler, less cynical, more honest, more loyal, and certainly much happier time. A time that lives now only in memory. But that's okay. The loss of the old ways is the price of progress. And the old ways were not necessarily the best ways, especially compared to the technological advances that have improved the quality of life and removed so much drudgery from work.

But technology cuts two ways. What it improves on one hand it aggravates on another. I've always been a proponent of working smarter, not harder, and have attempted to upgrade and improve the Allen farm operation at every opportunity. And I was able to do so, making us one of Wisconsin's largest and best, until the operation was crippled by a new technology: the WPS reconfiguration of the electrical distribution system. A current that ran through our property like a dagger through the heart.

CHAPTER 3

A CURRENT AFFAIR

F armers wear many different hats in the course of our working lives. We're alternately veterinarians, accountants, buyers, equipment operators, breeders, mechanics, electricians, plumbers, carpenters, and truckers. We're also skilled problem solvers and shrewd businessmen since our livelihood depends upon how efficiently we manage and increase productivity while reducing costs. This means keeping our herds and crops in optimal condition. Unlike businesses where managers manipulate data and fudge statistics, our alternatives are simple: produce each day or go under. March, or die.

Because we place our products into human bodies our business is heavily regulated, as it should be, by a number of local, state and federal regulatory agencies, including the USDA and the FDA. Readers will surely remember *E. Coli* and *Mad Cow Disease* outbreaks of recent years. If not for the knowledge, caring, commitment, and rapid reaction of American farmers in isolating and correcting the problem, these diseases might have resulted in epidemics of bacteria-caused deaths, as has too often been the case in other countries.

If any of our products prove harmful to people or animals, we should be held accountable (morally as well as legally) and compelled to pay damages. So, should a public utility like WPS be less responsible if it harms the consumers of *its* products? To ask the question is to answer it. And yet, when WPS' product—electricity—sickened, injured, and then killed my cows, the utility simply denied the facts and instead accused me of mismanagement and incompetence.

But stray current in the earth, electricity seeping through the ground and into my animals, is what poisoned them. But how WPS got away with murder, and how I finally managed to dig out from under their avalanche of lies, well, therein hangs a chilling tale. Chilling because they can do it to anybody. And they are.

Stray current—actually not stray at all but coming deliberately off the wire—can be defined as the continuous flow of any current over the earth that harms the health of humans or other living things.

In the tranquil, bountiful days of the '60s and early '70s, our farm was one of the two or three largest, most advanced, and most productive in the entire state, which is saying something, because Wisconsin has been the nation's leader in dairy production for well over one hundred years. Wisconsin milk and cheese is rightfully renowned for its high quality and distinctive flavor.

I remember feeling immense pride in our operation and my family. Thinking back on it, I recall one particularly warm sun-filled August afternoon some thirty years ago. We were outside the new barn, my brothers Bob and Cletus and I, having just finished milking and feeding the herd. Dripping sweat, we leaned against the door of the barn and looked out together across acres of fertile cropland, at the tall, thick, unending rows of corn and alfalfa gently undulating in the summer breeze.

No one spoke, but we all had the same feeling: awe and gratitude. That fleeting, insignificant moment is for some reason frozen in memory. As though it were yesterday, I can still hear the buzz of bumblebees hovering lazily above the snowball bushes outside the house, and the contented lowing of the cattle. I can see the high sapphire sky, cloudless and blue as the deep blue water of Green Bay sparkling in the summer sunshine. The sky that day appeared bluer than ever before. That blue profundity seemed to me like the color it must have been on the first day of Creation.

The Allen farm in 1976.

And then disaster struck. In 1976, during the same period in which we built a new free-stall barn and milking parlor, Wisconsin Public Service, WPS, reconfigured its distribution system, connecting many miles of distribution system beyond our farm, a seemingly harmless event. This resulted in putting the Allen Dairy Farm in the path of their neutral return current on its way back to the substation.

Because of the poorly designed distribution system, current flowed down the ground wires that were connected to the neutral wire—the one that took the current back to the substation—driving current into the earth and then used the earth itself to take the current back to the substation. It doesn't take a genius to realize that some of that current would stray. Had problems occurred right away, we would've understood the cause. However, the issue took much time and anguish to identify.

WPS was well aware of the design flaw, and had been all along, of what the repercussions to the farm would be. But they were banking on the fact that whatever negative consequences occurred, they would not happen overnight. It would take years. It was like the tobacco companies, lacing cigarettes with nicotine and tar, which could cause cancer, but continued for decades to deny this embarrassing fact because cancer took years to develop.

You should know that this design flaw is present all across our country, and may very well be at the root of many of the cancers that Americans develop and die from each and every day. You could say that utility companies are guilty of committing the same criminal actions that tobacco companies were found guilty of, but on a much larger scale.

But I digress.

Now, there are a number of difficulties that dairy farmers face each day. Utility companies know this and use the concepts of "farm mismanagement" and "multi-factor herd health" problems to confuse and to shift focus away from itself.

Having an elevated somatic cell count is one thing that can go wrong on a dairy farm. These are white blood cell counts found in the milk and are produced as antigens by a cow to fight infection. The higher the count, the greater the chance disease may be affecting the whole herd.

When mastitis, a bacterial infection of the udder, is present, the somatic cell count skyrockets. When the count climbs beyond a certain number, the milk cannot be sold, and cows with high counts are frequently pulled from the herd. Mastitis can be caused by numerous factors, but high counts are attributable to things like poor milking procedures, bad sanitation, *stray current*, long lactation periods, and various types of infection.

When our cattle became sick, we always quarantined them,

separating them from the healthy ones and starting treatment immediately. The sooner you can start treatment, the quicker you can nurse the cow back to health, providing she doesn't die first. But some cows didn't show signs of being sick at first, other than just getting weaker and weaker and soon, didn't even get up anymore.

Declining milk production is another thing that can go wrong in the course of business. Under normal conditions a cow will be calm and docile as its milk is removed. But because of the effects of electric current on the animal, calmness and docility go by the board and the animal becomes nervous and agitated, frightened.

As time passed after the reconfiguration, over several years in fact, we began to perceive increased behavioral problems throughout the herd, even among new cows we imported, and among calves. They would become skittish and balky when entering the milking parlor and continually kick off the milkers, sometimes injuring myself and the people that worked for me. Milking times drastically increased, since sterilizations and cleaning procedures constantly had to be revisited. Production decreased, and nothing we tried in the way of medicines and supplements seemed to help.

Other troubling signs were the development of sore hooves. It was hard to get cows pregnant and many would abort several times. And of the pregnant animals, many could not carry to term. No medicines prescribed by our vet, no feed or supplements or vitamins established by our nutritionist, seemed able to alleviate the symptoms.

At times, we had a 50 percent cull rate; the cows either died or were sold for slaughter before they died. Needless to say, those twin horsemen, sickness and death, were seriously reducing our farm's income.

Living with a deteriorating herd, it was clear that we had a major crisis on our hands. Our family's future was in jeopardy. Yet we felt we were doing everything in our power to heal the cows.

After all, we had several lifetimes' worth of dairy experience on which to draw from. We ran the gamut of emotional states. At first, we were merely frustrated; later we became depressed; eventually, we grew angry and spiteful, turning viciously against one another. Mutual recriminations flew around the place like boomerangs.

Early one September morning, Dad and my brother Les were in the kitchen awaiting breakfast. We had already milked and fed the cattle, and the conversation began typically enough, the three of us chattering on about small matters. Les happened to be in charge of the milking operation in the new barn. At that moment, we were undergoing a violent outbreak of mastitis.

With all his experience, Dad knew this was abnormal and unnatural, yet had no clue (as none of us did) that electricity was shocking and sickening our cows. The only thing Dad could imagine as being the cause of the problem was improper herd management. The conversation took a harsh turn when Les brought up the subject of mastitis.

Although generally a calm, quiet, and thoughtful man, my father was never one to beat around the bush when making a point, and now his point was that Les was royally screwing up. Les did not take kindly to Dad's accusation, and got loud and belligerent.

One of the saddest aspects of what WPS did to us was that Dad went to his grave without ever learning the full truth. For that, I blame myself. I wish I could've uncovered it much sooner. It would have restored Dad's faith in us, proven to him that we were good at our jobs.

And so the partnership we'd developed with so much amity and optimism began to disintegrate under the strain of dying cows and the financial pressure of plummeting productivity. The number of sick cows overwhelmed Cletus, whose responsibility was doctoring. He felt a bond with his animals, loved them. He became deeply depressed by their plight and his inability to cure them.

We first became aware of stray voltage about 1988. Back then we were like everyone else in America. We did not know that our utility companies were using the earth to return their current back to their substation. Naive and gullible, we thought along the lines of how utility companies had propagandized everyone into thinking, believing that stray current was just a smoke screen used by dairy farmers who were poor managers and bad businessmen to evade personal shortcomings and escape responsibility. Though we considered the idea of stray voltage affecting our cows to be ludicrous, we took measures to rule it out, since nothing else we tried seemed to be working.

We got our first taste of dealing with Wisconsin Public Service when we asked them to come out to our farm and check for stray current. They came, they saw, they reported...no problem. Just as we'd expected. We went back to the drawing board to figure out new possible causes and come up with new medical treatments.

For the next few years, we got really creative, and devised a whole host of solutions. In 1991 we bought a new state-of-the-art feed mixer to create a perfectly balanced food mixture for each cow, each day. With this piece of equipment, we could be certain that the animals were receiving the correct amounts and proper nutrients one hundred percent of the time. Every cow would receive the optimum quantity and quality of feed.

The new feed mixer was a sleek, expensive piece of perfectly engineered equipment. And it did zero to correct the problems. Milk production didn't improve and the cows didn't get better. They still balked at entering the parlor and refused to permit milkers to be attached. The death rate was high, and sore hooves and other mysterious maladies continued to torment them.

Everyone—veterinarian, nutritionist, other farmers— told us our countermeasures were correct and proper. Yet, there were years that at least 50 percent of the herd left the farm, either dead died or sold off. There was only one occasion in over 20 years that we were able to start culling for production. It happened to be when I had WPS' down grounds cut or disconnected. It did not last long. After a year and a half, WPS reconnected their down grounds and my world went insane again. I do remember a time when 75 percent of the herd was limping.

An equipment dealer I had spoken with about the problems suggested we consider remodeling the parlor, going from a double-twelve polygon to a double-twelve parallel, thereby decreasing the number of milk-unit kickoffs and preventing employee injuries. An additional benefit would be that we could improve productivity by needing only one person to operate the parlor instead of several.

We decided to take his advice, at considerable expense: $85,000. We'd leave no stone unturned to solve the problem once and for all. At about this time, the U.S. Department of Agriculture, after conducting a study on stray current, decreed that a new requirement for milking parlors was that they had to have what is known as an equipotential plane.

This plane essentially used the steel bars that reinforced the concrete floor and connected it to the metal of the parlor. This was supposed to make everything equal like a bird on a wire. Supposedly, this would prevent stray electricity, then thought to be caused by power spurts and spikes through milking equipment, from shocking the animals.

The new parlor was a work of art, a thing of true beauty. Fully computerized, it could gauge and measure output for every cow, allowing us to concentrate our attention on animals whose production lagged behind. With all of the new equipment in place and functioning—we had balanced nutrition, productivity measurements and tight physical control of the cows—we felt confident we'd taken every possible step to ensure success and were on the path to pinpointing the problem and overcoming our misfortunes.

We were dead wrong. As with the feed mixer, the new parlor was an expensive bust. Cows continued to sicken, production plunged, and fatalities increased. To those of us in the partnership who analyzed things realistically, it became apparent that the bottom had fallen out of our once-thriving dairy operation and that the business was doomed. Our farm was going under.

It died a slow, agonizing death. After ten years; the loss of my infant nephew to leukemia; the suicides of two sisters; the heart attacks of two brothers; my own heart attack; the death of another healthy brother, 44, from a massive coronary; the death of a slim, healthy brother-in-law, 50, and the death of a good friend, 43, a neighbor, slim, and working for the county; all from the same causes and the deaths of scores of cows, the dream died hard. All of the above-mentioned family lived in the vicinity of the farm and of the rampaging ground current. It wrecked us all in one way or another.

Throughout those years, all members of the partnership remained at each other's throats. Everyone accused everyone else of laziness, arrogance, incompetence, stupidity and greed. By 1989, the partnership had dissolved. I plugged along paycheck to paycheck, robbing from Peter to pay Paul.

It reached the point where I could no longer stomach the acrimony, and in desperation, I contacted the salesman who'd sold us the new parlor and took everything out on him. Mike was genuinely stumped, because he had placed identical parlors in a number of other farms that were humming along nicely. The only theory he could think to offer, which fit the facts of the case, was stray current. He promised to put me in touch with a man who had assisted other farmers with similar problems.

Still skeptical regarding the idea of stray current, but at my wit's end, I decided that I had nothing to lose by revisiting the subject. I asked Mike to set up a meeting with his man and began to read up on the supposed phenomenon.

I found out that the most well-known and widely circulated

piece of literature on the subject is the Department of Agriculture's so-called Red Book of 1991, titled *Effect of Electrical Voltage/Current on Farm Animals*. (Lefcourt, A.M., *Effect of Electrical Voltage/Current on Farm Animals: How to Detect and Remedy Problems*, USDA Handbook 696). It braced me immediately when I came across this passage:

"The first farms in which stray current problems were identified were suffering severe losses of milk production and income. The producers were generally aware they had problems and had spent considerable time and money attempting to improve their feeding program, the milking equipment, their milking procedures, and hygiene. But nothing seemed to help."

This description was exactly what we'd been going through. The handbook went on to describe how stray voltage shocked and panicked cows, which were highly susceptible to its effects as their environment was usually wet, aiding electrical conductivity. And much of the equipment surrounding them is made of metal, also an excellent conductor. Yet none of us could feel anything like an electrical shock anywhere on the farm, except for when we would put a unit on the cow. Occasionally we would feel a little tingle on our elbows when our elbows would touch the stainless steel curb. Therefore, it seemed highly unlikely to me that current was to blame. However I did not want to leave the subject before I had an expert come to the farm to assess the situation.

Mike set up a meeting for me with the owner of the Concept Electric company, master electrician Larry Neubauer. Suspicious because utilities were spreading rumors that there were legions of self-styled stray voltage "experts" roaming the Green Bay area who were nothing but flimflam artists, I became even more leery when I found out that Larry required a $1,200 retainer before he would even agree to set foot on the farm.

Larry looked more like a Packer lineman than a master electrician. Burly and taciturn, a no-nonsense type who spoke little, as though words were jewels to be hoarded, I discovered that the gruff exterior belied his deep sense of morality and feelings about right and wrong. As quick to laughter as to anger, Larry was smart, experienced, and conscientious about his work; and he didn't suffer fools gladly. Knowing him the way I now do, there's no doubt that Larry would've reamed me out like a Dutch uncle if he'd suspected or seen any evidence of farm mismanagement or maltreatment of animals.

Larry spent a few days investigating throughout the property. I spent time with him when I had any, which was seldom, for the press of problems in the dairy operation consumed all my attention. I didn't know a lot about electricity, but started getting an education in a hurry.

Larry called to me in his gravelly voice one afternoon when I passed him in the milking parlor. He had an electronic meter clipped to an archway. Built of metal pipe, the archway connected to a plate that fastened to a stall in the parlor that held cows for milking. I went over to him and squinted at the meter, nodding as if I knew what I was looking at, which I didn't.

"Eight hundred milliamps," Larry said and shook his head. "That's 0.8 amperes."

Then he did something startling. He shut down electricity coming into the farm from the pole and took another reading: "Still eight hundred milliamps."

Although I knew little about electricity, I knew enough to understand that something was wrong. Cutting power incoming from the pole meant the meter should have read zero. But the juice was flowing as forcefully as before. Then Larry did something else that astonished me— he disconnected WPS' neutral wire. Then, and only then, did the meter dip to zero.

Unless Larry Neubauer's instruments were malfunctioning or completely broken down, something was pumping current into the Allen Farm after he'd shut the switch. And the source of the current was WPS.

CHAPTER 4

SECRETS OF THE GODS

I n writing about electricity and how it destroyed us, I have a mental picture of the god Zeus in a loincloth, bearded and tall as a skyscraper, perched on his mountaintop, hurling down lightning bolts at my farm like flaming javelins.

Had that happened, it couldn't have been worse than what actually occurred. In fact, it might have been better, for we would have seen the fiery bolts raining down and taken action. As it stood, we saw and heard nothing and only comprehended the problem through its deadly results. No wonder, then, that the unseen mysteries of electricity, of fire, of magnetism, of lightning, of the aurora, were regarded in ancient times as god-like secrets, obtained by humans through theft or luck.

Contrary to the idea that an understanding of the nature of electricity is recent, originating with Benjamin Franklin and his famous kite, it's startling to discover that people have been experimenting with electrical power in one way or another since at least a thousand years before the birth of Christ.

According to several legends, in 900 BC, a Greek shepherd named Magnus walked across a field of black stones that pulled the iron nails out of his sandals. The area around the field became known as Magnesia. Much later, in the year 1269, an Italian named Petrus Peregrinus discovered that round lodestones aligned needles with lines of longitude pointing between two pole positions on the stone.

In 1638, Rene Descartes, the famous French philosopher, conceived the theory that light is a pressure wave. Stephen Gray in 1729 proved that electricity need not be limited to a stationary spot but is transferable from point to point by means of conducting wire. The aforementioned Ben Franklin propounded, in the year 1747, the theory of one-fluid electricity, proposing the idea of conservation of charge and positive current flow.

In 1800, Humphrey Davy invented a battery. 1825—Ampere publishes the results of his experiments with magnetism. 1841—Joule proves that energy is conserved in electrical circuits involving current flow and chemical transformations. 1876—Rowland's experiment proves that moving electric charge is identical to current. 1879—Edison re-invents the light bulb using lower current electricity and a small, carbonized filament. 1895—Roentgen discovers X-rays. 1905—Einstein publishes the general theory of relativity. 1915 (circa)—the concept of quantum mechanics is born. 1970—string theory is comprehensively developed.

I mention these pioneers and inventors as another way of pointing out that the accumulated knowledge in the field of electricity is such that American utility companies possess abundant means of safeguarding the transmission of current so it does not harm living things. We get all our electricity, which is a secondary rather than a primary power source, from converting other energy sources such as oil, nuclear power, gas or coal. In the past, towns were frequently built near waterfalls, which drove wheels and provided mechanical energy. Later, as technology improved, hydroelectric power plants went into operation.

An electric generator works by converting mechanical energy

into electrical power, based on the relationship between magnetism and electricity. When a wire moves across a magnetic field, an electric current runs through the wire.

The giant generators that utility companies use contain stationary conductors. A magnet attached to the end of a rotating shaft is positioned inside a stationary conducting ring that is wrapped with a long piece of wire. As the magnet rotates, it creates an electric current in each section of wire as it passes. Every section is itself a separate electrical conductor. All the small currents running through the individual sections make one big current. This big current is then used to generate electrical power.

A utility's power station employs either a turbine engine, water wheel, or some other type of device to drive an electric generator that converts mechanical energy into electricity. Steam turbines, wind and water turbines, and gasoline engines are commonly used in the process.

What electricity boils down to is this: it's a form of energy involving the flow of particles called electrons. Electrons (hence, electricity) are subunits of atoms, of which all matter in the universe is composed. An atom has a center, a nucleus, which contains positively charged particles called protons, uncharged particles called neutrons, and negatively charged particles called electrons. There is balance in that the number of electrons is normally equal to the number of protons. If the balance is disturbed, an atom can add or lose an electron. Once electrons are lost, their free, unrestricted movement is what creates an electrical current.

At this point, things get interesting. Because if some outside force, like a dynamo or generator, disturbs the equilibrium and electrons are lost, the loss is only temporary. The lost electrons must return either to the original atom or to another in the same system. This constitutes a closed circuit, which permits current to flow.

As an example, if a copper wire were attached to a battery

terminal on one end and to a bulb on the other end, no power could be generated because there would be no circuit. Yet, remove the wire from the bulb and attach it to the other battery terminal and the wire will become hot to the touch: a circuit has been completed and electrons are flowing between terminals via the copper conducting wire. The current has returned to the source that created the imbalance.

What's often called "earth current" occurs spontaneously in nature, due to the collision of the solar winds with the earth's atmosphere. "Ground current," or neutral wire-to-earth current, is made when a utility company's return wire to grounding wires creates a secondary circuit to earth. Earth current is normal, and natural; neutral return current should go back to a utility's substation on a wire. However, utilities instead prefer using the earth as much as possible for one simple reason: it's far cheaper.

This return current is what surges through my property to this very day, wounding and killing all creatures great and small, both animal and human.

The Public Service Commission of Wisconsin, that fount of un-wisdom, uses the following definition to assist utilities in fighting off lawsuits by enraged farmers:

"Stray voltage is defined as a natural phenomenon that can be found at low levels between two contact points in any animal confinement area where electricity is grounded. Electrical systems— including farm systems and utility distribution systems—must be grounded to the earth by code to ensure continuous safety and relia- bility. Inevitably, some current flows through the earth at each point where the electrical system is grounded and a small voltage develops. This voltage is called neutral-to-earth voltage (NEV). When a portion of this NEV is measured between two objects that may be simultaneously contacted by an animal, it is frequently called stray voltage..."

This gibberish purports to show that stray voltage, a "natural phenomenon" found in an animal confinement area, is fine. Calling it a natural phenomenon is where I have a problem. It's completely unnatural. And it's lethal.

CHAPTER 5

OF CLAIRVOYANTS AND
SOOTHSAYERS

As I learned later, most of the methods universities employ for researching and investigating stray current are akin to those of clairvoyants or soothsayers, who diagnose and predict using Tarot decks and Ouija boards, or by studying animal entrails or casting horoscopes. In defense of soothsayers, at least they believe their own mumbo-jumbo. Stray current researchers play shell games, attacking the problem by studying something unrelated. They make experiments in laboratories, controlled environments that have nothing in common with conditions found on dairy farms. They then trumpet their findings as the last word in science.

The question that leaps to mind is: why are the researchers not out investigating in the barns and in the fields and pastures where cows are dropping in record numbers? Could it be that the researchers are involved in covering up the issue? Do they have a vested stake in doing so?

University "experts" contend that their findings demonstrate nothing is wrong, that stray current can't possibly be causing my problems and those of other farmers. The state Public Service Commission, overseer of utilities and supposed protector of public welfare, has set a "level of concern" stating that nothing below this level need be addressed. "Level of concern" is a brick wall behind which WPS and other utilities hide.

As an experienced farmer, I would never deny that a certain number of animals raised on a dairy farm will die of natural causes like disease or infection. Birth or breeding difficulties, even accidents or mishaps, account for more deaths as well. As much as it hurts to lose even one cow or calf, every farmer realizes that animal deaths are inevitable and a part of the cost of doing business.

In 1996 the U.S. Department of Agriculture surveyed cattle mortality rates in Minnesota and Wisconsin. It stipulates heifer mortality rates at 15 percent. My herd suffered a 40 percent annual rate, and a high rate that is irreducible by any treatment indicates that stray current is the culprit. It is an all-too-common occurrence, becoming more and more widespread across the dairy belt.

The utilities and their paid "experts" dispute this conclusion, though, with all their might. According to them, their studies prove without a shadow of a doubt that "stray voltage" does not affect cows. But then, their research ignores everything that challenges their foregone conclusions. Never yet has there been a study that pumped in electricity and electrocuted cows in the same fashion as on the farms, and for good reason. The blowback of protests by PETA and the ASPCA, and the resultant media outcry, would be intolerable.

However, a real study would *have to* result in just such high death rates, because if the study didn't kill cows, then it wouldn't recreate environmental conditions.

Despite the massive propaganda efforts by utilities to convince the world that stray current is no problem, dairy farmers know full well that manmade electrical current is gushing from utility wires into the earth of their farms and into their livestock. Because help hasn't been forthcoming, some farmers have gone so far as to cut off all electricity from the utility and generate their own power using a generator, thinking that generating their own electricity is going to solve all their problems. They don't realize that they can't fix it because thanks to the poorly designed distribution system, current will continue to flow through their property whether they use a generator or not.

Others simply cut the utility's down grounds. In fury, but with great satisfaction, I personally cut eighteen of them, and my cows never had it so good as during the year-and-a-half interim between the cuts and wire restoration by WPS. The animals made a remarkable recovery. Milk production skyrocketed to a record high of 85 pounds per cow per day. Still, other farmers drained ponds, pools, and manure pits, anything with heavy liquid or moisture that was a conductor of electricity. Some were able to reduce current and get a herd response; other farms were simply destroyed.

The sad fact is that none of this—not the cutting of down grounds nor changing feed nor buying new milking parlors nor replacing equipment—was necessary at all. The true necessity was for WPS to quit using the earth of my farm, and others, as a return path for their electrical current.

Forty-nine of the fifty states employ this exact distribution system, all except California. Unsurprisingly, California has no problems with deadly utility earth current on its dairy farms, unless there is a serious on-farm problem. Not coincidentally, California has overtaken Wisconsin as the number-one dairy-producing state in the nation. These facts alone should prompt immediate intervention by both state and federal agricultural and environmental regulatory and oversight agencies, to say nothing of the USDA. However, the truth is that more than a few politicians owe their elections to hefty contributions from utility companies.

Back in 1975, just prior to WPS' reconfiguration of the system, our farm was one of the top dairy producers in the state, and Wisconsin in that year was number one in the country. Following the redesign, for the next twenty-five years or so, I had to sell and ship out to other, safer farms most of my cattle, and today I own not a single cow. I also had to sell off all of my equipment, including auctioning off the beautiful, state-of-the-art milking parlor. When they came and tore it out, it felt like they were tearing out my own innards, heart, liver, lungs. Although I still own the farm, 375 acres, and still raise crops, none of us, not I nor any of my surviving family members live on the farm today— the stray current is far too dangerous. Which is why I decided to take WPS to court.

WPS tried to rob me of my day in court by declaring, first, that stray current did not exist, and then by claiming that the seven-year statute of limitations on stray voltage suits had run out. But if, as they asserted, there is no such thing as stray current, why try to muzzle me with the statute? To properly appreciate these issues, we must peer briefly into the nature of electricity. Which, by the way, was the force behind the creation of the Frankenstein monster.

CHAPTER 6

OPENING ARGUMENTS

The night before the trial opened, I didn't sleep a wink. I was tossing and turning while dreading the results of defeat: paying court costs including attorney and expert witness fees, which would send me to debtor's prison for a thousand years. I'd lose my home and freedom.

For a few hours, I toyed with the idea of phoning my lawyers and ordering them to drop the case. But the morning arrived and I didn't call. I dressed in a rather handsome suit and tie, gulped down some black coffee and drove grimly over to Green Bay to meet my fate. Never having seen a trial except on *Perry Mason*-type TV shows, I had no clear idea of what to expect. That unknown scared me almost as much as the possibility of losing.

The trial took place in the historic Brown County district courthouse in Green Bay, the Honorable J.D. McKay, Circuit Judge, presiding. Designed by architect Charles E. Bell of Minneapolis, who also designed the state capitols of South Dakota and Montana, the courthouse is constructed of Marquette raindrop stone, with polished terrazzo floors and four large entrances surmounted by two-story ionic columns. Above the roof is a copper-covered dome, clock and bell tower. Portraits and wide, colorful murals adorn the walls, one of which depicts the historic landing of the explorer Jean Nicolet in 1634. The courtroom where the Circuit Court met is one of the smallest of the building's various chambers. Judge McKay's bench, the wood backdrop, witness stand and spectator seating are built of solid oak and are original vintage (1911). Beautifully and brightly lit by gold chandeliers, the Brown County Courthouse is listed in the National Register of Historic Places. Overall, the impression I had was of The Law's grandeur and overwhelming power.

In my suit for damages ($13 million), I had claimed three things: one, that WPS was negligent in providing electric power; two, that WPS created an unnecessary nuisance through that negligence; and three, that the utility acted willfully and recklessly by failing to provide adequate service to my farm.

Employing a battery of lawyers headed by their best, the tall, thin, nattily dressed, perpetually nervous-looking Trevor Will of Foley and Lardner, the largest law firm in Wisconsin, WPS had brought in the heavy artillery to pulverize me. They could not tolerate losing for fear of setting off a chain reaction of tobacco-like suits. Because I owned one of the largest farms and was doggedly persistent in pressing my claims, refusing to be put off or discouraged by their stall tactics, the utility was hell-bent on making an example of me as a warning and a lesson to other farmers who might get a notion to mess with WPS.

Hammarback Hammarback and Dan Murray Scott represented me. Hammarback, a lean, handsome six-footer in his mid-fifties with thick, salt-and-pepper hair, was a partner in Hammarback, Murray and Jacobson of River Falls.

I was jittery and tense as the proceedings got under way. Seen objectively, a loss for WPS would be little skin off its nose. Sure, they would receive bad press and lose money. But the negative publicity surrounding the case would quickly dissipate and they would simply raise rates to recoup their payout. In a real sense, me and the other victims of stray current were subsidizing the enemy.

WPS would go on without missing a beat. But if I lost, the way of life I inherited from my parents would vanish forever. So, I was staking everything on this one throw of the dice. I would not have dared to take on such a powerful entity, though, if I were not confident in my facts, assertions, witnesses, attorneys, and, most important of all, in the justice of my fight.

Still, I felt uneasy as I leaned forward in my most uncomfortable of spindle-backed chairs on the first day of trial, toe-tapping against the table's metal foot and concentrating on the Court's instructions. Judge J.D. McKay, sixtyish, tall and husky as a pro wrestler, his jowls clean-shaven and the iron gray of his hair matching a stolid demeanor, was asking prospective jurors a series of questions.

I nearly laughed out loud when he inquired of one red-faced fellow, "Can you be impartial?"

"No, absolutely not," the man asserted, sliding low in his seat.

"No?" McKay growled, as if he might bite into someone who showed so little regard for the jury system. "And why not?"

"Because my father-in-law lost thirty-five cows to stray voltage."

The judge grunted and nodded. This was good enough even for him. "All right, you're dismissed."

As might be expected in a state like Wisconsin, many in the jury pool had family who were, or had been, or knew people in, the dairy business. McKay dismissed another juror because she had filed a stray voltage lawsuit against WPS, and Scott Lawrence had been her attorney. Several others were dismissed because they had relatives employed by WPS. Then, of course, there were the usual suspects who simply wanted off, especially since the judge had said he expected the trial to last about one month.

Some of the excuses were priceless. One man asked out so he could go bowling in a tournament. Another claimed his mind would be muddled if he were forced to serve, since he would worry nonstop about his job. Another asked to be excused to coach his son's Little League team. Still, another begged off so she could schedule dental appointments in advance.

For his part, Will used his challenges to remove jurors who indicated even slightly that they just might possibly be sympathetic to the idea of stray current. Through clever questioning, Will got jurors to say that they knew people who knew people who knew other people who claimed to have been harmed by electricity. In this way, he obliged McKay to do some of his work for him by dismissing those folks, thereby allowing Will to save precious challenges. Hammarback employed similar tactics for our side.

Though fidgety and constantly fiddling with his pen, Will was very polished and skillful. After mentioning that stray voltage was really no more than a theory, he shrewdly, almost offhandedly, asked the jurors, "How many of you carry a lucky charm?" More than a few hands went up. "Anybody here believe in UFOs?" The planted idea was that a belief in stray voltage was pure superstition, equivalent to a belief in aliens.

I admired the man's skill even as I detested him for it. But by the time the jury was finally seated, I felt a bit calmer. Despite Will's best efforts, the underlying assumption among most of the jurors seemed to be a sense that stray voltage was real enough.

Hammarback's opening statement on that sunny May morning penetrated to the heart of the matter.

"Ladies and gentlemen, good afternoon," he said, looking from juror to juror. "We all know that electricity in the wrong place can injure and kill, and this case is about how electricity from WPS Corporation's utility lines came onto and is coming onto the property and is causing problems to their animals, causing early deaths in their animals and substantially reducing the milk production on that farm."

He pointed to his right at a photograph of our family farm, nestled atop the hill southeast of town, beyond the TV station's antennas on Little Apple Road. The picture could do little to describe the beauty of the farm, its unique smells and sounds, the sense of peace I felt when I arose and started my day in the morning. A peace that the power company shattered, releasing an invisible menace that stalked the property, more lethal than coyotes or wild dogs.

"It's a fairly large farm," Hammarback said. "It's got capacity now of about 400 milking cows and about another hundred dry cows, so about a 500-cow capacity up there. It used to be a big farm. It's not so big anymore, as you'll hear. Dairy farms are getting bigger and bigger and smaller dairies are going away. As time has gone by, the evidence in this case will show that the Allens have done and are doing everything they can to keep up with the modern trends. They started out with 32 cows, as I recall, and for a while actually milked them by hand. This was before World War II. In fact, when they first started, I don't think they even had electricity out at their farm, but it wasn't very long before—it was in the, I think, early 1940s electricity came up the hill and came out to the Allen farm and of course once it got there, they started using electricity for the things you do on the farm, for the milking equipment mostly. There are 11 children all together. It started out with Larry, who I think was born nine months and one day after they were married, at least according to us, then Leslie. Larry was born in 1939. Leslie, Jim, Cletus, Bonnie, Bob, Kevin and then came Russ, then Josie, Yvonne and Geri Lynn, the last one, who was born in 1959."

At the mention of my beautiful sisters, Josie and Geri Lynn, who had died by their own hand, I nearly broke down. To me, it was WPS' stray current that killed them. If the cows could only stand so much stray current over time before it took its toll, then my sisters suffered the same, until they had no strength left for life.

"Their father Alvin and their mother Alice helped them to learn to milk cows, and how to properly manage and feed animals. Russ actually started when he was about six years old," Scott continued. "Now, the way you milk a cow, then and even now, is you clean the cow's teats off. You put the milker unit on. You need to massage it at some point, and you need to get the milk out of the cow, and that's the same today as it was yesterday. Now, of course, there are parlors where the cows come to you instead of you going to the cows out in the stanchions like it used to be, but that's the way they started out. Well, it wasn't very long with the children coming along when the facility they had there got a little bit too small for them. So, in 1962 they had one of the last barn raisings here in Brown County. The family got together, and they had big meals spread out in the basement and everybody came over and helped..."

Yes, I still remember that day. People came from all over the state to help us, at least a few hundred friends and relatives. It was one of the last barn-raising bees ever held in Wisconsin. That barn was the featured story in the *Hoard's Dairyman* that Yvonne and Geri Lynn graced the cover of when they were girls in '64. I was only ten years old. That barn still stands decades later. But it's empty now, dead silent, without cattle. All that's left in there is the flotsam and jetsam from the ripped-out equipment we had to sell when we couldn't save the animals and continue milk production. Now only the cats wander in and out of the hay loft.

Hammarback paced in short circles, drawing the jurors back to the photograph again and again. "The barn that was put up in 1962 would house a hundred animals to be milked," he said. "So, they worked their way up from 32 animals in 1937 to 100 by 1962. As time went on, the operation increased in size. Then they had about 230 cows milking toward the end of the '60s, and in 1972 started thinking that, gee, you know, maybe we really need to expand. Maybe they really wanted to have a state-of-the-art facility. So, they went all over the place. They went to extension services. They went to different fairs to see people. They went to WPS Corporation to get information on the proper ventilation to use in the barn, and together the family actually built most of the barn. By 1976, late '75, they built what's now called the east barn. It was a free stall type of barn with a parlor in it. Now, as you probably know, a free-stall barn is where the cows have certain areas that they can roam around in on their own. They're not confined to the little stanchions anymore. They have stalls and their own area, and they can go into those stalls. Eventually, they would be able to handle about 500 cows, milking and drying. As the cows are being milked, of course, once they have a calf, they start giving milk. That's how this whole process works. The idea is to have a cow have a calf about every 13 months or so, 12 or 13 months, right in that range. By keeping them having calves in a nice regular manner then the milk production stays up. They have a calf. It keeps the cows healthy, and, of course, they reproduce. As these cows get older and are replaced, there is culling. That is that some of the cows that are sick or don't produce quite as much are taken out of the herd and these new cows come in. It takes about two years for a new heifer, as they're called, to come into the milk stream..." Hammarback went on in some detail and I watched as some of the jurors seemed to grow a little restless.

I knew Hammarback wished to clearly make the point that we were more than competent farmers. Those Holsteins were healthy, and they were big and solid and clear-eyed and beautiful. The farm was well organized and well run. Pa had taught us how to do that, and we could grow. Still, even though it's been my life, the details of farming are not to everyone's taste. I watched one juror close her eyes, and I worried that she'd fallen asleep.

"...When they moved into that barn, about 1975, what they did was consolidate this other heard from GV, move them up there, so they started with about 230 animals up there in about 1974, '75. Now, at the same time that they did that, and unbeknownst to them of what was going to happen, they had three-phase electricity from WPS Corporation brought up to their farm," Hammarback said with a horrified inflection as if he were telling of an army of fiends filing out the gates of hell and marching in ghastly formation onto the Allen Farm. "If you look at this exhibit, I'll point it out to you, it's 1004 C, but it comes down Little Apple Road here which goes to the southeast and the three-phase stops right at the Allen Dairy, and from the Allen Dairy outward, it's only a single-phase line."

Awash in memory, at this point I started to get really worked up. Hammarback was leaning on one elbow against the railing of the jury box telling my story, and telling it well, when he mentioned electricity. My jaws clenched and I balled my fists under the table, thinking of how my father had died believing the lie that we had screwed up the operation he built.

Hammarback continued by telling the jury how "troubling" it was that the down grounds from the three-phase transformer on the pole pumped heavy juice into the steel of our barn, tormenting our animals. But a nervousness began gnawing at me and I grew agitated, feeling Hammarback had made a big mistake by understating the problem. I shot a look at the jury to see if the truth of what I knew was registering with them: That the torture and death of cows by electricity, and the executions of the Rendering Plant rifleman was beyond "troubling" to the animals. I felt like vaulting over the table to the jury and shouting those very words at them.

As Hammarback persisted, striding up and down in front of the jurors and speaking more animatedly, I calmed down a bit. "Back in 1975 and '76 they didn't know about electrical problems. They were just milking their cows. One of the things Russ will tell you is that they always had a problem with cows kicking, and they wouldn't milk right. Now a cow needs to be contented," Hammarback was saying, "and the evidence in this case will show that the animals in the Allen barn were anything but. They would go into the milking parlor and what would happen is they would jump and kick their milkers off into the manure."

Hammarback now switched over to discussing the partnership and pointed to Exhibit 1010, a milk-production chart, something I wanted the jury to become familiar with for what was to come later. He moved his wood pointer across the easel the way a maestro waves his conducting baton, showing them an average of the past twelve months. Production was lower than it should've been. To my satisfaction, Hammarback focused on the insidious nature of stray electricity, a theme we needed to pound home. Every time the farm made a small gain, we would quickly lose it and more. One step up and two steps back. They were killing us on an installment plan.

Though the day was bright and beautiful, the May sunlight streaming in the courtroom windows, a sadness overwhelmed me as Hammarback recounted the destruction of the partnership. And my dead brother. The current did him in. Ruined his heart. Age forty-four.

Pausing to let this sink in, Hammarback shook his gray head somberly. "Russ Allen was the last one there running the farm. His brother Bob still worked for him, works for him today, and Bob's son Scott, who does the feeding, came on as soon as he was old enough. Cletus, one of his brothers, started a farm down the road, but dropped out because they could never figure who is causing these cows to get mastitis and why milk production wasn't what it should be. They would argue about it."

Hammarback refocused their attention on the production chart, comparing ours to the Wisconsin average. Then he introduced the villain of the piece, told the jury how I'd gotten WPS to come out and test the milking parlor for stray current.

"WPS didn't test anywhere else on the farm," he continued. "Didn't test the line. Didn't change out any split bolts or fix any of the 1940 series wire. They simply told Russ and his father that there wasn't a problem. And Russ believed them."

I looked over at WPS' lawyer, Will Will. He showed no reaction. Just kept twirling and playing with his ballpoint pen.

"But there was a problem, and Russ and his father desperately tried to find a fix to it. Mike Hoerth, a dealer who sold milking equipment suggested Russ should build a new parlor that they could run with just one person. That it would pay for itself in labor, and add a layer of safety. Patty Bowers, their herdsperson, nearly had her brains kicked out by shocked, unruly cows many times as she was milking."

But then Hammarback brought up a painful subject: The death of my sister, Geri Lynn, who had done the milking before Patty. Geri Lynn couldn't bear to go on any longer after her baby boy Jesse, fifteen months old, died of childhood leukemia. To this day I wonder if stray current played a role in his death.

"Geri Lynn, his sister, also did some of the milking," Hammarback continued, " but she passed away—actually, it was a suicide..."

They found Geri Lynn's body in a car, a shotgun in her lap. I shuddered in horror at the image. But then another image, a beautiful one, replaced it, that of Geri Lynn in her wedding dress, young and vibrant and beautiful. Her sweet voice calling to me, reminding me of why I was here, strengthening me for this ordeal. *Russ,* she said. *Remember: The reason you're in this place is not simply to get money for the death of our cows and business. It's to get justice for the death of our family harmony, the partnership, the death of our mental and physical health. Remember me,* she said. *And Les. And Jesse. And Josie. And Pa.*

Hammarback's voice abruptly interrupted my reverie and brought me back to the here and now.

"After that, Patty stepped in. They put in a double-twelve, parallel parlor so they could milk the cows from behind. Between the back legs. There's a kick plate up there so the cows can't kick you. But frankly, the cows were worse than ever. Russ and his father had gone through milking equipment. Housing. Nutrition. Everything they could think of. But more cows got mastitis. Frustrated, Russ called up Mike Hoerth who came out right away and tested the equipment, finding everything in good shape and functioning properly.

"You should check on stray voltage, Mike told Russ when he saw that the equipment he installed was all in good order," Hammarback recounted. "So, he did. Russ brought Larry Neubauer out and he measured the current at 800 milliamps. The testimony will be that the ground fault circuit interrupters in bathrooms when you push that button, they trip at six milliamps. At six milliamps, 6/1000 of an amp, a child cannot let go under some circumstances. That's the strength of that shock," he paused for effect.

"The testimony will be that utilities in Wisconsin can't contribute more than one milliamp of current in cow contact areas since about 1989. So, what we're looking at then is 800 milliamps or 800 times the contribution. What happened next is Mr. Neubauer disconnected the connection to WPS' transformer, called the neutral, and this 800 milliamps went away. So, he recommended an isolation transformer that keeps the neutral from bringing current onto the farm. So, on April of 1997, Russ called WPS and had them come out. Supposedly they tested extensively. They showed him a bunch of scribbled numbers, computations, and said they couldn't find a problem. But they offered to install a neutral isolator. Strange that they would offer him a solution to a problem they claimed was nonexistent," again, he paused for effect.

"So, WPS installed the Dairyland Isolator. The weather forecast for the upcoming weekend called for extreme heat and humidity, which meant that loads on the electrical system would be immense. Sure enough, the cows went wild. Larry came out and put a meter on the pole, demonstrating that the Isolator was closing—shutting down—under the stress of peak usage. Desperate for a solution, Russ decided to take matters into his own hands and buy the isolation transformer Larry Neubauer had described. Problem was, no one would lend him the $58,000 it cost. He was faced with the difficult decision to sell part of his property to obtain funding. Thankfully, it didn't come to that as one banker was kind enough to just use the farm equipment for collateral. So, in December of 1997, Larry Neubauer finished putting in this isolation transformer."

Hammarback went over to the easel. "If you look at the production graph here, Exhibit 1010, what happened—we're looking at these dates—there's December 1997, the cows were producing, on a monthly rate, 15,000 pounds of milk. By the end of 1999, the cows were producing almost 27,000. To a degree, the severity of the current is a function of weather, of hard, dry or frozen ground, which doesn't conduct electricity nearly as well as soft, wet earth. That's why when the spring thaws arrived, resistance to the current was much less; it passed easily through the ground and into the metal structures of the barn. The herd became miserable and far less productive."

Hammarback moved from the exhibit past the judge and slowly crossed the room back over to the jury box. "The testimony will be that there is *still* current from WPS on that line that they've asked many times to have removed. WPS does nothing. Except Russ and his family that it's not a problem. Now, in order to understand what was going on electrically, I hope you'll bear with me. I want to talk about electricity."

"Electric current is like water flowing from a hose. Voltage is like the pressure pushing the water, so that the water either trickles out or shoots out. Depending on how open the spigot is, the water is under high or low pressure, or perhaps somewhere in the middle." Hammarback said, speaking very slowly and carefully, as he showed them another exhibit, 1067.

"Here's our neutral wire coming from the substation." He tapped it with the black rubber head of the pointer. "Here's our two wires running to the transformer on the farm." He tapped again. "Here's the neutral that carries it back, and here's the down ground that goes into the earth. Here's that little inner tie that goes from the primary to the transformer, and you can see that here's the current coming down into the service entrance panel here and then into the grounding block, and into the earth, but more importantly, onto the steelwork, onto the milking unit, by, through and on the cow, back to the earth, all to get back to its source, which is now a ground rod at the substation. Once this electricity's in the earth, it's got to get back to the substation, but how much or how far it goes, they don't have a clue. There's no way to aim or control it. It's uncontrolled electricity, current going into the ground. It's going to flow back." His tone was one of a man who recognized a potent menace threatening the biosphere.

"The dose isn't important. The fact is that there's electrical current in the vicinity of these cows. Studies done by science advisors in Minnesota verify that if currents in the ground, step potentials as low as seven millivolts, 7/1000 of a volt, they affect the productive capacity of those herds."

Hammarback pursed his lips. "There's electrical charge on the water. The cow puts her tongue in the water, she gets a shock. Cows have been trained from birth that electric fences are bad, so a cow doesn't drink. Doesn't eat. Doesn't produce milk. Everybody says 'stray voltage,' but it's really, stray current."

Pausing for a moment, he looked around the courtroom at the spectators in the wooden benches, then meandered across the carpet and sidled up to the jury. "Dr. Andrew Johnson will be here to testify that the cows on Russ Allen's farm are definitely affected by the current. The electrical folks will tell you that this happened the minute they—WPS—put that down ground next to the feed room. The current rises and falls depending on soil conditions and loads, but the current's been there ever since."

"Why should WPS be responsible? They're using wire used in WWII. It's still supplying all of these loads. They don't do the maintenance. The only records they showed us were that they tested the poles out there just to make sure they didn't break! We've got an exhibit of the dozens and dozens of split bolt connectors sitting out on Little Apple Road. We've asked that they be removed, and WPS has said no. They won't listen. Russ Allen has sent a letter to Mr. Weyers, the president of WPS, saying, 'please stop putting current on my ground.' He got a letter back saying, 'We always put current there. We're going to continue to put current in the ground. And by the way, quit cutting our ground rods.'"

"The bottom line is," Hammarback said to the jury, his eyes narrowing, "what do the cows say? Because there will be lots of studies that come up, *funded by utilities*, very suspicious, and we'll dig into some of the details. Lots of college professors are making millions, I'm not kidding, testifying for utilities on studies that we don't think have any merit at all. We submit that WPS knows it because their *own* expert told them."

"Ladies and gentlemen, stray current is a cause of all this. WPS is simply not maintaining their line. They don't follow their own procedures. The state requires a maintenance program. There's not a shred of evidence that the line has been maintained since the time the second barn was built in 1974. These split bolts on the line are failing. They leak current in the ground. They're not providing adequate service to the Russell Allen Dairy Farm, and that's what the testimony in this case will be."

He fell thoughtfully silent. The courtroom was silent, too; even the spectators stopped whispering with one another. Nervous though I was, I was glad to see he had the full attention of all twelve, plus alternates.

"This is the last time I get to talk to you until the end of the trial, at which point we make closing arguments. I hope you'll find this case interesting. It is complicated. Please bear with us on that and thank you for your kind attention," and with that Hammarback ended his opening arguments.

Will Will of the high-powered legal firm of Foley and Lardner rose from behind the defense table and positioned himself center stage, halfway between Judge McKay's polished oak bench and the jury box. Tall, thin and elegant, sandy-haired with some distinguishing gray about the temples, he wore an expensive, charcoal pinstripe suit and a pale blue shirt. His navy and gray polka-dotted tie exactly matched the folded handkerchief peering out from the chest pocket of his unbuttoned suit jacket. Black wingtips buffed to a high gloss, he looked as if he were preparing for a spread in *Gentleman's Quarterly*.

Will had a reputation as a legal titan, one of the brainiest, winningest attorneys in the region. My palms felt sweaty and I rubbed them against my knees. That Will had not previously argued stray voltage cases in no way reassured me. WPS was not paying him massive fees just to watch him lose.

"Good afternoon," he said to the jurors, and I had to admit that he had a pleasant, friendly, Midwestern voice. "It is my great privilege and responsibility, with Mr. Maassen, Mr. Meckstroth and Mr. Whaley, to represent Wisconsin Public Service—WPS—in this matter. Our job here is to bring you the *whole* story. What you heard isn't the whole story. I'll try to be entertaining enough to keep you awake. We have some things to look at on the computer screen over here, which is why we have the lights off." Everyone's attention shifted to the monitor as Will quickly sketched his case.

"There are three things I am going to talk about. One is Wisconsin Public Service's conduct, since that's been made an issue. Two, is stray voltage really affecting Mr. Allen's cows? And three, what actually happened at the Allen farm over the years."

He pointed with his index finger to a spot on the diagram up on the screen. "This case is not about transmission wires," he said. "You've all seen these big poles, called H-frames. This is about the distribution system— 14,400 volts. That's the voltage of the lines that serve Mr. Allen's farm. There's a picture," he pointed out. "On the left side, there's a three-phase. You've heard about the primary neutral. The low wire is the primary neutral. These wires on top that have the insulators, those are hot wires or phase conductors. This is the kind of system, three phase, that goes from the Mystery Hills substation to Mr. Allen's farm. Past Mr. Allen's farm the distribution line changes to a single phase." He paused to give the jury a chance to study the picture.

"There is one hot wire on top. The primary neutral is right here, on which the current flows back to the substation called Mystery Hills. This is a picture of a pole on a single-phase line," Will Will said, pointing. "A green arrow shows the grounding wire. It is attached to a long, steel rod driven into the earth. When you heard of Mr. Allen cutting grounding wires, that's the wire."

Will explained that a multi-grounded system was designed for protection against accidents like lightning striking a pole, or a car slamming into a pole and knocking down a hot phase conductor. It was designed to protect voltage stability so that equipment like computers or motors was not damaged by voltage surges. And he made a key admission, one I hoped the jurors would pick up on and really think about.

"There is current that will flow down from the primary neutral, into the earth, through the earth and back to the substation. The multi-grounded system is designed to protect people, property, and you'll hear why it is standard," he paused and turned to the jury.

"So, what is this case about then? The central issue is current being put into the ground-flowing through the earth, up the legs of Mr. Allen's cows, through the cow, and out the other side." His tone was one of deep skepticism.

"This is not a case about how much current is on the ground wires, how much is on the primary neutral, because those things don't affect the cow. The evidence is going to be clear you have to have current *through* the cow."

"Now, let's talk about my client's conduct and what the evidence is going to show. It's going to show that the company acted properly. The second thing it's going to show is that we acted reasonably and appropriately under the circumstances." Will still had the ballpoint pen in his hand and tapped it against his palm. "WPS is a public utility. That means it is regulated in the state of Wisconsin. It has to comply with laws passed by the legislature."

I felt anger surging upward in my chest and lodging in my throat like an indigestible pit. WPS, a huge, rich corporation, gets laws passed—buys them—to its benefit by contributing cash to the campaigns of Wisconsin legislators and politicians. It's an old story; he who pays the piper calls the tune. As an example of how things actually work around here, Governor Jim Doyle recently accepted $41,550 in contributions from two utilities after a state panel controlled by Doyle appointees approved the controversial $220 million sale of the utilities' Kewaunee nuclear power plant. WPS and Alliant Energy asked the Public Service Commission to approve the sale. Over half the campaign contributions were accepted by Doyle one week before the sale was approved. These facts are in the public record. Money makes the Wisconsin political world go 'round. Just maneuver your hirelings into positions where they can ram through laws to enrich you.

"It has to follow those laws whether it likes them or not. How does that apply to a multi-grounded neutral distribution system? Well, the Public Service Commission essentially complies, and Mark Cook from the commission will be here. Is he trying to tell us that it is illegal to install a safe system that doesn't leak current in the earth, exposing everyone to it each day?"

Hammarback rose to address the Court. "Your Honor, I object to any statements of law imposed at this point."

Judge McKay suddenly sprang to life, glad, I supposed, to have something to do. "Well, I haven't heard any yet," McKay said judiciously. "I don't know what direction Mr. Will is going in—I certainly understand your objection, but your objection is overruled because I haven't heard any such statements."

Will continued. "There's a specific regulation that applies to multi-grounded systems. You need a ground at every transformer and not less than nine per mile on poles in rural areas such as where Mr. Allen's farm is. Wisconsin Public Service has always complied with this. The second legal requirement," Will said, "is an order of the Public Service Commission called docket number 115. The Public Service Commission commenced a hearing in 1996—the subject was stray voltage and what should be done about it. There were scientists, farmers, utility representatives. Based on evidence offered, the commission issued an order. That order established what's called the *level of concern*. Cow contacts voltages flowing through the cow, which is permitted under PSC order. The utility's contribution cannot be more than one milliamp. You will hear from Mr. Cook that this is not a level of harm. For purposes of measuring current through cows, the Public Service Commission said assume cows have a resistance of 500 ohms."

Will went over and placed both hands against the rail of the jury box. Smiling cheerfully, it looked like he was attempting to bond with the jurors. "So if we know that under the level of concern, the utility can contribute one milliamp, that translates into half a volt. When you go out on a farm, you take measurements and check the voltage differential. You divide it by 500 ohms to find out how much current is flowing through the cow. Has WPS taken measurements on the Allen farm? Yes, they have. In 1988, for the first time taking measurements in the parlor, they didn't find anything problematic."

"Remember the comment by Mr. Allen's lawyer—they only measured in the parlor. And the comment was made that Mr. Neubauer found 800 milliamps in the barn. In fact, when Mr. Neubauer *supposedly* found the 800 milliamps, that was on an arch in the parlor. It doesn't tell you if 800 milliamps was flowing on the metal, doesn't tell you what the voltage differential is. You need to know what the voltage is on the floor to know whether or not you're going to have current flowing through the cow. Mr. Neubauer didn't do that. We've been out to the farm. We didn't find evidence we were violating that standard. What if we violate that standard? We'll get to that."

Will now shifted and assumed an injured rather than accusatory tone. "You heard criticism of the company's maintenance procedure. It's not accurate, as the evidence will show, to say we haven't done maintenance on that line since World War II or before. In 1975, the line was upgraded. It's had pole inspections two times since then. And as problems occur it is maintained. It is inspected the same way as any other line. Mr. Allen is being treated the same way the company deals with all its distribution lines. On the topic of how we behave, it was reasonable and appropriate under the circumstances. Every time we were asked to come out to Mr. Allen's, measuring for stray voltage, we did that for no charge. We were asked out on three different occasions."

He walked over to the dry-erase board, picked up a red marker and started writing. "I'm going to write these down because they're important. First was in about 1988. There is a record of the readings taken. Next was in April 1997. Mike Moore, who you'll hear from, was out there. They did an investigation in the parlor, took spot checks in the barn. The spot check numbers were so low that Mr. Moore didn't even write them down. They didn't actually have a chance to talk with Mr. Allen because he was out somewhere. They left a report for him," he continued. "They didn't find anything that suggested a stray voltage problem."

"The next time was July of 1997. Two people visited—Vern Peterson and Jerry Held. Mr. Peterson is the engineer. They were there to install the Dairyland Isolator you heard described, the one Mr. Allen asked to have that would separate the primary neutral from the secondary. They installed the isolator, started testing again, and were getting some strange readings. The reason they were getting strange readings was that the reference rod they were using to take readings had been placed, unbeknownst to them, near a pipe that served the manure system from the old barn. Mr. Neubauer came out the next day and figured out what the problem was."

I nearly fell off my bench. I looked up at Hammarback and he just smiled. Larry Neubauer, my electrician, had to figure it out for them. Will had belittled the "supposed" readings of 800 milliamps that Larry had registered, but now trusted Larry's explanation of these readings over WPS' own expert engineer, Peterson?

"Mr. Peterson verified the problem. They went to move the reference rod and take new readings. You'll hear that Mr. Allen was fed up with them. Told them to go home. They never completed their testing because he said he had had enough."

This blatant lie was, for me, a red cloth in front of a bull. I took several deep slow breaths. This was only the barest of beginnings. My blood was up because Peterson had outright lied, without even having the tiniest grain of truth behind the lie. I never told them to leave. Said nothing of the kind. WPS had all the notes from the Peterson visit that day, taken by his assistant. And there was no mention of my kicking them out or impeding them in any way, as there would have been had I done so. These were the kind of people I was up against.

"From then on," Will said, pacing slowly in front of the jury, "Mr. Allen was working with Mr. Neubauer. However, that wasn't the end of the story. WPS people still continued to call on Mr. Allen to assist him with, for example, a wiring program that offers money in the event a farmer needs to rewire his system. The company was to come back out and test the Dairyland Isolator in early winter 1997, but Mr. Allen said he wanted it removed."

The damn thing didn't work; it was useless. So, why would I want to keep it?

"Are we saying Mr. Allen is a bad farmer? No, but he has certain limiting factors that prevent him from getting where he thinks he may be. Over time he's had consultants make suggestions he has not implemented. Another factor is the barn, which has a slatted floor. It can cause herd health problems with pneumonia. It's dim. He has not put in brighter light, which has been shown to increase milk production."

"Statistics," he went on, firing away, "show that if you go to artificial insemination instead of using bulls, that produces an increase in milk production. He has not done that either. So, to the extent his herd is not performing, it's not due to any electricity but to the decisions he's made himself."

"And that brings up the topic of damages and the $13 million. I need to say a bit about that. I'm not going to tell you who Dr. Behr is. I'll let you be the judge of that when he's here and we can talk with him about his qualifications. But you should know what he did. To prepare the damages estimate, he spent less than a day at the Allen Farm, between five to eight hours. Looked mostly at milk checks, receipts that say how much milk Mr. Allen sold to the dairy. He got some cow count numbers, some of which were missing..."

Suddenly, Hammarback shot up and cut him off. "Your Honor," Hammarback said sharply to Judge McKay, "at this point I'm going to object. Argument should be reserved for the end. This should be what the evidence is going to show."

"This is," Will Will retorted with irritation, "what the evidence will show."

Judge McKay bent a steely gaze on Will, indicating his intention to ensure proper legal conduct in his courtroom. "Mr. Will, restrict yourself to what the evidence will show."

Will nodded deferentially. "I will, Your Honor."

He turned back to the jury. "I think that the evidence is going to show that some time in 1997 or 1998, Mr. Allen and Mr. Neubauer decided that Mr. Allen was going to file a lawsuit."

He was implying a conspiracy. It was so ludicrous that I laughed out loud. Everyone turned and looked at me and Hammarback shot over a dirty look that said, *keep quiet, this is serious.*

"The evidence is going to show that since that time they have been operating the farm and installing electrical changes, ditch wires, managing the herd in a way intended to show that there is electrical damage."

Standing two feet away from the jury, his voice rose to such a volume that I was certain people out in the hallway and the offices could hear every syllable.

"When you listen to all the evidence, you're going to conclude that there is no evidence that current has been flowing through his cows at anywhere near the level required to damage them. The explanations for production changes are mundane. Things like nutrition, feed, cow comfort, vet care, temperature, weather. You'll see how those correlate with his cutting the ground wire. And when you're finished hearing all the evidence, you will conclude that WPS is not responsible for any injury to Mr. Allen's cows."

"Thank you very much for your attention and patience. I'll have an opportunity to talk with you again at the conclusion of the case."

So, there it was. The battle lines were drawn. The case would put expert versus expert, engineer versus engineer, electrician versus electrician, agronomist versus agronomist. Or at least until it was my turn to take the stand. I was no expert, only a simple farmer trying to make a living and preserve an 80-year-old family business and way of life. Though tense and uncertain of the trial's outcome, I was dead sure of one thing. I was in for what promised to be one hell of a ride.

CHAPTER 7

DR. ANDREW P. JOHNSON

As court opened the following day, another warm bright flawless May morning, our strategy was to employ the very best witnesses first. Hammarback believed that the jury's first impressions would be critical. Early witnesses and experts from various fields would provide an overview of the case and prepare the way for my own testimony. It was Hammarback's belief that the expert witnesses on both sides would cancel each other out, and that in the end, it was my credibility that held the key to victory. Or defeat.

Though my resolve to fight WPS was firm, I felt the burden, like a weight, of seeking justice for the dead: relatives, animals, dairy business. Though testifying and getting raked over the coals by WPS figured to be extremely unpleasant, akin to undergoing a root canal, I was eager to take the stand, make my case and get it over with. If the outcome of the trial depended on my words, so be it. I could live with that, regardless of how things wound up. At least I'd be active, instead of just sitting around letting the world make up its mind about what to do with me.

But it was not yet my time. My first crucial witness was Dr. Andrew P. Johnson, a.k.a. the "Udder Doctor," whose testimony,

I hoped, would be powerful. The doctor was a renowned veterinarian who had consulted for over twenty years in twenty-six countries and almost every state in the U.S. He was one of the foremost dairy experts in the world and I was honored to have him on my team.

In his mid-fifties, Dr. Andy Johnson was a physically commanding presence. Over six feet tall, with a full head of thick, gray hair and an iron-gray beard to match, the doctor weighed more than three hundred pounds, and every ounce of his bulk was majestic and imposing. But as learned as he was, Dr. Johnson had a knack of making specialized knowledge easily understandable for lay people.

"The source of that glut in your briefcase there that you brought up?" Hammarback, standing about five feet from the witness box, asked with a smile.

"My file on the Russ Allen case," Dr. Johnson said in his deep, clear voice. Bulging with a sheaf of papers thick enough to choke an elephant, the briefcase could be neither completely closed nor latched.

"You don't have a leather one?" Hammarback said.

"I couldn't find one big enough," the doctor replied, and the jury chuckled.

"How long have you been consulting?"

"From about the mid '80s to current."

"Who do you normally consult for?" Hammarback asked.

"Farmers form the vast majority of my work."

"Do you consult in litigation for just plaintiffs or also for defendants?"

"There's a mix," Dr. Johnson told him. He went on to say that having been raised on a dairy farm, he was always interested in cows and had been on his high school dairy-judging team at their FFA.

Hammarback wanted to drive home to the jury that this witness, unlike the university professors who would be testifying for WPS, spent his time in the real world, in the field on farms, and not in controlled, air conditioned laboratories.

"Have you evaluated dairy farms looking for problems with production?" Hammarback inquired.

"That's what I do. My expertise is milk quality, cow comfort. I also look at nutrition, disease, housing, milk quality, records management. I have the ability to look at most aspects of a dairy operation."

"After you've looked, what do you try to do?"

"Generate a report or have a discussion with the farmer, prioritize items I think are affecting profitability and a game plan of how to address those items." He rubbed the side of his nose with his forefinger.

"Has the work you've done taken you to national organizations?" Hammarback asked.

"I belong to the American Association of Bovine Practitioners, and I'm currently on the board of directors. I'm active in the National Mastitis Council. I'm active in the Wisconsin Veterinary Medical Association, and past president of that association. Dr. Graeme Mein and myself worked on the national standards protocol to evaluate milking equipment—our protocol was adopted by the ASAA."

"What types of awards have you received?"

"I was awarded Wisconsin Veterinarian of the Year, the top honor our state gives. I was awarded the Dairy Preventer Medicine Award by the Bovine Practitioners, the highest honor in North America."

Hammarback stood silently, letting the jury absorb the information.

"Bovines," Hammarback said, "for those of us that are veterinary-challenged, are cows, right?" Everyone in the courtroom laughed.

"Yes."

Hammarback paused for a moment and then moved nearer to

the witness box. Like a thunderclap on a clear day, he said loudly and from nowhere to Dr. Johnson, "What is stray voltage?"

Taken aback by the sudden change of subject, the doctor hesitated a moment. Then he slowly shook his head. "Stray voltage is a huge can of worms. There's a lot more we need to learn. Especially about nontraditional stray voltage, which is earth currents. It's an issue where there's some type of electrical phenomenon causing cows discomfort."

"From a veterinarian's point of view," Hammarback said, "can you explain what stray current does to cows?"

Dr. Johnson nodded. "We get dairies where it may only access cows at certain areas and only affect the water they drink, which affects the feed they eat, which affects the milk production they give. On other dairies, it irritates them in the parlor and they don't let their milk down. Don't milk out, and it causes mastitis. On some dairies, it causes immune stress and cows are susceptible to diseases. So, there's a wide variation of what it does. The cows are the ultimate answer as to whether the level is bothering them or not. My level of concern has never changed."

Hammarback nodded and turned toward the jury. "About a level of concern when it relates to voltage, what do you mean?"

"Well, how much voltage does it take to bother a cow? The level is whatever makes the cow change to an abnormal behavior, from the way she eats, drinks, walks, milks. The level is what bothers the cow. I'm not an electrical engineer, I'm a cow veterinarian, but the way I look at traditional stray voltage is what we use to measure cow contact points or AC voltage—we would simply take a voltmeter and test between cow contact points, say, hoof to mouth, and see if we get a voltage reading, which might be caused by live wires or loose, unshielded cables. Now we have something called ground currents, a different issue I'm not sure anybody has a complete understanding of. In my opinion, it's going to be a much huger issue than traditional stray voltage ever was."

"Why do you say that?"

"It's causing much higher levels of damage. With traditional stray voltage, you went in, you measured it, you found it, you fixed it. Life went on. With the new stray current, man, it takes a long, long time to figure it out. We haven't even been able to fix it."

"Let's say," Hammarback went on, beginning to pace slowly, "you go to a farm and measure for traditional-type stray voltage and don't get anything, but you see the cows are nervous and don't milk right. Does your investigation end there?"

The doctor shook his head vigorously. "Oh, absolutely not. On most farms that I deal with, we don't measure voltage, but the cows clearly tell me there's something wrong. I will refer the farmer to somebody to measure for ground currents. Because like I said, I'm not an electrical engineer."

Hammarback left the vicinity of Judge McKay's bench and went over to the jury, leaning with his back against the railing of the jury box and facing the witness. "The cow tells you these things," Hammarback reiterated. "They can't speak, or maybe they can, but how do you tell they're suffering?"

The doctor glanced up at Judge McKay, looked at Hammarback and smiled puckishly. "You know, I'm not Dr. Doolittle, I don't talk to cows directly."

Everyone laughed, even stone-faced Judge McKay. "But they talk to me in what—I've never seen a cow lie."

"You told me that you once consulted for WPS," Hammarback resumed.

"They had me do staff training, who then went to farms to give them ideas of issues they could look at to help the farmer determine if there are other problems on the dairy."

"When?"

"Early to mid '80s."

"Anybody from WPS come and tell you, 'Get out of here? You don't know what you're talking about?'"

The doctor grinned. "Not yet, anyway."

"When there's a thought that stray current might be causing a problem," Hammarback said, "what are the differentials, as you say, used in the diagnosis?"

The doctor's brow furrowed. "Housing, cow comfort, milk quality issues. My mastitis triangle would be: The man, the machine, the cow, nutrition, disease, labor and management."

"Management?" Hammarback asked.

"Labor—I would put those together, employees and management, both. Records, if available."

"Water?"

"Water, you could throw under nutrition."

"Why is water an issue?"

"Because," the veterinarian said, "if they don't drink, they don't eat feed, and don't make milk. It's 97 percent water, you want to make sure the cow has adequate water."

"If the cow doesn't drink water, she doesn't eat feed either?"

Will Will rose from behind the defense table. "Object to the question, Your Honor," he said in a nasal twang. "Leading."

Judge McKay nodded, and a small shock of gray hair tumbled over his forehead. "That is," he said.

"I'm sorry?" Hammarback said directly to Meckstroth, displeased.

"LEADING," Will retorted, and his voice rose and dripped with arrogance and condescension.

"Mr. Hammarback," Judge McKay said, "try not to lead. I'll sustain the objection."

Hammarback frowned and said sarcastically, "I'll see if I can." He said and turned to Dr. Johnson. "Have you heard the term 'limiting factor?'"

"Sure. Another easier way to refer to it is 'bottleneck.' Where does the bottleneck occur that keeps that cow—that farm—from getting to the next level of production, of success? The limiting factor may be the type of housing they're in or the feed quality or some disease preventing them from reaching goals."

"Can you give me an example of a bottleneck?"

"All those would be examples, obviously bad housing, improperly balanced ration, not breeding cows properly, having sore feet. Electricity could be a bottleneck."

"Dr. Johnson, you've done reviews and examinations of research in the area of stray voltage?"

"Yes."

"Back when you did your training at WPS Corp., tell me what you explained to the WPS personnel about things you looked for in housing when trying to evaluate stray voltage."

"Things like bedding, stall design, ventilation, different types of housing and how to identify potential bottlenecks," the doctor said.

"Bottlenecks caused by electricity?" Hammarback asked pointedly.

"Right."

"What understanding was given to you of what was going on at Russ Allen's?"

"That he had an unresolved electrical issue. I was to look at the facility and the dairy management and render an opinion as to whether I felt stray voltage caused damage to his dairy. So, I did a complete evaluation of the system," he said.

"And?"

"Everything checked out normal, except the regulator was dirty and needed service. I told Mr. Allen he needed his dealer to service his regulator."

"Can you tell me what effect, if any, the regulator that required cleaning would have on production?"

Dr. Johnson shrugged. "I don't think any."

"Did you see anything about nutrition or water that figured into your differential diagnosis?"

"I did not see anything that concerned me," the doctor said.

"In terms of labor and management," Hammarback said, "what observations did you make?"

The doctor answered quickly, and with an intensity of feeling that surprised me. "He had some really *good* people, key people very good at helping run his dairy. He had very good people and the farm was well managed."

"You have been called on to evaluate damages in lawsuits resulting from stray voltage, have you not?"

"Yes," the doctor replied. "I have."

"You feel you're qualified to do that?"

He nodded. "I'm qualified to show the actual damages. On cases, I've been able to show a dollar loss. I can stand behind my numbers."

"In terms of electricity on the Allen farm, did you look into the history of that?"

"All I did," Johnson replied, "is look at history, because you had electrical experts, and I was there well after isolation."

"Was there anything in the electrical history you found significant?"

"A whole lot of things. Mainly the response they got when they isolated the farm in '97 and the responses they got by putting the rings around the dairy. So, when you look at the significant increase in milk production, *that was something never achieved except at the time of isolation.*"

I could not tell if the jury grasped the significance of this point. They seemed attentive; only a few looked away from the witness or from Hammarback.

"Based on the evaluation you did and taking into account your differential diagnosis, do you have an opinion to a reasonable degree of certainty as to whether or not stray voltage had been affecting dairy cows?"

Will suddenly leaped up, "Object to the foundation," he said. "Dr. Johnson was not on the farm in '97."

Hammarback did not deign to look at Will and instead

addressed the court. "He's reviewed the history, Your Honor," he said with weary patience, and waited.

"Mr. Hammarback, it's a multiple question. I think you're going to have to break the question down. Then re-ask the question if you would, please."

Hammarback nodded, shoved both hands deep into his pants pockets, and refocused his attention on the witness. Again, he went to the heart of the matter. "Dr. Johnson, based on the examination, evaluations of historic records, and the on-farm evaluation you made, and taking into account the history of changes in the electrical system, do you have an opinion, to a reasonable degree of certainty, as to whether or not current has been affecting the Allen cows?"

"Your *Honor*," Will moaned, "there's no foundation for Dr. Johnson ever having reviewed any records from 1997. His testimony was that he looked at some records, a little before, a little after. I think he needs more foundation." He sat down with a thump.

McKay sustained him. Again. I was beginning to think the judge was sympathetic to WPS and against us. If that was right, we had big, big trouble on our hands.

"Dr. Johnson, since you were on the farm, have you received records concerning production?" Hammarback asked.

"Yes, I have."

"Have you looked at those records?"

"Yes."

"And are they the types of records you would normally look at coming to a determination of whether electricity had an effect on cows?"

"Yes."

Hammarback drew a deep breath, took his hands from his pockets and crossed his arms. "Okay," he said. "And based on all you've gathered and the history you've gathered, have you developed enough information to come to an opinion as to whether electricity had an effect on the Allen dairy?"

Dr. Johnson nodded. "I believe I have. Yes."

"And what is that opinion?"

"I believe that voltage did indeed have a negative impact on the Allen herd."

Hammarback paused to let it sink in. All fourteen jurors sat staring at the veterinarian, riveted. He then turned and faced the jury. "The record-keeping system, is that a limiting factor?"

"No," Dr. Johnson replied. "It would be nice to have more records, but I think they can manage."

"In terms of electricity on that farm, in your opinion, is that a limiting factor today?"

The doctor replied without a moment's hesitation. "Absolutely. Until we eliminate all current, this herd will be constantly fighting that battle to get where they need to go."

Hammarback said nothing. He did not move. Dr. Johnson sat still, quietly awaiting the next question. You could hear a pin drop in the courtroom. There was no sound, not from the jury, lawyers, bailiff, stenographer or spectators.

Finally, Hammarback broke the silence with an anticlimactic question. "The reproduction program on the farm today, and the feed, are they limiting in any way?"

Again Dr. Johnson shook his head. "No," he said softly, and nothing else.

"I have no further questions, your Honor," Hammarback said as he took a seat.

It was Will's turn now to question Dr. Johnson. His line of questioning started amicable enough, just stating facts about Dr. Johnson to the jury, asking about his credentials and whatnot. Reminded me of a fighter sizing up his opponent, gauging distance, waiting for the right moment to strike. When Will felt there was nothing for him in this line of questioning, he turned his attention to the milker communication sheet on which a frustrated worker of mine had written that he had beaten balky cows. Which never happened. But it seemed that Will was going to blame cow hysteria not on current, but on animal abuse by my employees.

"The comment made," Will said, looking at the communication sheet and then reading from it (Exhibit 1743), "was this: 'We had to milk—we had to milk again. No fucking notice. So the fucking cows got a good beating because they pissed us off.' Correct?" he asked, showing the sheet to Dr. Johnson.

"That's what it says," Dr. Johnson answered.

"And the milkers identified themselves as 'fuck this' and 'fuck that,' correct?"

"At least they're not initials," Dr. Johnson said, and the entire courtroom burst out laughing.

"And," Will continued, not cracking a smile, "they added the comment, 'Next time we want notice.'"

"I guess they hated to milk twice in a row." He meant working a double shift.

"And, Dr. Johnson, you don't know if they got adequate notice about the next time they had to milk, do you?"

"I've never met either one of these milkers, 'fuck this,' or 'fuck that,' so I wouldn't be able to answer," the doctor said dryly.

The courtroom roared.

"So," Will went on, his faced pinched like he needed a laxative, "you don't know if the milkers beat the cows next time because they were upset for not getting adequate notice, do you?"

Hammarback objected to the question as being argumentative and McKay sustained him. So, Will tried a different tack.

"Dr. Johnson, you consider the design of the free-stalls in Mr. Allen's barn, to use the words you used in your deposition, to be pretty shitty. Don't you?"

The doctor grinned. "You sure seem to be doing a lot of swearing," he told the lawyer.

"I apologize," Will said, red-faced, and the jury burst out in laughter again. "All my swearing has been in quotes, though." Then he quickly changed the subject.

"Dr. Johnson, you testified about differential diagnosis. And the idea was to take every limiting factor on a farm and rule them out to see what was holding the herd back, right?"

"Tried to, yes."

"Milk quality is another one of your factors besides housing and cow comfort, isn't it? And a key component is the milking practices followed by the milker, right?"

"Yes, sir."

"Another item is nutrition, right? You didn't see any rations from before the fall of 1997, did you?"

Dr. Johnson shook his head. "I only looked at rations prior to and after isolation."

"You think nutrition is a matter of art rather than science?" Will ambled over to the jury box, looked at the jurors, and then turned back toward the witness.

"A lot of it, sure."

"You don't know Steve Root, do you?"

"Not personally. I don't think he's the nutritionist for any of the people that I work for."

For a moment, Will stared silently at the doctor. I got the strange feeling something was going on under the surface but had no idea what it might be. I turned to Dan Murray and whispered, "What's up?" Dan simply shrugged.

"You testified," Will said, "that you were impressed with the quality of the people that worked for Mr. Allen."

"When I was there, yes."

There was a pause. "Did Russ Allen tell you that within the last month, his head milker pled guilty to reckless homicide?"

Hammarback immediately jumped up and requested a bench conference. The spectators were buzzing and it seemed bedlam might erupt in the courtroom. McKay ordered the jury out. When they were gone Hammarback demanded that the question be stricken from the record. He also demanded a mistrial, which the judge refused to grant.

What had happened was this: My head milker, Sergio, a Mexican who'd been my employee for about two years, had, along with two others, beaten a man to death. When I learned of it, I was dumbfounded, as Sergio had always been polite and quiet and was a conscientious worker. Evidently, there was bad blood, some sort of vendetta or family feud going on. After a night of heavy drinking the three had offered the victim, also Mexican and a drunk, a ride home from a bar. They drove to a desolate spot, dragged him from the car and beat his head in with baseball bats. By mentioning this, Will was looking to refute Dr. Johnson's claim that my workers were excellent. He wanted to portray them as brute savages responsible for abusing the herd, causing cow misbehavior and lack of milk production. His contention, as he told McKay during the bench conference, was that a man capable of murder with a baseball bat was quite capable of animal cruelty. The ploy worried me because, while untrue, it had a certain plausibility.

"If this were a vehicular homicide," Will argued to the judge, "it may not be pertinent. But given the nature of this homicide, it is pertinent. A person capable of doing that to a human being would certainly be capable of hurting cows. That's an issue, whether these cows were mistreated in 1997 or at any other time affecting the performance and health of the herd. It is relevant, and whatever prejudice Mr. Hammarback may feel it's going to present, it does not override the materiality of the testimony."\

The judge opened his hands and invited Hammarback to respond.

Hammarback said to him very deliberately, "I've been practicing law quite a while in Wisconsin, and I consider even the thought of this type of testimony as being outrageous. Furthermore, in light of the Court's pretrial order that such types of conduct be screened before presentation to the jury, it goes directly against the order in this specific case."

Will then made a counterargument that the issue for him was Dr. Johnson's assertion about the exemplary character of my employees, and the question of what type of information (or misinformation) I was feeding the doctor. This sent a nervous shiver down my back. I wondered if the entire case might hinge on this point.

Judge McKay hedged his bets and split the difference. Rejecting Hammarback's motion for a mistrial, he agreed with Will that Dr. Johnson's reliance on labor/management issues as part of his differential diagnosis left him open to questions about the character of my staff. He then decided to strike the inflammatory question and would instruct the jury to disregard it.

"I think," the judge told Will, "there is an area of inquiry which is appropriate. I don't think it's necessary for dramatics. You can make your point, I'm sure you know how, without referring to the homicide. A homicide of a human being and the manner in which cows are treated are far apart."

Will protested, but it was too late. Just before McKay ordered the jury brought back in, there was a short break. When I returned to the courtroom, I caught Will and his co-counsel laughing that they got the damning evidence in. They knew it would be hard to erase from the jurors' minds.

Dr. Johnson resumed his place on the witness stand. Will began revisiting areas of the doctor's differential diagnosis, arguing briefly with him about small points from his direct questioning by Hammarback. It seemed to me that Will's idea was to challenge and try to chip away at many of the doctor's conclusions about the electrical problem on my farm, to create numerous small points of doubt in the jury's mind as to the actual source of the problem, all of which would add up to one big doubt. It wasn't a bad strategy for a defense attorney who did not need to prove anything; all he had to do was create enough uncertainty to prevent them from finding in my favor.

"Dr. Johnson, there's something called 'on-farm stray voltage,' right? That's caused by the electric system that the farmer's responsible for, right? And then there's off-farm stray voltage, the kind that comes from the distribution line, right?"

"Yes, sir."

"You don't know whether that entire measurement Larry Neubauer made was caused by on-farm stray voltage, do you?"

The doctor admitted he did not know, and I squirmed on my bench. Will was scoring.

"Dr. Johnson, the only conduct of cows on the Allen farm that you attribute to stray voltage was that you thought the cows weren't comfortable going in, or while in the parlor while you were there, right?"

"Yes."

"You never saw the cows lap water, right?"

"No, sir."

"And you don't recall them being steppy when you saw them in December of 2001, do you?"

"I do not recall that," Dr. Johnson said.

"So the bottom line is," you've never seen the cows appear steppy on his farm, have you?"

Dr. Johnson pushed out his lower lip. "All experts have that problem."

"So the answer to my question is, no, you've never seen them act steppy?"

"That is correct."

Will wanted to know whether the doctor thought a cow could feel less than one milliamp of current, and did he always use a 500 ohm resistor to replicate the animal when testing at farms. Dr. Johnson explained that the literature on the subject suggested this. Will next tried to show that the udder doctor was behind the times when it came to contemporary thinking on the subject, as demonstrated in the Public Service Commission's raising of the level of concern.

"You consider yourself one of the few people who refuse to change your view of what the appropriate level of concern is, don't you?" Will said.

Dr. Johnson smiled. "Yes, sir," he said. "Until the cows show me something different, that's exactly where I'm going to stay."

"Well, by not changing your level of concern, you've been able to preserve your expert witness cash flow, haven't you?"

"Yeah," the doctor said with sarcasm. "If you consider my cash flow significant. My yearly income is a tenth—less than 20 percent of what your expert charged just in one case. So that's ridiculous. My percentage—is minimal. I don't enjoy these cases," Dr. Johnson said. "I turn down more than I take, and the bottom line is, we have a problem in the dairy industry that you people spend millions—"

"Your Honor—" Will interrupted, unhappy about the accusation the good doctor was about to hurl at WPS.

"—trying to fight," Dr. Johnson finished.

"Your Honor, I move to strike the answer as nonresponsive!"

Hammarback now chimed in. "I think it's responsive."

Behind me, I could hear a number of spectators chattering. They too seemed to be hoping for fireworks.

"I think," Dr. Johnson added, before Will could get in a word, "it's *very* responsive to your question."

"Next question," Judge McKay said, indicating agreement.

Will's face reddened. "I do move to strike the last portion of his answer!"

McKay peered down from the Olympian heights of his bench. "I'll strike the editorial comment, not the answer itself."

This seemed to satisfy Will and he quickly moved on. "Earth currents aren't new, are they Dr. Johnson?"

"Been there a long time, but we're learning more about them as time goes forward."

"Wisconsin has had a multi-grounded distribution system for over 50 years, hasn't it?"

"Unfortunately, yes."

"The only thing new is that vets like you who have refused to change your level of concern have encouraged farmers to bring lawsuits, right?"

"Completely argumentative, Your Honor," Hammarback interjected.

"Am I allowed to answer?" Dr. Johnson asked McKay, and I knew from his tone that, if allowed to respond, he was going to tear into Will. Will may have sensed it too because he left the vicinity of the witness stand and scooted over to the jury box. Maybe he figured there was safety in numbers.

"Not yet," the judge told Dr. Johnson.

"You're charging $200 per hour for your testimony here today, aren't you, Dr. Johnson?"

The doctor looked him in the eye. "Yes, sir."

"Now, you don't know how much Russ Allen paid Larry Neubauer for things Mr. Neubauer has done that's purportedly limiting adverse electric currents on his farm, do you?"

"I don't really care," the doctor said.

"You've never calculated conception rates for the Allen farm, have you?"

The doctor drew a long, deep breath of impatience. "I did not."

"It takes a long time to review all those vet records, doesn't it?"

"Yes, it does."

"Takes a long time to do analysis of vet records, doesn't it, Dr. Johnson?"

"Yes, it does."

"And it takes a long time to analyze milk production records, doesn't it?"

The doctor clucked his tongue. "You already asked that two questions ago."

"No," Will said. "My question now is, it takes a long time to analyze—"

"That's exactly what you asked two questions ago," Dr. Johnson reiterated.

"Let's not argue about it," Judge McKay growled. "If your answer is the same just say your answer is the same."

"You left that work," Will said accusingly, "to be done by Dr. Mellenberger, didn't you?"

"No," Dr. Johnson shot back, "I left that to other people. As I said in my deposition, other people were looking at that. I did not see a need to duplicate efforts."

"Dr. Johnson, BVD is not caused by earth currents, is it?"

"Not that I'm aware of."

"And Johne's disease is not caused by earth currents, is it?"

"Not that I'm aware of."

"And milk fever is not caused by earth currents, is it?"

"That's correct."

"Dr. Johnson," Will intoned, smiling wanly, "you're not aware of any scientific research that associates acidosis with electric current, are you?"

"Not that I'm aware of."

"And you're not aware of any scientific literature that associates laminitis with electric current, are you?"

"Not that I'm aware of."

"Dr. Johnson, do you have an opinion as to when Russ Allen's herd first became adversely affected by electricity?"

"An estimate based on the records, it was several years prior to isolation. But I can't give you a start date."

"Did I ask you that question on the day of your deposition April 17, 2003?"

"Yes."

"And did you tell the truth on April 17, 2003?"

"Based on the material I had at that point in time, absolutely."

"Now, Dr. Johnson, you've had an opportunity to meet with Mr. Hammarback since April 17, 2003, haven't you?"

"Yes," Dr. Johnson said.

"And you knew that unless you changed your testimony it was likely that the Court was not going to permit Mr. Allen to recover any damages for any time period before 1997, the time the isolator was installed. Didn't you?"

Dr. Johnson glowered. "No, I did not."

"Can you narrow your visit to that certain farmer you mentioned in the deposition who had cut his grounds down any closer than in the last ten years?"

"No, I can't. Like I said in the deposition. Sometime in the last ten years."

"Do you at least remember his name?"

Dr. Johnson sighed loudly, blowing air out his nose like a bellows. "If I could narrow it down to the exact time and date, I could remember the damn farmer's name!

"Your memory fails you, is that what you're saying?"

"If I could tell you it was one and a half years ago in June of 2001, I would tell you that. I go to so many farms, more than probably any other dairy consultant you will ever run into. I can't remember. I'm just telling you what I can recall. If you would like —I thought it was unethical for a lawyer to answer my questions, but if you want to go there, from now on I will ask you, Kurt, what you would like for an answer. I've done the best I can. I am not trying to hold anything back. I just flat-ass don't know the exact date!"

"I didn't ask you the exact date, Dr. Johnson!" Will sprang up out of his chair, head low and arms outstretched, looking for all the world like he intended to dive across the table into the udder doctor and ram him like a tackling dummy.

Dr. Johnson clearly read the movement that way. Bug-eyed, prepared to defend himself, the doctor vaulted up. I thought the two would collide like Sumo wrestlers, right in front of the stunned court reporter.

"Come on, mister!" Dr. Johnson roared, goading him on. "Don't you treat me unprofessionally. Don't you dare get up like you were going to attack me! Or, I'll flatten your ass!"

The readiness to rumble shown by the normally genial doctor stopped Will dead in his tracks. He whined, "I move to strike. I did not get up!"

"You did, too!" Dr. Johnson yelled, assuming the stance of a fighting cock with his legs apart and his chest thrust forward.

"Record should reflect he started to get up," Hammarback said to the stenographers.

"Yes, he did!" Dr. Johnson hollered.

"I take exception to that," Will said prissily. "I did not start to get up out of my chair!"

"You did too, you threatened me!" Dr. Johnson bellowed. "You don't like the answers, don't you dare threaten me again. If you come out of that chair next time—you have been warned. I have the court reporter as a witness, three other people here. I will deck you if you attack me again."

"I move to strike Dr. Johnson's entire response as being nonresponsive," Will griped.

"You have gotten an answer," the doctor snapped.

"You can't narrow the time span down?"

"No, I can't." The doctor nearly spit the words out. "Would you like to put in a number?

"Are you that unethical? Pick a number between one and ten."

Everybody laughed except Will. He paused, stepped away from the jurors, and went over near Judge McKay. "Your Honor," he said, "I have no further questions."

And so Dr. Johnson ended pretty much where he'd begun, by reminding the jury that when it came to cows reacting to current, the proof of the pudding was in its taste, not in the recipe ingredients. In my opinion, Dr. Johnson had testified effectively and built a very strong foundation for me. It didn't seem that Will had laid a glove on him in the cross. If that was the best Will could do, I felt a growing confidence that we were in good shape. But then again, what I felt didn't matter. All that mattered was what those twelve folks in the jury box felt, and that I would not know until well after the fact.

As it was late afternoon, Judge J.D. McKay adjourned for the day. As I lay down in bed that night, I could only pray that the rest of my witnesses would testify even half as well as Dr. Johnson had. And that included me.

CHAPTER 8

MIKE BEHR

M ike Behr was an agricultural economist and the man who had calculated my damages. He was sixtyish and very fit, a handsome six-footer with short, sandy-gray hair and a deep, melodious voice. He was going to be raked over the coals by the defense, but for now, Hammarback had him on direct. The doctor began by explaining that he was a forensic economist, one who determines a likely course of economic events under varying circumstances, such as what my production would have been but for stray current. He had two master's degrees in economics and a PhD in agriculture. He had grown up on a farm in Minnesota, taught college economics in Duluth, and later emigrated to Wisconsin, where he taught business and economics at the university in Superior from 1969 to 1983. After that, he had opened his practice as a full-time forensic economist.

Hammarback began by asking him about the types of matters that fell under his domain. "The bread and butter of this business," Dr. Behr said in a twangy, Minnesota accent, "has been personal injury and wrongful death cases where persons have to take lesser employment...determine what the loss is there. Beyond that, most of the work is where small businesses have been disrupted in one way or another. Most of that has been farm business, such as here."

He mentioned that he'd evaluated some 1,400 separate agricultural losses of one kind or another, and had received a great deal of insight into farm problems as a result. He reeled off an impressive list of organizations to which he belonged: American Agricultural Economics Association, American Law and Economics Association, International Atlantic Economic Association, American Statistical Association, American College of Forensic Examiners. From each of these bodies, he had received prestigious fellowships.

Dr. Behr explained why he had been summoned by Hammarback to my farm. "To determine the amount of damage, economic loss, associated with the presence of stray voltage," he told the courtroom.

Hammarback rose from his counsel and slowly made his way toward the jury. "How do you go about figuring damages on a dairy farm?" he asked.

"The manner is the same," Dr. Behr said, "whether it's a dairy farm or someone injured in an auto accident. It is to compare the resources in monetary terms that were preserved after the injury or event and compare that value with the probable value that the person or business would have produced without the injury or damage. The difference between the two—the actual and the normal—is the amount of damage; There's no other way to do it."

Hammarback nodded. "Dr. Behr, what information did you gather to perform your analysis of the Allen farm?"

"First, information about what actually happened, the presence of damage; Second, information about the economic environment of the farm—that is, what similar farms are doing, by which we evaluate what the Allen farm could have expected to accomplish without stray voltage. The sources of information are twofold: Farm budgeting—data compiled by universities in agricultural parts of the country where farms send in their records for analysis, whether it's hogs or cattle, and what can be expected by way of profits. The secondary category is statistics—price information on products used in farming, which is from the US Department of Agriculture. The third category is people of various types. A farmer would provide some information, and others associated with operation over the years such as veterinarians, electricians and dairy scientists. That pretty well sums up the types of information that go into the mix."

"We've got Exhibit 1010 here," Hammarback said. "Explain what that is."

"That's a chart," Dr. Behr responded, "constructed from data in my report. The yellow area is a measure of milk production per cows, called 'rolling herd average.' The darker black line also measures milk production per cow, but month to month as opposed to year to year. The straight line is a trend of milk production per cow by year for the state of Wisconsin. The upper line is the normal trend, 'normal' defined as probable conditions on the farm without damage. So I'm saying the upper line is my opinion about the probable milk production on that farm without stray voltage."

Hammarback paused, allowing the jurors to digest the information on the graph. Then he said, "Dr. Behr, taking into account your experience, training and expertise in agricultural losses, and taking into account the information you worked with on the Allen farm—assuming stray electricity affected animals on the Allen farm from 1976 to the present—do you have an opinion to a reasonable degree of certainty as to whether or not the Allen farm sustained economic damage?"

"I do."

"What is that opinion?"

"It is that it did."

"And based on your evaluation, do you have an opinion to a reasonable degree of certainty as to the total amount of those damages, leading to the present any effects that inflation may have had?"

The doctor looked straight at Hammarback. "Yes. I do."

"And what is that opinion?"

"That amount is $11,043, 387."

"In today's dollars?" Hammarback asked.

"That amount," the doctor said to him, "would be $13,870, 967.

"What types of things does a dairy farm produce, Dr. Behr?"

Dr. Behr folded his hands together in front of his chest. "My approach is to view a dairy farm—a dairy enterprise—as producing three things. Milk, of course. It also produces beef in the form of milk cows that get turned into hamburgers when they no longer give enough milk. And the third thing the farm produces is other dairy animals: Heifers who replace the culled cows when they're sold, and usually in numbers that exceed the number of cull cows so there will be extra heifers to either increase the herd or to sell to other dairies."

"When you did your analysis, were there losses in these categories?"

"Yes."

"Would you explain to us what a trend line is?"

Dr. Behr shifted in his seat and crossed his left leg over his right. I noticed that his black wing-tip shoes were polished to a high gloss. "A trend line in the case of the Wisconsin state average is calculated by a procedure called regression, which computers do easily, and takes values year by year and calculates a general relationship between them giving an overall picture."

Hammarback leaned back against the front rail of the jury box. "In your opinion as an economist, is it fair to compare a trend line with actual production?"

"Sure."

"On your report, once you've gathered all the information

about what the farm has produced historically, what is the next step in milk loss analysis?"

"To determine what the production would have been without the damage, and this goes to the normal trend. My understanding that the events that relate to the onset of the issues here go back to 1976, when there were electrical installations. I did not start the damages directly in 1976."

"And why not?" Hammarback asked him.

The doctor shrugged. "I give the cows a couple of years to adjust to the new situation. So, I waited until 1978 where the cows dropped, came back up, could not keep going, dropped some more. At the second drop I started calculating damages. The point is that the normal trend line says production is going up at 100 pounds per month per cow, 1200 pounds per year per cow. The reason I picked 100 pounds is that although it varies from farm to farm, about a hundred pounds per cow is a good average."

"I have no further questions, You Honor," Hammarback said as he sat dawn.

Judge McKay nodded toward the defense table. "Cross-examine, Mr. Will?"

"Certainly, Your Honor," Will rose and walked slowly toward the witness box, tall and elegant in his navy-blue suit and Gucci loafers.

"Dr. Behr, I want to ask a few questions about your background because that's where the examination started," Will began. "First of all, you have one PhD, not two?"

"Right."

"And you're not a veterinarian, right?"

"No, I'm not."

"Not a biologist?"

"No, I'm not."

"Not an electrical engineer?"

"No, I'm not."

"You're not trained in dairy housing?" Will asked.

"I'm not."

"Or animal behavior?"

"No, sir" the doctor confessed.

"Or an animal reproductive expert?"

"No, sir."

"You've described what you've done in this case as acting as a forensic economist, is that right?"

"That's correct."

"And you've defined that as someone who makes a living testifying in litigation. Fair?"

The doctor smiled. "I don't think I included, quote, 'making a living' doing it. But some people do, and some do it on a lesser basis."

"Since you're still here body and soul," Trevor Will told him, stone-faced, "I guess you're making a living at it. Fair?"

"I guess so," Dr. Behr conceded.

"Now, you don't have a degree in forensic economics, correct? You're not aware of any school that offers a degree in forensic economics, are you?"

Dr. Behr shook his head. "I'm not sure there is, although some courses are offered in this the last few years."

"In fact," Will said, "anybody who's an economist can call themselves a forensic economist, correct?"

"I suppose," the doctor said.

"There isn't any test you have to pass? And no state licensing or regulations?"

"No," the doctor said.

"In fact," Will said pointedly, sliding over toward the jury, "there isn't even a continuing education requirement, is there?"

"No."

"You said you're the only full-time self-employed forensic economist that you know of. You draw a distinction between academic economists and forensic economists, correct? Isn't there a difference?"

"It's different, sure."

"And what you define as an academic economist is somebody who typically has an appointment at a university or other institution, teaches or does research. And a forensic economists' work is also done by academic economists, in their spare time, outside normal hours. Fair?"

"That's the way I got started, right," Dr. Behr agreed.

"You mentioned you did more than 1,400 cases, correct? And isn't it true that more than 95 percent of the cases are for the plaintiffs or the claimant?"

"For the claimant, yes. Without regard to the legal configuration, yes."

Will smiled at the jurors. "Basically, the person is trying to get money?"

"You could say that."

"And in the stray voltage area, you've been hired to work on over 350 cases, haven't you?"

"Yes," the doctor said.

"All but one was brought by the farmer, right?"

"Yes."

Will nodded several times. Then he turned again and faced the jurors. "You've been hired for over 100 cases by Mr. Hammarback and his law firm, correct?"

"That's correct."

"I'm not getting any younger." Hammarback broke in.

This lightheartedness annoyed Trevor Will. "Maybe I would ask Mr. Hammarback to discontinue editorial comments because I didn't do that during your examination," he said sourly.

Grinning, Hammarback apologized.

"You estimate," Will said to Dr. Behr, "that about two-thirds of your income is from testifying in stray voltage cases. And you typically spend about 1,750 hours a year providing professional services?"

"You're probably reading off my deposition, and that's fine. It sounds reasonable."

"That would mean," Will said, "that you're spending around 1,200 hours a year on stray voltage, fair? You went out to the Allen farm in September of 2000, and at that time there was not a lawsuit filed, correct?"

"That's correct."

"You were at the farm for about five hours. And the only person you remembered talking to, for anything substantive, is Russ Allen, right?"

"Right," Dr. Behr affirmed.

"And you didn't tour the facility?" Will asked.

"Correct."

"Didn't take any feed samples?"

"Correct."

"Didn't observe milking?"

"Correct."

"Didn't see any cell count testing or data?"

"I probably did, but did not make any particular note of it."

"Didn't inspect cropping operations or observe field hands, right?"

"That's right."

"Didn't review any electrical measurements?"

Dr. Behr shook his head. "I don't believe so."

Trevor Will turned to face him. "The place where you were for most of these five hours was at the kitchen table in the home, correct?"

"Yes."

"And you were—you were basically going through records that Mr. Allen had assembled for you to review?" he said in a skeptical tone.

"Yes."

"Now, you are of the opinion that the three most common causes of dairy farm damages in Wisconsin are

Smith harvesters, milking equipment and stray voltage. Correct?"

"That's correct."

Trevor Will spread his arms theatrically. "And yet when you went to the Allen farm, you didn't even ask to inspect the milking equipment?"

"That's correct."

Trevor Will shook his head slowly and somberly, as if in disappointment. "And you didn't even realize there was a Smith harvester on the premises, did you?"

"I don't know," the doctor replied. "But if that's what I said in my deposition, I guess that's true. I know they're not a big issue in this case."

Again, Will shook his head incredulously. "You didn't even remember that Mr. Allen had one. Is that fair?"

"That's very possible," the doctor told him.

"All right," Will said. "When I asked you at your deposition, you weren't even able to describe his barn, correct?"

The doctor smiled. "Well, I was not in it."

"And," Will said accusingly, "you also told me that your conclusions in this case would have been no different even if you had never gone to the farm! Correct?"

"Certainly, at that point. Probably even as I sit here today," Dr. Behr said forthrightly.

"At that point," Will said, "you had already identified 1978 as the time at which you would start damage calculations, correct?"

"At least tentatively so, yes."

Once more Will struck a pose of disappointment. "Even though you hadn't spoken to any other experts?"

"That's correct," Dr. Behr replied.

Will paused for several moments. "Doctor, in the stray voltage work you do, often there is an electrical event involved such as isolation, correct?"

"That's often the case."

"And then what you do is look at production data that precedes the date of isolation?"

"Among a lot of other things, that's correct."

"What you look at is the production graph, for an area in time where either production fell or stopped rising at the rate it had been. Is that fair?"

"Those kinds of things. Yes."

"And then you start damage calculations from that point?"

The doctor shook his head. "Not always, but the point is the cows talk to me."

"And so we're clear on the record," Will said, "you don't speak Holstein?"

This caused a ripple of laughter.

"No. But I speak milk production."

"It's your view, isn't it," he said, "that starting in the late '70s there was a widespread stray voltage problem in Wisconsin and the Midwest?"

"Again," the doctor said, "there is a strong tendency of what the cows are saying. These problems began in the very late '70s, absolutely without question."

Will stared at him. "At your deposition, you said you could have started it in 1980 or 1976. You picked 1978, in the middle; you thought that was fair?"

"Based on what I just said in the late 1970s, probably so."

"But that was done," Will said, "without going out and doing any kind of analysis of what was going on at the farm in the 1980s or 1970s. Not at vet records, cow comfort, milking routines, et cetera. Correct?"

"In general, correct," Dr. Behr answered.

"Well," Will said, "if we simply 'listened to the cows' as you put it, one could look at the production graph and say, well, maybe it was here they were telling—in 1985, they were telling me stray voltage cropped up, correct?"

"You say 'maybe,'" the doctor told him. "And that's the question. I would still not select that point for reasons I have not had the opportunity to explain."

"Now, in your analysis of the Allen materials, you were primarily interested in the milk check records, correct?"

"I would say so. Yes."

"There were periods of time for which Mr. Allen did not have records that told how many cows were on the farm?" Will asked.

"That's correct."

"And that's part of where you and Dr. Mellenberger, my expert, had a disagreement about cow numbers. But the problem is, if you don't have actual cow numbers, you have to estimate or approximate them. And you went about it one way and he in a different way. You went about it by saying," and here Will again turned accusatory, "if I know the beginning and ending number of cows, you would approximate the intermediate numbers?"

The doctor replied defiantly. "That's true. I might make some adjustment beyond a linear progression based on large changes in milk sales at a given point. But generally, you are correct."

"Now, it's true, isn't it, Dr. Behr, that because you don't delve into some other farm records, you have missed important data?"

Dr. Behr opened both hands, palms facing upward. He shrugged. "That's possible."

"In fact," Will said with the harshness of an inquisitor discovering a new heresy, "there was one case where you missed—"

This brought Hammarback up out of his chair, and not a moment too soon. "I object," he said, "to what may have happened in other cases."

Judge McKay called for an off-the-record bench conference, from which Trevor Will returned duly warned. He remained standing near the witness box but seemed more slow and careful in framing his questions.

"Dr. Behr," he said, "you have missed data that indicated how much milk was being produced in a particular instance. Fair, in one case?"

The doctor looked at him with raised eyebrows. "Well, I don't know. I don't know what you're talking about."

"Do you remember a case where the son of the farmer was—"

"Your Honor," Hammarback interjected without rising.

"Right," McKay instructed Will, "Without going into specifics—and if the doctor doesn't remember, just go on to another question along the lines."

Will's brow furrowed. "Perhaps I have a way of refreshing his recollection, because we discussed this in deposition. If I could show him the deposition it might refresh his recollection."

"As long," Judge McKay cautioned him, "as you don't read it."

This whole exchange really bothered Hammarback. Will was looking to twist the rules. And that could only hurt me.

"I guess I object," Hammarback told McKay, and this time stood up to do it. He sounded impatient and annoyed. "I don't see how this is possibly relevant. He's admitted it's possible for him to miss something in a case, and where else are we going with this?"

"The problem," Judge McKay told Hammarback, "is that the witness hasn't specifically indicated that he misses things. If you're willing to stipulate there are times he does, then Mr. Will can go in a different direction."

"Absolutely," Trevor Will said.

"I think," Hammarback told the judge, "Dr. Behr is willing to admit it's possible that he could."

"Nobody's perfect," he said. "Including me. I don't dispute that. I'm sure I've missed something here or there, one time or another along the way."

"Would you be willing to agree," Will asked Behr, "that you've even missed how much milk was actually being produced on that unnamed farm?"

Dr. Behr chuckled. "Could be. I thought I knew when you started this what you were probably talking about. There's a good deal that can be said about that, but I'm not sure that's the right case."

"Doctor, is it fair to say that when you started on this project, your working hypothesis was that there was a stray voltage problem on the farm?"

"I'm going there with an open mind as to whether that is correct or not."

"You haven't tried to assess whether it's cow contact or earth currents or something else?" Will asked.

"No. Other people are better qualified."

"And you're not able to apportion—if you assume there was an on-farm electrical problem, you're not able to apportion any of these damages to that as opposed to some other electrical problem?"

This brought Hammarback up out of his seat with another objection. "That's assuming facts not in evidence, Your Honor. There's *no* evidence of any electrical on-farm problems."

"Well, Your Honor," Trevor Will said, "I disagree. Since—"

Judge McKay abruptly cut him off. "He's answered the question. The question and answer stand." McKay asked the court reporter if he'd gotten it straight; the reporter replied that he had. I felt McKay should've been doing a lot more of that kind of scotching of Will and Meckstroth all along.

"Would you agree," Will continued, "that in preparing the damage claim, the economist must exercise judgment?"

And then the obvious answer: "Sure."

"And the way in which that judgment is exercised can affect the damages result?"

"Sure."

"You told us in your deposition that you started as a full-time forensic economist in 1983, correct? You had been doing that for a little before that?"

"Yes," Dr. Behr said. "Beginning in 1978."

"And you were offering your services to lawyers at that point?"

"Yes."

"And in 1984 to 1985, you were in the process of building up your practice?"

"You could say that," the doctor told him. "Although prior to that time it was pretty well up to full speed during the last month I was at the university. But what you say is generally correct."

Will strolled over to the jurors and leaned against the center of the jury box, facing the witness. "There was an event—I don't want to get into the details—but an event in 1984 that caused a dip in your practice, correct?"

"You got that right," the doctor said with bitterness. Whether his bitterness stemmed from his memory of his divorce to his wife, Will's brass in bringing it up or both, I couldn't tell.

"And isn't it true," Will said to him, "that at that point you described yourself as a 'maximizer'?"

"Yes, I did," Dr. Behr said defiantly.

"And that was in a letter you wrote to an attorney with whom you were hoping to work?"

Dr. Behr shook his head vehemently. "No, not correct! That was in response to him having been on the opposite side of a case from me."

"So he was representing the opposition? And it was in that letter to him you described yourself as a maximizer?"

"That is correct."

"And isn't it also true, doctor, that the reference line in that letter is to your lottery ticket?"

Dr. Behr wrinkled his nose and snorted. "I've forgotten that. But I think that's correct."

"No further questions, Your Honor," Will headed back to his table, satisfied to have dented Dr. Behr's credibility.

CHAPTER 9

DOUG SUTTER

N ext up on the witness stand was Doug Sutter, an educated, articulate, and serious man. A former Brown County, Wisconsin, agricultural agent, Doug's main focus had been on applying university research on topics of importance to practical situations existing on farms throughout the state. He spent time holding public meetings, giving talks, and disseminating information about such things as barn lighting, bag silos, and mixing sites for calf feed.

Thirty-something and handsome, he was lean and fit, with sand-colored hair and light eyes. Aside from his warm and fuzzy personality, the thing I liked about Doug and what made him an important witness for me was that he was a disinterested, objective observer with a foot in two worlds: a university man and teacher as well as a farm boy and keen dairy farm observer. His testimony, I hoped and expected, would contradict some of the WPS expert testimony.

Dressed nattily in a light-gray, glen-plaid suit, with a white shirt and red silk tie, Hammarback opened, as he had with my other witnesses, by questioning Doug about his background and credentials, getting him to explain what the job of an agricultural agent entailed.

Doug smiled and adjusted the microphone in front of the witness chair as he settled in. "That would take a couple of days to fully explain. There's a lot of things. The overriding umbrella is that we're supposed to meet the needs of our clients. Primarily, that is farmers. But it could be a homeowner or somebody who owns land up north—anybody who wants information as it relates to agriculture."

"Do you have any interface with the university systems here in Wisconsin?" Hammarback asked.

"There are specialists we work with," Doug said. "Be it dairy, crops or other matters, there are specialists we work with for data."

"What's in your background," Hammarback asked, "that led you to this career as an agent?"

"My undergraduate degree was in agronomy. My master's was in integrated pest management."

"I'm born and raised on a dairy farm," Doug continued. "I worked for a consulting firm out of college, for a co-op after that, and was a tech rep for a company that produced organic fertilizers prior to coming here."

"The major area you list," Hammarback said to Doug, "is consulting regarding stray voltage, right?"

Doug affirmed this. Hammarback then wanted to know what particular areas of the stray voltage problem most concerned him.

"Initially, it was to try to resolve differences between what farmers are hearing from electricians, the utility and university research. More people would ask what I'd seen happen on other farms, to remove some of the grapevine rumor mill and have some verification of the reality of the situation."

"Would you say your role was primarily communication?"

Will objected to his "leading" the witness.

"What," Hammarback went on, "was the predominant issue

that arose with your work in stray voltage? Tell me what knowledge you gained."

Doug crossed his legs and adjusted his tie. "I was contacted by a farm with problems they couldn't identify anywhere else. Didn't appear nutrition-related, or cow-comfort-related, or—"

Will again, interrupted with an objection, and a bench conference took place. The interruptions were annoying. They made the testimony disjointed. But maybe that was the plan.

After the conference, Hammarback proceeded, "When was the first time you were on the Russ Allen farm?"

"I was hired in June of '95. That summer I visited the farm."

"What was the purpose of that visit?"

"Russ was interested in remodeling the old dairy barn, and I had brought a specialist up from Madison to look at it and give some ideas. Russ had picked up a parlor from the farm show in Green Bay and wanted to change a stanchion barn into a free-stall to accommodate cow comfort issues."

Hammarback circled the courtroom, moving slowly from the judge's bench over toward the jury box and back again. "Did you have an understanding of the reason for that modification?"

Doug nodded. "Better utilization of the facility made it more usable. It was a 'special needs' facility to support the main dairy."

"The next contact you had with Russ Allen?"

"By the next summer he had concerns with stray voltage. I got involved at that point as he was looking for a loan to pay the cost to have the farm isolated. I had to run a computer program that would make projections as to what a payback would be on that change."

Hammarback circled back toward the witness stand. "After Russ Allen found a
lender to loan him the money for the isolation transformer, did you have
another meeting on the farm?"

Doug nodded. "Prior to installation of the isolation transformer, there was a meeting at the facility. An electrician would have been there, the nutritionist, the veterinarian, a couple of people that worked there, and Russ himself."

"What was the purpose of the meeting?"

"To establish a team," Doug said. "This was a vested interest to get off their flat milk production. So everybody needed to be on the same page on what expectations were, and to establish goals."

"What's the term 'limiting factor'?"

"Something that would be in place," Doug replied, "that wouldn't allow

you to go to a higher level in the case of a milking cow."

"Give me," Hammarback said, "a practical example of a limiting factor on a dairy

herd."

Doug thought for a moment. "If you wanted 80 pounds of milk per cow per day and the ration was formulated to 60, the ration or the balancing of the ration was a limiting factor."

Hammarback nodded and went back over toward the jury. "Did you discuss the issue of limiting factors at that time with the folks at the meeting?"

Doug looked across the courtroom at Hammarback. "I don't know context, but everybody was asked, is there any reason we couldn't get up 75 pounds. Nobody felt, in their area, that they shouldn't be able to achieve that."

"What was your role at the meeting?"

"I was basically there for oversight. To document what had been going on—to track it through after isolation to see the response on the farm."

"Why was that?"

"Stray current was a hot topic. Quite a few people are concerned. I was getting calls from other farmers wanting some clarification, the agricultural agency, is supposed to serve as an unbiased third party. So I was trying to gather data and information, as other people were asking what was happening on a given farm, and to validate issues."

"And did you?" Hammarback asked.

"Yes. I did."

Hammarback nodded. "Did you follow up and go to the farm after isolation?"

"Yes."

"Now," Hammarback said, "before isolation, I think you made a videotape?"

"Correct," Doug told him.

"Upon Russ' request, I went through all the cows in one milking to videotape their feet, legs, hocks—just the condition of them."

"Before or after isolation?"

"Shortly before."

"I'll represent to you that the evidence in this case is that that tape is missing and cannot be found. Is that your understanding?"

"Right."

"What's your recollection regarding the condition of the hocks or what you actually saw?"

Doug sighed. "Cows get swollen up at what I guess is the equivalent of our knee. Certainly, there was swelling in the hocks on Russ Allen's animals."

"Anything you would consider surprising?"

As Hammarback and Doug discussed the cows' miserable condition, I again began to feel the sense of melancholy, of irreparable loss. Because even if the farm were to be restored to its former health tomorrow, that couldn't bring back my dead sisters, or baby Jesse, or erase the suffering and deaths of so many poor animals. I felt a lump in my throat and blinked back tears. I tried to concentrate harder on Doug's testimony.

"I would say," Doug told Hammarback, "there were more cows with swollen hocks than you would like in any given barn. That's a debilitating thing to a cow, where she can't get around."

"What about the behavior of the animals in the parlor?"

"Well, that wasn't the intent of the video, but there's another farm where kicking was an issue. So, that was something that came up. I would say there was a fair amount of dancing, what we call rocking back and forth as they're being milked. That was apparent."

"Based on your evaluation, what happened to the production of the Allen herd after isolation? Did you go out and verify production, with the records?"

"Yes. There was a straight-line increase the first six months, around 20 pounds. Then, over the next year or so, he picked up another 10 pounds per cow per day."

Hammarback thrust both hands into his pockets and came up near Doug. "After isolation occurred in December, did you make additional observations of the cattle?"

Doug nodded. "Water consumption became an issue. I did some visits to watch cows drink. Summer of 2002."

"In 2002," Hammarback said to Doug, "you looked at cows and water. Why?"

"Water consumption has always been a big issue on farms that suspect stray voltage. Cows are unable to drink the amount of water they want or need. I identified four farms that would be representative of high-production facilities, one of which was isolated, one of which was not, and two that were not or had been isolated but not responding, and Russ's facility, which was isolated, but not seeing high production continuously, had lost it. So, I wanted to look at how cows approached the drinking water. Do they go right up and drink? Did they stand there and just look around? Did they lap?"

"Did you make some of these observations on the Allen farm?"

"Yes."

"When?"

"Through the heat of summer—July, August."

"What did you see?"

"For the heat of summer, cows that would stand at the water and not drink, or put a nose down to the water and retract without drinking. As cows *would* drink, they would put their muzzles in the water, sucking in water—sounds like drinking through a straw. They'll stick their tongues out, and it's not lapping like a dog. They're testing the water, lapping."

They were getting ready for electric shocks, is what they were doing. Like Pavlov's dogs salivating to the sound of the metronome, my cattle had learned that drinking water brought pain. And so, they avoided it as much as possible. And got sick. And had to be shot. And died.

"You saw that at the Allen farm?"

Doug sighed and drew a deep breath. "I saw more standing around looking than I did lapping. If a cow is thirsty, she would go up and take her drink of water and go somewhere else, or lie down. Our rule of thumb is you like to see them either eating or laying around. The fact they're just standing at the water in the heat of the day is contrary to what you'd like to see."

"In your opinion, Mr. Sutter, was the installation of the isolation device in December of 1997 a substantial factor in the increased production?"

Will suddenly leaped up from behind his table with a protest. "Objection, Your Honor! There's no foundation that he knows anything about electricity."

McKay, as usual, sided with Will. "Mr. Hammarback, with regard to your question, I don't have a clue what he knows about electricity. I mean, there is no foundation for that question."

Hammarback turned to Doug, "Let me ask it this way: Assume there was testimony that the isolation device reduced ground current near the feed room. Based on your experience as an extension agent and your observations of the farm before and after verification of production records, do you have an opinion whether that decreased current caused the production to increase?"

Again, Will sprang up, breathing fire. "Objection, Your Honor! *Foundation*! Mr. Hammarback has not laid a *foundation* for the witness to render such an opinion. He's got a background in agronomy and pest control and his history consists of working with seed and fertilizer companies!"

McKay peered down at Will from the height of his bench and nodded sympathetically. "I understand your objection," he said in a soft voice.

Hammarback said, "This goes to weight, Your Honor."

McKay thought for a moment. Maybe realizing he had gone too far, he said, "Well, I'm going to allow him to answer based on the fact that the question was posed as a hypothetical, and to the extent of your knowledge, you can answer."

Doug glanced at McKay and then looked at Hammarback. "I would go back to my earlier statement: There was nothing else that happened on that farm that would have caused that production fluctuation. I can't tie it specifically to the feed room."

"Or to the ground?" Hammarback said.

"Your Honor, I object to Mr. Hammarback's question as leading and move to strike!"

Hammarback peered over at Will, grinned at him, and turned to the judge. "I described a hypothetical, Your Honor. He looked at the installation of the isolation system."

McKay shook his head. "I understand, but he's answered. Didn't you answer his question?" McKay said to Doug.

"I tried."

"Let me ask it to you this way, Mr. Sutter. In your experience as an extension agent and dairy farmer, and taking into account the actual evaluation you did both before and after isolation, and assuming the isolation reduced earth current on the Allen farm, do you have an opinion on whether or not the reduced current I'm asking you to assume caused an increase in production?"

Will bobbed up again. "Objection, Your Honor," he sputtered. "Asked and answered."

"Objection sustained," McKay said.

Hammarback went over near his counsel table, glanced at Will, and leaned against the table, facing Doug, with his back to the rows of spectators. "Is there a level of concern you used as an agricultural agent regarding electricity?" he asked.

Once more Will stood up and objected, claiming there was no foundation for the question. But this time McKay overruled him.

"I have a comfort level," Doug said sarcastically. "A zero. I mean I disagree with the current threshold that research would say is acceptable."

"Thank you, Mr. Sutter. No further questions," Hammarback finished his direct and

gave way to Will's cross-examination.

"Mr. Sutter," Will said, standing and walking up toward the witness box. "That summer, in 2002, when you went to the Allen farm, did you go inside the barn?"

"No."

"Hypothetically speaking, would you agree that if there was an excessive amount of ammonia inside the barn emanating from the pits beneath the slatted floor that could be a reason why cows would eat outside instead of inside?"

"There's probably some level of ammonia that would at some point drive a cow outside, yes," Doug said.

"And you don't know whether that level was present on the day you saw the cows eating outside, do you?"

"No, I do not," Doug said.

"When I took your deposition back in 2002, you made no mention of videotaping cow hocks and hooves, did you? And you didn't say you went down the line and looked at each individual cow, did you?"

"No."

"You taped milking for a couple of hours and weren't sure whether you taped even one complete milking, correct?"

"Not to say for certain, no."

"You concluded with respect to the cows' behavior there wasn't a major issue on Mr. Allen's farm, correct?"

Doug shrugged. "I don't know what it states in the deposition transcript but there was not excessive kicking on the day I was in there, no."

"And you told Mr. Allen that, didn't you?"

"I believe I did, yes."

"And he disagreed, right?"

"I don't know," Doug told him.

"He wanted the cows to stand firm while they were being milked?"

"Yes."

Will paused. "By the time you asked Mr. Allen that question about the whereabouts of the tape you had made, he had filed his lawsuit against WPS, right?"

"That's possible."

"And you had known that he filed the lawsuit, didn't you?"

"At the time of the deposition, I did, yes."

"You didn't press Mr. Allen at all about what he had done with the videotape, did you?"

Doug snorted. "Did I put him up against the wall and frisk him? I don't know..."

"You didn't even ask him who he loaned it to?" Will said incredulously.

"Probably not," Doug said.

Hammarback objected without rising. "Argumentative," he said. "And cumulative."

McKay sustained him.

Will sauntered over toward the jury box and stood several feet in front of it, facing the witness on an angle. "At the time I took your deposition in 2002, you didn't know whether Mr. Allen had a parlor camera or not, did you?"

"I get on a lot of farms," Doug said acidly. "I don't keep them all straight which ones have cameras and which ones don't."

But Will was nothing if not dogged. "When you learned that the videotape you made of Mr. Allen's cows had disappeared, you never thought to try to find out whether there were any parlor tapes available that would show the cows in the parlor?"

Doug chuckled. "Didn't know that it was an issue, no."

"Did you make notes pertaining to your observations on the Allen ranch?"

"No, I do not."

"Your observations lasted about an hour. You never counted the number of cows that drank water during that hour on Mr. Allen's farm, did you?"

"No, I did not," Doug told him.

"And you never counted the number of animals that seemed hesitant to drink water, did you?"

"No, I did not."

"And you never counted any number of animals that you believed lapped water?"

Hammarback stood up to object. "Cumulative," he said to McKay.

"Did you?" Will pressed Doug.

"I admit," Hammarback broke in and told the judge, "that they're very clever questions and they're all slightly different. But they're establishing the very same fact."

McKay held up a hand, palm outward, to Hammarback. "I'll allow him to answer the question," he said.

Doug said quietly, "There were no counts taken."

"You don't know whether it's natural for cows to lap water or not, do you?"

Doug grinned. "That's why I went to four farms. To try to establish some parameters."

. . .

"You don't do any electrical testing?" Will asked.

"I do not."

"Matter of fact," Will said, "you've made a point not to get involved in electrical testing, right?"

"That's correct."

"Because your background is crops?"

"Yes, that's correct."

"No one," Will said, "has ever told you that a cow contact measurement was made on Mr. Allen's farm that exceeded the Public Service Commission's level of concern, correct?"

"Correct," Doug told him.

"Mr. Sutter, did you not regularly receive from Mr. Allen production records for the farm? Production records which would be paper?"

"No."

"And you sometimes stopped by the farm and talked to Mr. Allen about milk production?"

"Correct."

"And Mr. Allen told you that his milk production increased after isolation, didn't he?"

"Correct."

"And he told you several times there were no management changes on the farm between the time of isolation and the time of his production increase, right? But you didn't play detective and try to verify anything he told you, did you?"

"I stated this before," he told Will, and I thought I could see smoke coming out of his ears. "I would go there when Russ wasn't there and talk to the employees. I didn't bird-dog every statement made, no, but there were times I did independent verifications."

"In fact," Will said in his best bully-boy voice, "you didn't play detective and try to verify *anything*, did you?"

"Your Honor," Hammarback said, "I don't think there's any statement in the record that he's ever played detective."

"I'm going to sustain the objection," the judge said.

"You didn't try to verify *anything*, did you?"

At this Hammarback sprang from his chair. "Objection, Your Honor! He's already been asked and answered that!"

McKay nodded. "Sustained. He's indicated, Mr. Will, that he had his own method of verification. That's what he's indicated."

"No, further questions, Your Honor," said Will as he finished his cross-examination, pleased with himself.

CHAPTER 10

DONALD ZIPSE

Donald Zipse, a straight-talking, no-nonsense, forensic electrical engineer who was brilliant, creative, and experienced, and who'd studied not only mine, but many others' problems with stray current, was taking the stand this morning. He was my biggest cannon of them all, a two-ton howitzer, and he was about to fire on my behalf.

Bespectacled and affable, a portly but dynamic 69-year-old, the top of his bald dome ringed by bushy hair on the sides, Don's direct testimony began with a summary of his background and qualifications, which were now up as Exhibit 1368.

"I started," Don said to Hammarback in his deep, clear baritone, "at Williamson Free School of Mechanical Trades in the power plant operation. From there I went to Atlas Chemical, which was previously called Atlas Power Company. They were bought out by ICI, and I worked for them as a senior electrical engineer."

"Did you design electrical systems at that company?" Hammarback asked.

"Not only come up with concepts, not only designed systems,

but ordered the equipment and oversaw construction and installation, participated in start-up of the projects."

"Since then what have you been doing?"

"I've had my own company, Zipse Electrical Engineering, an independent consulting company doing forensic work. I also sell time to a company called Discovery Systems."

"Do you investigate incidents involving electric shock as part of your consulting work?"

"I do. Zipse Electrical has been in business for approximately nine years."

Hammarback now went over to the jury box and took a turn at getting familiar with the jurors. "About how many incidents involving shock to living things have you investigated?"

"Over fifty."

"Do some involve cows?"

"They do."

"Would most of those incidents involve shock to humans?"

"Shock and electrocution," Don told him grimly. "Electrocution is death by electricity."

This menace is spreading steadily throughout the United States, metastasizing like a cancer. It's a new pollution, a new polio, a new plague. We're only just beginning to understand its deadliness."

"What's the National Fire Protection Association?"

"That association dates back to before the turn of the 20th century. It's an organization that includes firemen, fire chiefs, fire inspectors, people interested in fire protection. It also includes electrical inspectors and insurance personnel. I am a member."

"What's the National Electrical Code, and how does it relate to the National Fire Protection Association?"

"The Fire Association produces standards in the same way the IEEE does. The National Electrical Code is a standard that the

National Fire Protection Association administers. They're the secretary for it."

"Are you the author of a portion of an encyclopedia on electrical and electronics engineering?"

Don sat up straight in his chair. "I am, sir," he said proudly. "It is John Wiley, a large publishing firm. The volume I'm associated with is number eight. The editor is John G. Webster from the University of Wisconsin in Madison. Mr. Webster and his committee solicited my input for the grounding chapter. That chapter was peer-reviewed."

"Not to be modest, sir—are you an authority in that field?"

"I am, sir," Don replied.

"And what have you observed at the Allen farm during the course of your three visits?"

"I've driven the complete line from the substation, the total circuit."

"And have you discussed with Larry Neubauer, the master electrician, the work he's done on the farm? And reviewed the records of Wisconsin Public Service in this case, and the transcripts of witnesses both for WPS and Mr. Allen?"

"Yes, I have."

"Did you request that data be gathered on the single-phase portion of the distribution system in the vicinity of the Allen farm?"

"Yes."

"What data did you want and why?"

Don inched forward in the chair and adjusted the microphone. "The amount of current flowing out the line, the phase current. And the other reading I wanted was the amount of current coming back on the neutral, known as the multigrounded neutral. Current flowing out should equal the amount coming back. If it doesn't, that's an immediate, simple indication of the amount of stray current flowing over the earth uncontrolled." "And that's in evidence as Exhibit 1324," Hammarback said. "On 1324, can you

explain the graphs and traces and their significance to your inquiry?"

"Yes. As I mentioned, the primary current going out is in red, at a low of 5 amperes, and goes up to a peak of 19 amperes. This was on a little over a day and gives a good indication of the cycle. The blue chart or plot that you see is the amount of return current coming back on the neutral. I'm really interested in the red and blue. There is a difference: The amount of current flowing over the earth is the difference between the blue and red line."

Hammarback walked over near the jury box. "And what's the significance of that?" he asked.

"When I see something like this it immediately tells me there's a problem with current flowing over the earth."

Hammarback remained standing near the front of the jury box. "Were you able

to analyze how much is coming back compared to going out?"

"Approximately 70 percent of the current is flowing over the earth."

Don's answer was an eye-opener for the jury. A couple of them had to do a double take.

Hammarback was silent, allowing the courtroom to absorb this crucial piece of information. He then asked Don to explain the significance of the data on a new graph, Exhibit 1369. "This," Don said, "is the amount of stray current at any moment in time during the period that this was recorded, starting on April 30 at 9:32 a.m. and concluding on May 1 at 1:06 p.m. The amount of current flowing over earth ranges from approximately 3.5 amps up to 15 amps."

"Why do we see periodic ups and downs on the chart?" Hammarback asked.

"Well, that is the result of the amount of current being used by customers on the system beyond Mr. Allen's farm. As you can see, it occurs at approximately 6 p.m. on Wednesday and again at 6 a.m. or 7 a.m. on Thursday. And that is the time of milking, when the electrical load is at its maximum."

"Mr. Zipse, have you seen similar graphs of current versus time in WPS' records taken at any time?"

Don shook his head. "I don't recall seeing a plot."

"Would it be important for WPS to take such measurements near the Allen farm for any purpose?"

Don nodded rapidly and opened his eyes wide. "Very definitely. Because it's a quick way of determining the amount of stray current that's flowing uncontrolled over the earth."

"The wire on the WPS system to the east and south of the Allen farm," Hammarback said "What's the nature of that conductor?"

"The type of conductor is what's known as a No. 8 copper weld. That wire dates back to approximately 1935."

Hammarback again paused to allow the jury time to absorb this.

"Did that surprise you?" he asked.

"Yes. Copper weld has a tendency to deteriorate and has a higher resistance."

"What, if anything," Hammarback asked, "should WPS have done about that 70 percent of the current flowing over earth at the Allen farm?"

"There's several things they could've done," Don told him. "One would be to insert a transformer which would start a new system, in between transformers. The substation had a transformer, and this happens to be the end of the line, so that is a system, but they could have put a transformer at this location, on this pole. Would be what's known as a 'one-to-one transformer.' We would start a new electrical system, and instead of stray current flowing all the way across the Allen farm to the substation, the current would then flow back to that transformer."

"What effect would such an installation have on the percentage relationship of the phase and neutral current back at the farm, where Mr. Neubauer measured them?"

"It's my opinion it would reduce the stray current to a very, very small amount, because the only stray current would exist from the poles." He pointed out the various down grounds on the exhibit. "That would also go with this recommendation," Don continued. "That they change the conductor, use a semi-insulating conductor which is inexpensive, and the reason is to protect the line. It would not be grounded, so that would eliminate all those grounds there."

"Even if you left those grounds there," Hammarback said, "would such an installation improve the situation?"

"Yes," Don said.

"Is this costly?" Hammarback wanted to know.

"Not at all. It's one of the least costly solutions. The transformer itself is less than $2,000. I've estimated it would cost less than $10,000 to install, labor, et cetera. That's without installing new wire all over the system."

"Is the notion of ground currents being problematic anything new in the electrical industry?"

"Not at all."

Hammarback went to the table, picked up a document, walked over to the witness

and gave it to him. "Mr. Zipse, I've handed you Exhibit 1142. Tell us what that

document is, please?"

Don scanned it and said, "It's a United States Patent Office document entitled 'System Electrical Distribution.' It is specs forming part of a patent dated August 30, 1887."

"And who's the author of that patent?" Hammarback asked with a straight face.

"The author," Don said with a smile, "is Thomas A. Edison."

"Was he considered an expert in electrical distribution?" Hammarback asked, still

straight-faced.

McKay broke in here to say, "I'll recognize Thomas Edison for what he is."

"Objection, Your Honor," Will interrupted. "I'm not sure what the relevance of a patent from 150 years ago is, Judge."

Hammarback glanced over at Will and grinned. "I'll lay a little foundation, Your Honor," He said to McKay. "Mr. Zipse, how are these pages from the Edison patent relevant to the issue of current in the earth?"

"This discusses what should be done about current flowing in the earth. Now, the original patent for an electrical distribution system was in 1880. In the intervening seven years, Mr. Edison had a problem, and the patent talks about that problem. The problem was—"

"Objection, Your Honor. Relevance."

"Sustained," again, McKay sided with Will.

"Mr. Zipse, does the NESC have requirements with respect to inspection and tests of lines and equipment, and are they set forth on Exhibit 1370?" Hammarback asked.

"They are. There's five: 'Lines and equipment shall comply with safety rules; lines and equipment shall be inspected at intervals; shall be subjected to practical tests; any defects shall be recorded and maintained until the defects are corrected; lines and equipment with defects that endanger life or property shall be properly repaired, disconnected or isolated.'"

"Now," Hammarback said to him, and looked at the jury, "in your professional opinion, has Wisconsin Public Service Corporation complied with the requirements of Section 214 of the NESC with respect to the distribution system in the vicinity of the Allen farm?"

"No, sir," Don said loudly and clearly. "They have not. They have not complied with these requirements."

Hammarback waited. Then he said, "Do you hold that opinion to a reasonable degree of professional certainty, sir?"

Don looked him in the eye. "Oh, yes. I do."

"Mr. Zipse, do you have an opinion to a reasonable degree of professional certainty as to whether Wisconsin Public Service Corporation has been negligent in the operation and maintenance of its distribution line in the vicinity of the Allen farm?"

"Yes," Don said forcefully. "It has been. Yes."

Hammarback paused to let the jury digest the last remark. "Mr. Zipse, if a solution to the condition of the single-phase line past the Allen farm is not implemented, do you have an opinion to a reasonable degree of professional certainty as to whether Earth Current will continue to access Allen livestock housing facilities?"

"I do," Don told him. "It will continue until the line is repaired, changed, modified in some way to prevent stray current flowing over the earth in the vicinity of the Allen farm."

"I have no further questions, Your Honor," Hammarback said as he sat back down.

"Mr. Zipse, would you agree with me," Will asked Don, stepping up near the stand, one hand in his trouser pocket, "that for a dairy cow to be harmed by electricity, there must be current flowing through the cow?"

"That would be correct."

"If there's no current flowing through a cow, electricity, it will not cause the cow's milk production to decrease, correct?"

"Yes, sir."

"And if no stray current—a term you like to use—flows through the cow, the milk production will not be adversely affected by electricity, correct?"

"Correct."

"To determine if current is flowing through cows on the Allen farm due to earth currents, you take measurements, two points in the earth that the cow can touch simultaneously, correct?"

"Yes."

"One of the places is metal?"

"One of the places is a conductive surface, sir."

"And if," Will said, "you're trying to measure current flowing through a cow, you have to take into consideration the resistance of the cow, correct?"

"You do," Don told him.

"You have not taken any measurements on the Allen farm to determine how much current is flowing through the cows?"

"Correct."

"Let's talk about the multi-neutral distribution system. You understand that every

utility in Wisconsin has one, correct?"

"I understand that to be a fact," Don said.

"And you know that 49 of the 50 states in the US have exclusively or predominantly multi-grounded distribution systems? And since 1950 the multi-grounded system has been the predominant electrical distribution system in the United States, correct?"

"Unfortunately so," Don replied.

"You know it is an undisputable scientific fact that some current goes down a grounding wire that is connected both to a primary neutral and to a ground rod driven in the earth, correct?"

"That's correct, sir."

"And," Will went on, "it is an undisputable scientific fact that current flowing on the ground rod will then flow into the earth, correct?"

"Yes," Don said absently, as if to humor him.

"And that's what you call stray current, correct? And you believe the multi-grounded neutral distribution system itself is defective, don't you?"

"I certainly do," Don told him.

"And you believe it is always negligent for a utility in

Wisconsin to distribute electricity using a multi-ground neutral distribution system, correct?"

Don stared at him. "I certainly do from the information available in the public domain, sir."

"Because," Will said in a voice dripping with sarcasm, "that violates what you call 'Zipse's Law,' correct?"

"That's correct," Don said evenly.

"We have Ohm's Law," Will said, pacing slowly and continuing the sarcasm. "We have Newton's Law of Gravity. And you've named a law after yourself?"

"Yes, I have, sir."

"And so even if WPS operated and maintained its system near the Allen farm in a satisfactory manner, your position would still be that the multi-grounded neutral system is harming the cows. Correct?"

Don hesitated. "Well, sir, there is a possibility of having a multi-grounded neutral system where the current is at such low value that it is not harming cows—but that does *not* include the Wisconsin system."

"Now let me ask it again! Even if WPS operated and maintained its multi-grounded neutral distribution system in a satisfactory manner, your position would still be that it's harming the cows on the Allen farm. Correct?"

"I said that if it operated as elsewhere in the United States, that the amount of current would not be harming the Allen farm with a multi-grounded neutral distribution system."

Will shook his head and rolled his eyes. "Well, let me ask it differently. No matter what WPS did to the system in existence now, there is no way they can prevent stray current flowing over earth unless they remove all the grounds on their distribution system, correct?"

"The way you have rephrased, correct," Don told him.

"WPS is required to follow the law, correct?" Will said.

"Yes."

"And when there's a conflict between the laws of Wisconsin and the opinions of Donald Zipse, author of Zipse's Law, you know that WPS is required to follow the laws of

the state of Wisconsin and not your opinions. Correct?" Will asked in his most sarcastic and arrogant tone.

"Unfortunately, that is true," Don said.

"You believe the law—requiring a connection between the primary and secondary neutrals—is defective. That's the word you used at your deposition, correct?"

"Correct," Don said.

"You have never designed a utility distribution system, correct?"

"I have not," Don told him.

"You have never been a licensed engineer in the state of Wisconsin, correct?"

Don smiled at him. "That is correct."

"But for the purposes of this lawsuit, you think it's appropriate for you to term or declare Wisconsin law defective?"

"Not only Wisconsin, but the National Electrical Safety Code also," Don snorted.

"I'm going to ask about your five-wire system, one of your proposed solutions written on the chart over there by Mr. Hammarback."

Don held up a hand. "I object to you calling it my system. It's been in effect a long, long time. But I appreciate the compliment."

"What you aim to do," Will said, "is have 49 of 50 states switch from a multi grounded system to your proposed five-wire system?"

Don nodded. "Over a period of time. Just the way that a receptacle were to change from two poles to three."

Will shook his head theatrically and threw out his hands. "And you want 49 states to change over to this system, even though you have no idea how much it would cost?"

"As I said, it would be a period of many years, therefore cost would be a

nonissue."

"You are not aware of any utility that in the last 50 years has used the five-wire system of the type you are proposing?"

"Correct," Don said. "It is a uni-grounded system."

"Your five-wire system is what you call a 'ground conductor ground?' And that's in accordance with Zipse's Law, correct?"

"No continuous return current on it."

"So, now we know that in your opinion, Wisconsin law is defective and the NEC is defective, correct?" Will said, again sarcastically.

Don laughed. "That's correct! The NEC is revised every three years, and the reason is so that when we discover defects in the code, we can change the code and the public can act. We write a proposal to change the code. So, yes, the code is defective."

Will folded his arms and leaned with his back against the post of the jury box, facing toward the witness. "Now," he said, "you are aware that Mr. Allen has cut WPS grounding wires, correct?"

"Yes, I am."

"In fact, when WPS' lawyers faxed a letter to Mr. Lawrence stating that it was inappropriate and dangerous to cut grounding wires, you happened to be in Mr. Lawrence's office when the fax came through, correct?"

"That is correct."

"And you laughed at that part of the letter. Correct?"

"I don't know whether I laughed at that or not. Don't recall."

"Did you tell me at your deposition that you laughed?"

Don shrugged. "Doesn't sound like something I would say. But you can look it up if it will save you time. I accept that."

"And you *laughed* because you thought it was funny, because we didn't

know who was cutting the ground wires. But *you* did, correct?"

"No," Don said, leaning back away from the microphone. "If I laughed, it was because we were preparing an affidavit at the same time you sent in that fax. So I was probably laughing at the coincidence. I guess you had clairvoyance, knew we were preparing this affidavit and kind of cut us off at the corner."

"You assume it is illegal for somebody to cut utility ground wires?" Will asked.

"I can assume that."

"And yet you know that Mr. Neubauer cut grounding wires on WPS transformer poles, correct?"

"Sure, I was aware," Don told him.

Will walked over to his defense table, and looked at his pad for a moment. "I want to talk a little about this law of physics you've named after yourself, okay? You are a firm believer in Zipse's Law, correct?"

"I am, sir."

"And you think Zipse's Law is a fundamental law of physics?"

"It's a fundamental law of electrical distribution."

"You consider Zipse's Law as scientifically sound as Ohm's Law, correct?"

"For electrical distribution, I certainly do, sir."

"You agree your ideas on grounding requirements for utility distribution systems are outside the mainstream of electrical engineering?"

"At this point in time, yes."

"When I took your deposition in 2002, you told me that both the NESC and NEC had rejected all your ideas on changing grounding requirements, correct?"

"It took 21 years to get ranges and dryers, which are in everybody's homes, to be wired correctly. So, I expect it will take 21 years. And since I've been working about three years on this, I expect it will take another 18."

"You submitted to the NEC four to six new proposals relating to what you call 'stray current.' And these new proposals all related to what you call 'Zipse's Law'. And you consider Zipse's Law related to the issues in this lawsuit, correct?"

Don nodded several times. "Oh, I do. Yes."

"The NEC voted on your proposals in 2003. You made a proposal to Panel Five regarding your theory on Zipse's Law, correct? And between January 2003 and April 28, 2003, when I took your deposition, you could have called any member of the code-making panel to find out results of the vote, correct?"

"I was willing to wait until the publication was final, because the committee vote is not final until the document is published in July."

Will went up and handed Don a document. "I'm going to show you what's been marked as Exhibit 1738. Do you recognize it as an NEC test report prepared by the Edison Electric Institute, a member of the NEC?"

"Yes."

"This document," Will said, "sets forth your proposed changes to the NEC, correct? And in connection with those proposals, you submitted written substantiations, correct?"

"You have to."

"And the substantiation you submitted to the committee specifically refers to Zipse's Law, correct?"

"Yes, it does," Don said.

"And you know with this document in your hands," Will said, in full gloating mode, "what the vote of the committee was. Don't you?"

"It doesn't surprise me at all," Don said evenly.

"They rejected all five of your Zipse's Law proposals by a vote of 16 to nothing. Correct?"

"Yes," Don said. "That's correct."

"So, by a cumulative vote the NEC has voted on Zipse's Law and rejected it 80 to nothing. If we add up five votes of 16 to nothing, that equals 80, correct?" Will continued to gloat.

Don grinned. *"Liars can figure. And figures can lie."*

"No further questions, Your Honor."

Hammarback moved quickly to redirect as Will passed him on his way to the defense table.

"Mr. Zipse," Hammarback said, "you made reference in your deposition to three-pronged outlets in homes. Did the principles involved in three-pronged outlets on a 120-volt circuit in homes also relate to utility systems?"

"They do," Don told him. "In your home, you know, you have a three-pronged receptacle. That used to be a two-pole receptacle, and in the 1950s the NEC—which we've just been talking about—said it was safer if we had an equipment-grounding conductor. That's the green wire. The utilities have taken the two wires and twisted them together into one to save money and save installation cost. For the lineman's safety, it's required that it be grounded four times per mile so the voltage doesn't build up on that combination wire. I submitted a proposal to the NEC, in jest, to do just that for your home wiring, so they would realize the significance."

"Was one of your proposals to the code committees contained in Exhibit 1773 accepted?"

"Yes, sir."

"Mr. Zipse," Hammarback said to him, "are you on the NEC committee that writes Section 96 of the National Electrical Safety Code?"

"I am."

"And portions of that document are adopted in Wisconsin law?"

"Portions are," Don said.

"Mr. Zipse, with respect to Section 97 E-2 as adopted in Wisconsin, does that have to do with interconnection of neutrals between utility and customer on both grounded systems?"

"Yes, sir."

Hammarback looked over at the jurors and then slowly crossed the courtroom toward them. "Mr. Will asked you about your ideas on grounding being outside of the mainstream. In the city, in industrial applications, are your ideas out of the mainstream?"

"No, not at all," Don told him. "They've been used since 1950. That is the five-wire system."

"Mr. Zipse, given the electrical configuration of the systems at the Allen farm as of April 1997, have you seen any evidence indicating that the Allen farm wiring system was creating stray currents?"

"None at all," Don said to him.

"Mr. Zipse, who are the members of the grounding committee subsection of NESC who rejected your proposals? What industries do they come from?"

"The majority comes from the utility industry, sir."

"And has that been true generally during your 50 or so years on that committee?"

"That is correct," Don said.

"That's all I have," Hammarback said, letting Don's last answer reverberate through the courtroom.

CHAPTER 11

LARRY NEUBAUER

I figured that Foley and Lardner would do their damnedest to make a whipping boy out of Larry Neubauer. Larry was a crucial witness for me. He had spent more time on the farm helping me than anyone. Trevor Will indicated in his opening statement that Larry and I had conspired together to hatch this court case to get a big financial windfall out of WPS, so it was pretty clear that they intended to go after him hard.

Certainly, I'd never tried to hide the fact that I wanted a settlement to pay for all the damage they'd inflicted. That would be justice. But I also hoped the jury would decide that not only was WPS liable for monetary damages, but they must be forced to correct the deadly electrical menace so I could continue to run the family dairy business with a prospect of success. More than anything, I wanted the business to thrive.

This fine morning, Larry, a friend as well as an excellent electrician and idea man, was approaching the witness stand for his direct testimony. Looking like the proverbial Packer lineman—big and burly—Larry seemed ill at ease in his too-small blue sports jacket and crooked tie. And who could blame him? I felt exactly the same way about going up there, sitting in that fishbowl and testifying. If Larry felt nervous now, I could only imagine how he'd feel after Will started kicking him around.

Hammarback began by asking him about his occupation and background. An electrical contractor as well as a consultant, Larry held a master's license in Wisconsin as well as North and South Dakota, and a journeyman's license in Idaho. He'd started in the business in 1982, served a four-year apprenticeship through the International Brotherhood of Electrical Workers, and ran mostly industrial jobs in paper mill technology, installation of drives, and process control. In 1993, Larry created his company, Concept Electric, Incorporated and was currently doing consulting work on a nationwide basis. He went on to say that problems at dairy farms with stray current had begun to take up more and more of his time until it became the business' focal point. To date, Larry had performed stray electricity identifications on over 600 farms in 25 states.

Hammarback asked him how he'd gotten involved with me, and Larry explained that Mike Hoerth, my equipment dealer, knowing that he specialized in identifying electrical phenomena affecting dairy cows, had put us in touch. I spoke with Larry in 1997 and hired him to come out to the farm and conduct some tests.

"I explained to Russ," Larry was saying, "that I needed to monitor his electrical system, power steel voltages, currents, access, and the grounding network. I had Russ explain how his operation worked. I looked at a layout of the farm and commenced a design to come up with a testing procedure." Larry unbuttoned the neck button of his blue dress shirt and loosened the collar.

"Did you test various motors and electrical equipment in the free-stall barn?" Hammarback asked.

"Yeah," Larry said. "I set my machine on low parameters, but the filled memory meant something was happening electrically. Whether on the farm or off, at that point I didn't know.

Then I started checking equipment and panel wiring. I found large current-flow numbers present on the meter display screen on the grounding conductors. And it raised my alarm that my first premonition was right—that we had primary neutral, secondary neutral entries throughout the dairy due to the service laterals. Question was, was something on the farm wrong that was causing the current I was measuring on the grounded conductors, or was it just the loop from the primary neutral? So, I went through every circuit in the back and front equipment rooms one by one to identify if there was on-farm leakage."

"Did you find any?" Hammarback asked.

Larry shook his head. "No on-farm leakage, no defective equipment."

"How long did it take to do all that?" Hammarback asked, inching up a little closer to Larry.

"Standard test procedure in '97 was about a day. This dairy took two."

"Why?"

"Because I was confused by what was going on with the large amounts of current on the grounding conductors traveling through the dairy. And Mr. Allen was explaining his concerns about the adverse effects on his cows—a lot of them were in very poor shape."

"After checking out electrical equipment," Hammarback said, "what did you do?"

"Well," Larry said, turning his head side to side as if the shirt collar bothered him, "I used a four-and-a-half-inch-diameter clamp that I use for checking currents on parlor steel, where the cows would be. You use a scope meter with that. You set that on the one-volt amp range so you can get into milliamps; 1,000 milliamps equals an amp. Clamping the parlor steel, I found 800 milliamps. So, I shut the incoming electricity off, and it remained. So, it alarmed me."

Hammarback nodded. "Is a finding like that unusual in investigating farming?"

"Yes," Larry quickly answered. "In this dairy, it was highly unusual from what I'd seen in the past."

"What conclusions did you draw?"

"What I found," Larry told him, "was that current wasn't taking the neutral wire back to the substation. That current was taking the direct connection into the dairy's grounding field and traveling through the dairy into the earth."

"And who owns the primary system?" Hammarback asked.

"Wisconsin Public Service."

Hammarback paused for several long seconds. "What did you do next?"

"Well, I told Mr. Allen that I wanted to focus on removing the two services from this dairy and getting it down to one. Because, if we don't, this dairy isn't going to be around much longer."

"Did you tell him that would solve all his problems?"

Larry smiled. "Mr. Allen didn't believe me at first. He had a lot of good questions, and I told him to go get a second opinion. I told him to call WPS and have them test the dairy. So he did."

"What did you do after that?"

"Talked to Mr. Vern Peterson from Wisconsin Public Service, and asked him about bringing this dairy down to one service so that the primary neutral system wouldn't have adverse effects upon Mr. Allen's cows."

"What did he tell you?"

Again, Larry smiled. "That Mr. Allen didn't have a problem. He was below the level of concern set by the Public Service Commission of Wisconsin."

"Where did you leave it with Mr. Peterson after this conversation?" Hammarback asked.

"I had a meeting with him at the dairy. Basically, Vern Peterson does not believe in anything people like me do," Larry told him. "Because it's contrary to his protocols. I explained to him that my concern on this dairy was high current levels accessing the grounding conductors. He kept telling me that it takes two milliamps or so to affect a cow. I said we needed to get this dairy to one service—it had to be done. He kept reiterating there wasn't a problem. So, after a lengthy discussion, he offered Mr. Allen an isolator. My question to him was, where would you install the isolator? Because without relocation of the three-phase service out in the yard, an isolator would most likely fail."

Hammarback put both hands in his pockets and slowly paced back and forth in front of the judge's bench. "Why?" he asked.

"The proximity of the primary neutral down ground was less than eight feet from the side of the dairy wall which has an 8-foot-deep pit."

"Manure pit?"

"Manure pit. That's important because manure pits, beneath slatted floors, are highly conductive."

"Did Mr. Peterson agree to cooperate in getting the Allen farm down to one service?"

"Yes," Larry said. "He did."

"Did you," Hammarback inquired, "have the opportunity in 1997 to test whether the isolator was effective?"

"We did. The isolator was bypassing. An isolator is supposed to block voltage and current flow. Putting a current clamp on the neutral conductor of the secondary, basically when Mr. Allen didn't run electrical loads, it went near zero. But when loads were run, it increased dramatically. We measured over 60 milliamps coming in with an isolator installed. It meant the isolator couldn't handle the load or block aspects of the primary system."

"Is it possible," Hammarback asked, pounding away at what was sure to be a WPS theme, "that the 60 milliamps was from anything on the farm's wiring system?"

"No," Larry shook his head. "Because the load box is hooked directly to the transformer."

"Did you share your findings with Mr. Peterson or anybody from WPS?"

"Actually," Larry replied, "Mr. Peterson shared his opinion with me."

"Okay," Hammarback said. "Tell us what he told you."

"I received a phone call from Mr. Allen after they had tested the isolator, and Mr. Allen was upset. He said we had mis-wired the dairy and that WPS wanted to check out his house, because they felt it was an open neutral in the house that was causing the voltages they were measuring when they tested their isolator."

Hammarback stopped pacing, went over to the jury and stood near the first juror, the foreman. "What's an open neutral?" he asked.

"An open neutral is a situation where all the current has to return through the earth because it cannot take the insulated conductor back to its source."

"Essentially, a broken wire or a missing connection?"

"Correct. At that point, since we had Vern Peterson there we asked how come he wouldn't relocate the three-phase service. I had done a graph with a flute meter. And I actually measured not 60 milliamps, but well over 400. And I showed him the graph of the isolator bypassing. So, we pressured him if we could get this down to purely one service and relocate the three phase. Because otherwise Mr. Allen's dairy, in my opinion, was going to fail."

Standing beside the foreman with one hand on the rail of the jury box, Hammarback asked, "Did he agree to do anything to help Mr. Allen at that point?"

"After repeated discussions, he said, 'I'll agree to relocate but only where I want to put it.'"

"Did he tell you where?"

"Well, I requested that he relocate it across the street. He refused. He located it near the well casing on the farm."

"What happened next with respect to resolving the electrical concerns at the Allen farm?"

Larry sighed. "Well, at that point I told Russ to take it. I said, 'We've got to get this away from the parlor because we had an isolator on and it was being bypassed.' Mr. Allen was complaining things were worse for the cows. They were bad enough when I walked into the dairy. I knew he was in deep financial trouble. We knew," Larry continued, "the isolator wasn't holding because of conditions on the WPS line. The fact was, even if it did hold at some point, it would close and open depending on load orientations. What we needed was to get the three-phase transformer as far away from the dairy as we could. From that point, we installed the isolation transformer."

"Have you personally installed such systems on other WPS farms since then?" Hammarback asked.

"Within a year after that time," Larry told him, "WPS granted me two services of that nature on two dairies. They were also large dairies."

Hammarback next asked about some of the photographic exhibits of farm structures and utility wiring.

"Mr. Neubauer, tell us if, when you're making stray measurements, ones you consider important, if you double check your measurement with two different types of meters?"

"You should double and triple check."

"Is the farm not isolated in Exhibit 1331 when that measurement was taken?" Hammarback asked.

Larry leaned forward, squinted at the photo, and then took his glasses from his coat pocket and put them on. He shook his shaggy head. "It is not isolated. This is actual current coming into the dairy."

"Exhibit 1332," Hammarback said, "another photograph of a meter. What are the conditions under which measuring is being done?"

Larry craned his neck forward. "The utility isolator is now installed in the three-phase service pole which is the only service feeding the dairy. They've turned the load box on creating an artificial secondary power source, creating return current going on the neutral."

"And what are you measuring?"

"We're reading 60.4 milliamps showing isolator bypassing installation."

"How is it," Hammarback asked, "that you have current coming in with the load box on and the isolator in this place?"

"That was a tough one," Larry said. "But the down ground on the three-phase service is located less than eight feet from the dairy barn. There was over 180 milliamps accessing the dirt right there. The isolator is not blocking everything. It's allowing this amount to get through."

"Explain what's failing and why, please?"

Larry cleared his throat, took a drink and held on to the water glass with his right hand. "Even though we spent $57,000 plus on the isolator, when this piece of equipment hooked up and the transient at this level showed up on a grounding conductor, not even electrically connected to the dairy, yet I was able to measure it in the dairy, that told me it was traveling through the earth into the dairy."

"Did you do anymore testing after that?" Hammarback asked him.

"Mr. Neubauer," Hammarback said. "I'm going to shift gears a little. Did there come a time when you had discussions with Mr. Allen about the installation of what's called a ground ring?"

"Yes. Primarily in '97, '98. We did a lot of dairy farms that had electrical problems. And Wisconsin Electric used to, when they had an electrical issue on a dairy, dig around the dairy and drive a bunch of ground rods and connect a ring of wire. But, then they would also bond it to the primary neutral."

"On how many farms have you installed such a device, roughly?" Hammarback asked.

"Well over 30 or more; 50."

"Do they fully resolve issues of current in the ground?"

"No, no, they do not fully resolve them."

"How was it that one became installed on Mr. Allen's farm?"

"After we'd put in several," Larry said, "a lot of customers were happy. Mr. Allen knew this. He called and said he wanted one. He was complaining that spring had come, his cows were re-kicking in the parlor after all the work that had been done. So we put the ground ring in."

"Do you have information as to whether Mr. Allen cut ground wires on the WPS system in the vicinity of his barn at around that time?"

Larry looked over at me. He hesitated a second before saying, "When Mr. Allen saw the amounts of current on his ground ring, after that he removed WPS' down grounds."

"Does cutting ground wires on the WPS system in the imme-diate vicinity of the Allen farm affect current on the ground ring?" Hammarback asked.

"Yes."

"How do you know?"

"It's not only the current, it's the voltage, too. But the current is reduced because the down grounds are no longer able to inject current near the farm. It makes the neutral do more of its job."

Hammarback meandered up near Judge McKay's bench. "At some point a ditch wire was installed in the vicinity of Mr. Allen's farm. Did your company do some of that work? Tell us what the ditch wire was all about."

"It was actually a bypass wire," Larry told him. "I helped drive the ground rods. To reduce earth current, Mr. Allen ran a ditch wire all the way down to the corner about a mile south of his dairy to build a neutral.

"Is the installation of that wire causing any damage to WPS' system?"

"No."

Hammarback paused. "Did Mr. Allen put a ring of copper around his farmstead?"

"Yes."

"Did you have involvement in doing that?" Hammarback asked Larry.

"To a degree. Mr. Allen knew that when the surface conductor—surface condition of the soil was wet—that he could see adverse effects to his cows because electricity travels better on moist soil than dry. He attempted to borrow my trencher. He was going to cut a trench around the dairy, fill it with rocks and put in a pump to keep the water off his property; he was that concerned. After he went about 30 feet, he realized it was a very tough task. I told him, 'Why don't you put a surface ring on and see if it helps?' So he did."

"Will a surface ring result in reduced current flowing through?"

"Definitely."

"Why is that?" Hammarback wanted to know.

"Kurkoff's Law. It's basically a continuous loop similar to a rubber band. Break it, it's gone. Induction is purely magnetic fields, current flowing through or across the conductor creating it."

"If all the WPS return current stayed on the neutral conductor, what would happen to the current buried in the surface rings of the Allen farm?"

"It would go to zero!" Larry replied.

"Do you have any data," Hammarback asked, "to establish whether Mr. Allen's on-farm system is contributing to this current?"

Larry nodded. "Two days after Mr. Allen put a monitoring device on this ring, the power went out in the area. Mr. Allen then ran the entire dairy on a generator, with the same electrical loads of milking equipment, the feeding operation, everything that was running before was running again, but from the generator. *And the ring measurement remained at zero with the power company's line down.*"

"Thank you, Mr. Neubauer. That's all I have," Hammarback said, and went and sat at his counsel table.

"Mr. Neubauer, you've been a licensed master electrician since approximately 1995," Will stated for the record. "And you took the test four times and flunked it before you became a master electrician in Wisconsin?"

The faintest trace of a smile appeared on Larry's lips. He could see right off the bat how this was going to unfold. "Actually, five times, and passed it."

"Right." Will nodded, happily. "You flunked the first four and passed on the fifth time, correct?"

"Correct."

"And after that, you took the same test for a master's electrician twice in the state of Minnesota, correct?"

"Not the same, a different test, correct."

"And you flunked both times?"

"Correct," Larry said.

"And then you went to the state of Michigan and took a test there to be a licensed master electrician. And you flunked that one?"

"Correct."

"So, you've taken the licensing test to be a master electrician and you've flunked it seven out of eight times. Correct?"

"Correct," Larry told him.

"You know that the unit of measurement for current is amperes, correct?"

"Correct."

"But when I asked you at your deposition, you told me it was a joule. Correct?"

"Well, correct."

"You are not a licensed professional engineer and you are not an electrical engineer, correct?"

"Correct," Larry said.

Now Will made his way over to the jury box. "From April of

1997 through February of 2002, you charged Mr. Allen some $230,000 for work on his farm. Correct?"

"That's correct."

"And that was certainly the most you ever charged any single customer during that time frame, correct?"

"Yes."

"Would you agree," he said, "that your work on Mr. Allen's farm, given all the time and money and effort you've put into it, represents your best work?"

"That's correct," Larry replied.

"Mr. Neubauer, I'm going to show you a document we've marked as Exhibit 1606. Exhibit 1606 is an order from the Wisconsin Department of Commerce, entitled, 'Notice of Violations and Orders.' And you know who Tom Garvey is, a state electrical engineer?"

"Correct," Larry said.

"And you know that last month Mr. Garvey went on Mr. Allen's farm and conducted an investigation of the electrical system you are responsible for?"

"Correct."

"During and after that investigation, Mr. Garvey issued this report we've marked as Exhibit 1606. Mr. Garvey, on behalf of the Wisconsin Department of Commerce, found 22 code violations to the electrical system on the Allen farm that you're responsible for. Correct?"

"Correct," Larry said.

Will nodded with satisfaction. "As a master electrician, you are familiar with the fact that a code violation raises a safety issue?"

Larry shrugged. "Could go both ways. It does, generally."

"Now, I want to talk about how many times you've been on that farm. You were on the farm in 1997, 1998, 1999, 2000, 2001, and 2002 in connection with Concept Electric?"

"That's correct."

"I'm going to show you now, Mr. Neubauer, Exhibit 667.

We've listed year by year the invoices that Concept Electric and then Concept Services sent to Mr. Allen in connection with your work and Concept Services' work on the Allen farm. From the last page, Concept Electric invoiced Mr. Allen $219,211.41. When you add what Concept Services did, the total came to $229,846.97. Correct?"

"Correct."

"And invoices for your work since March 2002 total approximately $14,000. So that brings the total to just under $245,000, correct?"

"Correct."

"You told Mr. Allen in 1997 that to get rid of what you called 'loop current,' you needed to eliminate the single-phase service to the parlor and then rewire the farm?"

"Correct."

"You charged Mr. Allen $9,000 for that work. After you eliminated the single-phase service, you told Mr. Allen you had reduced the current flowing through the parlor and free-stall barn. Correct?"

"Definitely," Larry said.

Continuing to pace, Will said, "Have you seen any production records that show that milk production actually went down after you did this work in May 1997?"

"No."

The attorney stopped moving and faced Larry. "Assume for me that there are such records. If that were the case, would you attribute the decrease to the work you did?"

Larry frowned. "No."

Will's lips twisted into a small smile. "You would agree, though, that eliminating what you call 'loop current' had no positive benefits?"

"Correct."

"Is it fair to say you misdiagnosed the problem?"

"Yes," Larry confessed. "It was the three-phase unit that needed to be relocated. The isolator was bypassed."

"Did you refund Mr. Allen that $9,000?"

"Nope."

Again Will paused. "When you isolated the farm in December of 1997, how much did you charge Mr. Allen for that one?"

"$55,000," Larry told him.

"Did you take any cow contact measurements before that work to determine how much current was flowing through the cows?"

"No."

"And after that work, did you take any cow contact measurements to determine how much current was flowing through cows?"

"The only thing I addressed," Larry said, fiddling with the knot in his tie, "was current flow through grounding conductors."

"After installing the isolator, in 1998 did you take cow contact measurements to determine if the work had effect on how much current was flowing through the cows?"

"Other than the wave form analysis, I knew the current was pretty much absolved from the dairy. So, no cow contact or step potentials."

"Mr. Allen cut 13 grounding wires on April 21, 1999, correct? And you knew Mr. Allen was cutting the wires, didn't you?"

"After he had cut them. Yes."

"You knew Mr. Allen reconnected those wires at some point. Did you take any cow contact measurements after he cut the wires to determine if that had any effect on current flowing through the cows?"

"When Mr. Allen reconnected them, no. But when WPS reconnected them, yes."

"What you're talking about is, Mr. Allen actually cut

grounding wires a second time, didn't he? And after WPS sent him a letter telling him not to. Correct?"

"I believe so," Larry said softly.

Will stuck both hands in his pockets and rocked slowly on his heels in front of the witness stand. "You've had farmers tell you that the ground rings you've installed have done absolutely no good, correct?"

"I would agree with that," Larry said.

Will now proceeded to the jury box. "Do you remember that during your deposition I asked you about the surface ground ring, and you told me that Mr. Allen was being electrocuted through the earth?"

"If you looked up in *Webster's Dictionary*, the term electrocution, that's defined as that."

"And when I asked you what proof you had to back that strong of a statement, you mentioned that a light bulb could be lit off the surface ground ring. Correct?"

"Right," Larry said. "Which is uninsulated."

"The fact," Will said, his tone skeptical and testy, "that a light bulb as big as the eraser tip on a pencil can be lit off the surface ground ring is your proof that Mr. Allen is being electrocuted?"

Larry sighed, took a deep breath. "If a wire laying on the surface of the earth can light a light bulb, there's energy behind it! That light bulb is a resistance between that surface."

"But in your deposition, you testified that 84 percent of current on the ring is induced. Correct?"

"It's induced," Larry said with impatience, "by the imbalance of the WPS neutral. If it was balanced, it wouldn't light, sir."

"Not what you call 'earth currents'?"

"Well, the buried ground ring is earth-current based. The surface ground ring is more induction."

"When Mr. Vern Peterson of WPS told you that measurements at the Allen farm showed that the WPS Dairyland neutral isolator was functioning properly, you did not disagree with that, correct?"

"I disagreed. I didn't disagree that it wasn't functioning to his specifications."

"Now, you took measurements on the Dairyland Isolator for three days, but never after. And you didn't demand that it be removed?"

"I wanted a new service installed at the Allen farm, and I wanted it removed. Mr. Allen couldn't afford to have it taken down at that point."

"Were the cows more hesitant to come into the parlor after the Dairyland Isolator was installed?"

"At first, no," Larry told him. "Then it got bad again."

"Is it your claim," Will asked, "that all of Mr. Allen's problems are due to electricity from WPS' distribution system?"

"All of his problems? That would be impossible."

"Are you claiming that, in connection with this lawsuit, the problems regarding electricity on the Allen farm are all attributable to WPS' distribution system?"

"Yes," Larry said forcefully. "In this lawsuit."

Will now read a portion of a letter that Larry had written me back in 1997, Exhibit 668, when I was looking for that $58,000 loan to purchase an isolation transformer. After introducing it, Will said to Larry, "At the very end of this letter you wrote: 'Remember, any product WPS issues to solve a problem is always designed around their system's functioning and capability, and in that message lies their interests, friends, stockholders, costs, legal department, et cetera.' Did I read that correctly?"

"Yes."

"What you were telling Mr. Allen was, 'You can't trust WPS.' Correct?"

"No, I was telling him that the Dairyland Isolator that was going to be installed would likely fit their characteristics."

Will now whipped out another letter, Exhibit 1764. "This

letter," he said, "is dated January 18, 2000. And what this letter references is a meeting that's going to include Mr. Allen, yourself, and Mr. Hammarback regarding conditions on the Allen farm, and to prepare for the lawsuit to be filed against WPS. Correct?"

"Correct," Larry said.

"By July 28, 2000, you had received money, $5,000, for being an expert witness for Mr. Allen, correct?"

"I believe half that amount," Larry said.

"And this is five or six months before this lawsuit was filed, correct?" Will asked accusingly.

"I believe so," Larry told him.

"That's all I have, Judge," Will said. He turned on his heel and walked briskly over to the defense table.

Hammarback stood up to do a redirect. "Mr. Neubauer," he said, coming up toward Larry while he buttoned his suit jacket. "With respect to Mr. Garvey's report on code inspection on the farm, at whose request was that done?"

"Wisconsin Public Service."

"What's that about with respect to the code?"

Larry edged forward in his seat and folded his hands together in front of him. "The code states that at a building service or near the first panel you would run a grounding conductor from the ground bar—in the city it would be a water meter—and put a jumper on it. Therefore, you're tied into the plumbing system, so electricity could travel. On a dairy, if you have a building and a metal water pipe comes up, the code says you have to bond it. That was one of the issues—through the electrical system, they want a properly sized bonding conductor, copper wire connected to that pipe."

"If you have copper water lines not bonded with the wire, what can you do to solve that problem from the standpoint of the code?"

"At Mr. Allen's, they cut the pipes off as they entered the building, put on a piece of plastic, bonded it to the copper or water line to make it inaccessible to human touch, and it met the code."

"Can that lead to stray electricity concerns?" Hammarback asked.

"Yes!" Larry told him. "Because the water line is similar to the ground ring, it's return current that travels on the water line."

"In April of 1997, when you first met with the WPS reps, what measurements did you tell them about that you had made on the Allen dairy?"

Larry took a quick, short sip of water. "Told them we had loop current horrendously high and that the cows were being affected by the dual services. And it was reiterated then—by them —that there wasn't a problem, there was no current."

"How did it turn out with respect to the dual services?"

Larry shrugged his shoulders. "Didn't solve the problem."

"What didn't?"

"Relocating the service to the center of the yard and relocating that down ground to finally push it out to the road, and extensive on-farm wiring to meet codes."

"No further questions."

Hammarback walked over toward his counsel table. As Larry stepped down off the stand, I drew a deep breath and tried to take stock of the proceedings. My important expert witnesses, my big guns, were through testifying. I thought they'd presented themselves incredibly effectively and proven beyond doubt my contention that WPS' stray current was responsible for destroying the Allen dairy business. I could only hope and pray that this jury of my peers would see things in the same light.

CHAPTER 12

VERN PETERSON

When Vern Peterson of WPS took the witness stand for the defense, I felt we had a golden opportunity to win the jury over permanently. Peterson was a snake oil salesman who'd say anything, no matter how contradictory of the facts. What was true and right meant little; all that mattered to him was shunting blame from the utility and laying it off on me. I'd seen that up close and personal when he was out at my farm. In a sense, I understood; he worked for the company and had to toe the line.

Peterson, currently WPS' customer service manager, started his testimony by telling Will about his prior position in the company, when he was electric distribution engineering project supervisor. That was in 1997, when he first visited my place. He mentioned that he held bachelor's degrees in science and electrical engineering, and that he was a registered professional engineer in Wisconsin.

Under Will's questioning, he talked about his initial visit to my farm.

"What was the reason for going out there at the time?" Will asked, looking elegant as ever in a gray, three-piece suit, wearing a pale blue, French-cuffed shirt with silver cuff links.

"Russ Allen and Larry Neubauer wanted to discuss options, and Russ Allen's stray voltage concerns. Russ had concerns that his cows were jumpy and that he had overall low production."

Trevor Will walked slowly toward the jury box and stopped just short of the railing. "Did anyone tell you that Mr. Neubauer had measured .914 volts over a feed bunk? Did anybody tell you that Mr. Neubauer had measured 800 milliamps of current on the parlor steel?"

"No, they did not."

"Did they give you any test results?"

"No," Peterson said.

"Did you have a response to their request about moving the transformer out to the road?"

"Yes. That we were not able to, as a result of a declaratory ruling—an

order from the Public Service Commission."

Will nodded. "Is it typical to have discussions with the Public Service Commission staff about orders?"

Vern Peterson nodded back at Trevor Will. "They're our regulators, control what we do as a utility with the stray voltage program. I talked to Dan Dashal, head of the stray voltage program at the PSC."

"Under what circumstances," Will asked, "was WPS committed to move transformers at a customer's request?"

"When you were out on the Allen farm in summer of 1997, did you make reference to this PSC order, to Mr. Allen?"

"Yes."

"What did you say to him?"

"That the order told us we could not move the transformer at his request."

"Did you have options to offer him?"

"Isolation on demand," Vern Peterson said. "Where we install a neutral isolation switch otherwise known as a Dairyland Isolator."

"What did you say to Mr. Allen or Mr. Neubauer about the Dairyland Isolator?"

"That it was a very good solution," Peterson told him.

"Mr. Peterson," Trevor Will said, walking over to the exhibits. He picked one up and took it to the witness. "If you look at Exhibit 151A, seventh page, this was a load box test on the three-phase setting at the Allen farm, as part of putting up the isolator. Why did you use the three-phase at that point?"

"That's the setting that serves the parlor and free-stall area."

"Is there anything about those readings," Trevor Will said, "that indicates to you a stray voltage problem on the Allen farm?"

"No, there is not."

"What readings support that conclusion?"

Peterson glanced at the document. "The .0022 which is our cow contact reading with our load box on its highest setting."

"Are there any values or readings in this study that indicate there might be a stray voltage problem on the Allen farm?"

"No, not at all," Vern Peterson said, and I chuckled out loud.

"Was Mr. Allen present when you were installing the Dairyland Isolator?" "Yes."

"Was Mr. Neubauer?"

"No."

"At any point during the installation did you say anything to Mr. Allen about what you were finding?"

Peterson nodded. "I told him we were able to get isolation but I was concerned about the numbers."

"What did you tell him you wanted to do?"

"Well, we tried to isolate the single-phase service. I was able to, and get appropriate readings. We spent time going through some wiring, trying to figure out where that location was on the single phase on the services, to try and figure out what that interconnection was."

"Interconnection," Will said. "Are you talking about something on the utility system or the farm system, or somewhere else?"

"It would typically be through the farm system."

"How did you leave it with Mr. Allen at the end of the day?" Will asked him.

"I told him we would come back and try to pursue it further, or he could get his electrician involved."

"And when you left, where was the Dairyland Isolator?"

"On the three-phase setting," Peterson answered.

"And was it functioning?"

"Yes, it was."

"What happened after that?" he asked.

"We received a call either from Mr. Allen or Mr. Neubauer the next day. The idea was they'd found the source of the problem and asked us to come out to the farm. We went out right away."

"Did anybody go with you?"

"Jerry Held came with me," Vern Peterson said quietly.

"When you got to the farm, what did Mr. Neubauer say?"

"That our reference rod was over a pipe that ran from the back of the old
barn to a manure pit, and he felt that was affecting our reading."

"And what did you find?"

"That he was correct," Peterson said. "We moved our reference rod, and
readings looked better."

"What did the readings show about whether the Dairyland Isolator was working?"

"It showed it was working."

"Did Mr. Neubauer raise any other issue?"

"Yes. He claimed the isolation switch was closing."

"Did he offer evidence of that?"

"He showed me a scope, a current level he'd measured over several hours."

"Was there any way of determining when and where that reading had been taken?"

"No, there was not. I was concerned, but I also questioned the reading."

"Why were you concerned?" Trevor Will wanted to know.

Vern Peterson smiled. "Well, I was very concerned because Mr. Neubauer had a reputation of taking readings—"

"I object to this, Your Honor," Hammarback said to McKay.

"Your Honor, reputation of the defendant goes to how he reacted to what was presented to him." Will retorted.

McKay called both lawyers to him. After a bench conference, McKay allowed—what else?—the witness to answer, but limited him to stating his own perceptions and nothing more. A partial overrule was better than a total one, I supposed.

"Mr. Neubauer had a reputation of taking claimed readings that were elevated and no one else would be able to duplicate those readings. He also had a reputation of taking readings in locations that didn't make any sense." Peterson said.

"Did he specifically show you where he took the reading that he claimed was on the scope?"

"No. I told him I wanted to do a complete load box test and a 24-hour chart."

"What was his reaction?"

Vern Peterson opened his eyes wide. "He was very upset by that."

"Was Mr. Allen present at that point?"

"He was."

"After Mr. Neubauer got upset, what did you say?"

"That I wanted to test," Peterson told him. "To verify those readings myself. We got into a conversation about the Dairyland Isolator—the claim that the isolator was closing didn't make any sense to me. The device will not close unless the voltage across it exceeds 31 volts, and the testing we had done previously was nowhere near that level on our primary system. I found it very unlikely that the isolation switch was closing. Then the conversation turned to Mr. Allen."

"What did Mr. Allen say at that point?"

"Mr. Allen was very upset," he told Trevor Will. "He came over and said, 'You know, Mr. Neubauer is telling me that this isolation switch has a load on the feeder, that the switch cannot handle the voltage and current coming from our system.' "I told him I didn't believe that was true. He got very upset and said he was done dealing with us. He was going to go with Mr. Neubauer. He was going with an isolation transformer, and he wanted us off his farm immediately."

"Almost six years ago," Will said, "how is it that you can remember so clearly?"

"It was the first and only farm I have ever been kicked off of."

"And how did that make you feel?"

"I was very upset," Peterson muttered.

"Why was that?"

"Because Russ didn't believe me. I also felt I had been set up, and it was upsetting to get kicked off that farm."

"When was the next time you remember being back on the Allen farm? And who was involved in that meeting?"

"Late summer, early fall. It would have been Mr. Neubauer, Mr. Allen. Jerry Held was with me."

"At the point when you had agreed on the location of moving the transformer, what seemed to be the atmosphere?" Will asked.

"Everyone was pretty happy we had come to an agreement."

"Mr. Peterson, we were talking earlier about when the subject of an ungrounded 480-volt delta system to service the farm came up." "Yes. Mr. Allen and Mr. Neubauer requested we provide a three-wire, 480-volt service."

Trevor Will unbuttoned his jacket and crossed his arms. "What did you tell them about their request for 480-volt ungrounded service?"

"I denied their request."

"Why?"

"I did not feel it was appropriate voltage for a dairy facility. I was concerned about safety."

"What are those safety issues?" Trevor Will asked.

Peterson coughed, cleared his throat and gulped from his water glass before answering. "The ungrounded service—if you do get the first ground fault, nothing, no breakers trip. Problem is, unless you clear that fault, before you get a second one, that second is a 480-volt fault, which is very high energy. In that wet dairy environment, it's very unsafe, both for humans and the cows."

"Did there come a time when WPS did provide 480-volt ungrounded service to a farm in this area?"

"Yes. We viewed that farm as a different type, large dairies, over 1,000 cows. A 24-hour operation. We felt there would be a responsible person there around the clock.

"How many farms actually got the 480-volt ungrounded delta service?" Will asked.

"Two."

"Have other farms requested it?"

"Yes."

"Did you see Mr. Allen again before this lawsuit was filed in November of 2000?"

"Yes," Peterson told him. "In November of '99."

Will thrust both hands in his pockets and walked a few paces nearer to the witness stand. "Did Mr. Allen ever approach you to talk about possibly resolving the claim he had?"

"No."

"Based on your experience, did you see anything on the Allen farm that indicated a stray voltage problem?"

"No, I did not."

"Have you found stray voltage problems on other farms you've tested?"

"Sure."

"And when you found them?"

"We've corrected them."

"That's all I have," Trevor Will said to Judge McKay.

"Mr. Peterson," Hammarback said, standing close to the witness and clasping his hands together below his waist. "On those 1,000 cow dairies where this ungrounded secondary was provided, the purpose was to reduce the current through the dairy?"

"That was what Mr. Neubauer requested, yes."

Hammarback nodded. "In fact Mr. Neubauer was the electrician for both of those farms?"

"I believe both."

"And you considered him a qualified electrician?"

"No," Peterson snorted. "I did not."

"But you provided the ungrounded 480 regardless?"

Peterson shifted uncomfortably in his chair. "They were working with their regular electricians," he explained.

"But Mr. Neubauer performed the isolation work," Hammarback reminded him. "Correct?"

"Yes, he did," Vern Peterson acknowledged.

"And those farms have parlors with equipotential planes?"

"Correct." Hammarback went up closer to him. "The cow contact voltages in those parlors were very, very small, were they not?"

"That's correct."

"And yet," Hammarback said, "the owners of those 1,000 cow dairies thought they had a problem. Correct?"

"In one situation, yes."

"Was the subsequent course of milk production at either large dairy reported to you after the isolation work was done?"

"I was not given specifics."

"Now," Hammarback said, walking over to the jury box, "in the system Mr. Neubauer installed at the Allen farm, isn't it true that by design, customer current on that secondary neutral was totally eliminated?"

"Yes."

"And he did that by installing sub-transformers toward the load in the barn that made the farm system look like a phase-to-phase load to the utility system, correct?"

"Correct."

Hammarback nodded again. "The second item in the Public Service Commission's order in which you felt you had to deny Mr. Allen this service was that placement should be outside animal confinement areas, correct?"

"Correct."

"And," Hammarback continued, "Mr. Allen and Mr. Neubauer were not requesting a transformer that was in the cow yard, correct?"

"No, they were not," Peterson agreed.

"The last of the Public Service Commission concerns," Hammarback said, "is, and I quote, 'The customer's preference must also be considered in placement.' Correct?"

"Correct."

"And there was no doubt about Mr. Allen's desire for placement, correct?"

"That is correct," Vern Peterson answered.

"So," Hammarback said, "we're three for three. There's no problem moving the pole?"

"Yes, there is a problem moving the pole."

Hammarback did a double take and raised an eyebrow. "And in your estimation, that's the Public Service Commission's position?"

"Correct. And that's who we have to answer to."

"And who has no jurisdiction over farm wiring. Correct?"

Vern Peterson shrugged. "In the declaratory ruling, which said we could not rely upon the customer's devices to take care of that secondary neutral drop. In the future, that system would be changed back to a more normal operation and secondary neutral voltage drop wouldn't be a concern."

Hammarback leaned both hands on the rail of the box and faced the jurors. "Mr. Allen was not party to that proceeding, was he?"

"No," Peterson said. "He was not."

"But you permit this kind of move now?"

"Yes, we do."

Next Hammarback showed Vern Peterson Exhibit 151A; this document recorded various contacts WPS had with me. Hammarback dug through a number of entries

until he was able to unearth some real gems.

"Third entry down, step information," Hammarback said, "refers to meters being set in the milk parlor. Do you know when that happened?"

"The entry date is 4-22-97. I don't know which one that refers to."

"The next entry," Hammarback told him, "says 'pulled meter.' And you weren't

involved in that either?"

"Correct."

"The following entry says, 'Customer notified, data discussed with Russ. He wanted farm isolated on 7-10-97. Vern P. and Jerry H. hooked up isolator and tested switch. It was functioning properly.' Did I read that properly?"

"That's correct."

Hammarback nodded and continued, "Page 11, first entry says, 'Required action by

WPS, none.' Correct?"

"That's correct."

Again, Hammarback nodded. "And the next entry is 'order complete.' Correct?"

"That is," Vern Peterson said.

Hammarback nodded once more, then left the jury area and went over to the witness. "And neither on page 10 nor 11 do we see an entry indicating that *anybody* was refused permission to test. Do we?"

Vern Peterson took out a handkerchief and wiped his forehead. "No, you do not."

"We don't see an entry indicating that anybody was kicked off the farm. Correct?"

"No."

Hammarback's brow furrowed as if he was confused. "And yet," he said, "there are items entered on here that occurred the very same day you indicated that happened. Correct?"

"That's correct," Peterson admitted.

"And that to you was a very memorable event, being kicked off the farm," Hammarback said to him. "Correct?"

"Yes, it was!" Peterson exclaimed, and I almost burst out laughing.

"Now, what's Mr. Held's reputation for truthfulness in reporting voltage readings?"

"It's very good," Peterson said with a straight face.

"Is there a reason," Hammarback asked, "that he's no longer employed by WPS?"

Trevor Will suddenly leaped up and objected. Somehow, he had to find a way of defending Held's dishonor. And the only way was to prevent the jury from hearing about it at all. Judge McKay, in full coddling mode, sustained him. So Hammarback went a different route.

"Isolation on demand is provided in part to give farm customers answers on whether eliminating electricity below the level of concern may help them, correct?"

"That is correct," Vern Peterson told him.

"And in the case of the large farms you discussed a moment ago, they wanted to isolate with a Dairyland transformer, correct?"

"Correct."

"And that's a fast device, will close on short impulse?" Hammarback asked.

"The duration of impulse will determine how fast it will close."

"Have you ever seen any measurements by Mr. Neubauer in January of '98 after the isolation system was put in?"

"No."

Hammarback moved a step nearer to the witness. "Your company never received an order from the Public Service Commission directing that it could not change transformer locations on the Allen farm, did you?"

Peterson shook his head. "Not specifically related to that fact, no."

"Isn't it true that the system Mr. Neubauer proposed to install included an alarm system?"

"It could have. I don't know."

"The systems installed on those other two farms have an alarm system, do they not?"

"I don't know that for a fact."

"In addition to providing the ungrounded service, you did some other things to help those other farms. You loaned one farm a generator. Correct?"

"We paid for a generator," Peterson said.

"Mr. Peterson," Hammarback said, again going over to the jurors, "before you went to the Allen farm, you didn't get any records from WPS on the condition of the line in the vicinity? You didn't get records on the age of the line? Or records of inspections of connections on the line? Or any measurements of phase and neutral current recorded on the line?"

"No, I did not," Vern Peterson replied.

"You've never seen copper weld conductors on a customer service order?"

"Correct."

"And you haven't seen knob and tube wiring from the 1930s installed on a 500-cow dairy?"

"I would say no."

Hammarback went over to his counsel table and looked at some notes on his pad. Then he went back to the witness. "Mr. Peterson, there's no regular inspection program where a state inspector will come out and do a line inspection on a WPS distribution system, correct?"

"No, there isn't."

"And there never has been. Correct?"

"Not in my career, no."

"Mr. Peterson, you're familiar with the principle of four and five-wire systems on farms?"

"Yes, I am."

"Those systems separate the functions of the ground from the neutral?" "Correct."

"The hardware you have to use for high voltage is different than for low voltage?" Hammarback asked.

"Correct."

"The concept of a four or five-wire system can be applied to a utility system as well as a farm system?"

"There's certainly a lot more consideration on the utility system."

Hammarback turned sideways to the witness stand and placed his hands on his pants pockets. "You have no experience with four or five-wire systems that separate ground and neutral?"

"No," the witness said. "I do not."

"Keeping connectors in good repair is a good thing to do on any electrical system?"

"I would agree."

"Keeping the conductor size adequate on any system is a good thing todo? And upgrading the conductor size as time and experience and electrical loads dictate is important? And all of that applies to utility systems as well as farm systems?"

"That's correct," Peterson told him.

That's all I have," Hammarback said, and Will rose quickly to start his redirect. He seemed in an awful hurry and more nervous than usual. A sign, to me, that he felt he needed to rehabilitate this witness.

"Mr. Peterson," Trevor Will said, buttoning his jacket and going up close to the witness stand. "You were asked a series of questions about the order and docket 106 as it relates to the metering pole. Who owns the metering pole on the WPS system? The customer or the company?"

"The customer," Peterson told him.

"The transformer pole," Will said. "Who owns the pole there?"

"The utility."

"When Mr. Allen and Mr. Neubauer were talking about moving a pole on the farm, which pole were they talking about?"

"The transformer pole," Peterson told him.

"You were asked before by Mr. Hammarback about providing a generator to a farm. Why was it the company provided that?"

"That was part of experiments we were doing on the farm."

Will nodded. "You were asked about the isolator closing. After it was removed from Mr. Allen's farm, was it tested?"

"Yes, it was."

"What were the results of the test?"

Peterson craned his neck forward to get closer to the microphone.

"The isolator closed in at the 32 volts just as the specifications call for."

Trevor Will nodded and walked over near Judge McKay's bench. "You were asked if you got any line inspection data before you went out to the Allen farm. What was the practice of WPS before you went out to do a stray voltage investigation?"

"We did not do that."

"And you were asked whether you completed additional

testing in July. Why didn't you complete the phase-two testing and primary profile in July 1997?"

"Because," Peterson told him, "I was kicked off the farm."

"That's all I have," Trevor Will said and went back to his seat.

And that was it for Peterson, a witness who went out with a whimper instead of a bang; Trevor Will had nothing else. Maybe he was saving his best for the next witness, the quarter-million-dollar man, Roger Mellenberger.

CHAPTER 13

DR. ROGER MELLENBERGER

Roger Mellenberger was a key witness for the defense, an intellectual heavyweight who would present their arguments and theories with the same kind of force that Mike Behr and Don Zipse had done for me. He had the reputation of being as slick as they came, as well as articulate and personable. I felt my heart begin beating faster as the man slowly rose, walked to the witness stand, took his oath, and sat down in the chair.

Mellenberger knew his stuff. He'd published lots of articles and papers on the dairy industry, agriculture, and stray voltage. From my vantage point, the problem wasn't that he lacked expertise; it was that he placed his expertise in the service of a bad purpose. He drew all the wrong conclusions from his studies. Just as his paymasters demanded.

Will began with the usual, having the witness present his bona fides and report his background. Mellenberger had received his bachelor's degree in agriculture from the University of Wisconsin, had been raised on a 50-cow farm, and performed every variety of work there. He'd recently retired from teaching dairy and animal science at Michigan State University and become a "dairy consultant."

"Are you familiar with something called the Kellogg Biological Station?" Will asked him.

"That's one of three research dairy farms we had at Michigan State University. There was a dairy herd there that W.K. Kellogg started back in the 1930s. We replaced that in 1986 with a 140-cow Holstein herd and built new facilities. From '86 to '98 I was faculty supervisor for that facility."

"What did that job entail?"

"I would sit with the farm and dairy manager and make decisions whether we'd milk three times a day, use BST, how many acres of corn we needed, what research project might get done. And I used Kellogg to train people, from milk inspectors, field personnel and laborers."

"Dr. Mellenberger, you were retained by Foley and Lardner in this case. What were you asked to do?"

"Look at the Allen farm—the time of the complaint period. Look at records, just see what happened from a dairy herd management standpoint over those years."

"What years were you looking at?" Will asked.

"1976 through 2002."

"What methodology did you file to conduct this analysis?"

"My normal methodology is to take all records from the farm or businesses that have sold to that farm. Enter the information into the computer and develop a spreadsheet so that at any point in time I can evaluate the mastitis situation, reproduction and milk production. When I was first called in February of 2002, there were 46 boxes of documents waiting for me, records about anything: milk checks, feed invoices, vet records, herd production records, bank records, sales slips to stockyards—everything imaginable."

"How were the records organized?"

Mellenberger sighed. "Totally mixed up—the years all mixed up. No order whatsoever."

"What did you do?" Will asked in a tone of sympathetic surprise.

"Painstakingly went through page by page. And I arranged it category by category. Had to take all the years and sort by category, by year, box by box by box."

"Did you encounter problems collecting data from the documents?"

"From a couple of standpoints," Mellenberger whined. "For instance, from 1984 through 1989 we had no cow numbers. No records. Same for '96, '97. Same thing from September of 2000 to February 2001. And then when he went on his computer system in 1997, there was no way to extract the information back out, so I had to hand enter all of that. That was very laborious."

"Dr. Mellenberger, in conducting your analysis why didn't you just rely on the information presented by Mr. Allen and his expert witnesses?"

"If I'm asked to assess what happened to this herd over time, I need specific numbers, based on numbers from the farmer's records."

"What information were you provided by Mr. Allen and his experts in that regard?"

Mellenberger smiled across the width of the courtroom. "None that I can think of."

"Have you worked on any other stray voltage cases? If so, how many?"

"At least 60."

"How does the amount of time you've spent on this case compare to other cases?"

"The maximum I've spent on any other farm is maybe 400 hours. So, it's three times higher, 1200 hours."

"Why have you spent so much time working on this case?" Will asked.

"Because," he said, "the records were in such disarray. I had to put them in a form that I could use them."

"Doctor, what do you understand to be Mr. Allen's main contention in this case?"

"That milk production on his farm was adversely affected from 1976 through 1997, and after the farm was isolated and the transformer moved in December of '97, that production increased substantially, indicating to him that voltage had been the main determinant to milk production for that length of time."

"Dr. Mellenberger, do you have an opinion as to whether Mr. Allen's herd has been adversely affected by stray voltage during any period of time since 1976?"

"Yes," he said emphatically. "I do."

"What is that opinion?"

"No, the farm was never affected by stray voltage or any electrical event."

"In making your assessment of Mr. Allen's farm, what period of time have you looked at?"

"1976 to 2002."

"What is Exhibit 1781?"

"The Allen annual milk production year by year. I needed to see what happened over time as part of my analysis."

"What conclusions have you drawn?"

"Well," Mellenberger said slowly, "as you can see, there's years it goes up and down. With the death of Russell's sister Geri Lynn in 1991—who had a lot of responsibility for herd management, specifically lactating cows—somebody else had to assume responsibility. Therefore, we see a drop when that occurs. And then from '91 until '98 or '99, there's a steady increase in milk production."

"Dr. Mellenberger, do you have an opinion as to whether the annual milk production is indicative of a herd affected by stray voltage?"

"If we take," Mellenberger said, "just going from 1976, that increase is a little over 8,000 pounds, especially when we get to 1996 for the almost 8,000-pound increase, that's more than a doubling of milk production in those 20 years. And I wouldn't expect that if there had been objectionable current or voltage accessing these cows."

Will went back over to the jury box and stood near the end of the rail. "What about the period after 1996? Do you have an opinion to a reasonable degree of certainty as to whether production during that time is indicative of a herd affected by stray voltage?"

"It has not been affected by stray current after 1996 either."

"Have you looked at milk production for the period 1996 to 2002?"

"Yes, I have."

"Dr. Mellenberger, I'm showing you a blowup of Exhibit 1782." Will put it up on the monitor. "Is that the graph you prepared that relates to the period 1996 to 2002?"

"Yes. It goes from January '96 through December 2002."

"Why did it do that?"

"The main reason is that Mr. Allen started using BST on a continuous basis."

"What did milk production do in 1997?"

"Decreased."

"Why?"

"Essentially," Mellenberger said, "he stopped using BST. Also in '97 there was a major crop failure, a winter kill in '95 to '96 which affected alfalfa on a lot of dairy farms including Mr. Allen's."

Still standing by the jury, Will folded his arms across his chest and leaned back against the rail. "Let's turn to 1998. What did the production do on Mr. Allen's farm?"

"It increased substantially."

"How much?"

"Twenty-three pounds of milk per cow per day."

"Why?"

"Several reasons. If we allow for BST, about six pounds of

increase is due to it. In early '98, Cow Group 3 started milking three times a day. Group 2 was already on three times. So, we're going to get an increase. That's four pounds approximately. There was a change in ration in April, an improvement, that brought the high cows up six or seven pounds more. The forages Mr. Allen harvested from his spring seeding were absolutely excellent. Really good material."

"In your opinion is the production increase in the spring of 1998 indicative of a stray voltage fix on the Allen farm?"

With a sly smile, Mellenberger said, "No. The current had nothing to do with it."

"What was your understanding of what occurred on December 31, 2001?" Will asked.

"My understanding is that Mr. Allen cut some grounds around his farm."

"In your opinion, did cutting those grounds have any effect on the herd's milk production?"

"None!" Mellenberger exclaimed.

"Dr. Mellenberger, how would you rate Mr. Allen's management decisions as reflected in the material you've reviewed?"

"I would say average. Some good, some bad."

"What decisions would you characterize as bad?"

Mellenberger rubbed his chin and licked his lips. "Overcrowding the dry cow facilities, not adding more waterers to the east free-stall barn, not changing the stalls in the east barn. He could disagree—I do not like slatted-floor barns. It's hard on the feet and legs of cows. Unfortunately, the slats are there, so it's tough to take care of them. On the feed, I didn't like the feed that was put up in '97. It wasn't very good feed."

"How would you rate Mr. Allen's supervisory skills?" Will asked.

Mellenberger was silent for several moments. He stuck out his lower lip. "Things in the milker communication sheets concerned me," he said finally. "Seeing manure pits and slatted floors overflowing. Sometimes that comment occurs for a week, sometimes two. There are comments that some of the waterers sit empty for a week or two, or are overflowing. Seeing cows getting hung up on post railings or breaking through the slatted floors. I saw things that should have been taken care of. Whose responsibility is that? Ultimately, Russ Allen. He's the last man standing."

Next, Will played videotapes that Mellenberger had made in June of '02 at my farm. The witness pointed out what he considered defects in the free stalls, their dividers, the neck-rail pipes, and cow housing and milking routines.

"Could you please explain to the jury," Will said, "what you saw the cows doing during that last milking?"

Mellenberger nodded happily. "On the milking routine, they take a foamer—this has a brush to add iodine to clean the teats off. This is where the teats are first touched and the cow is what you would label as 'kicking'. I could call it 'steppy,''dancing,' whatever. But this occurred essentially on every cow they milked either midday or night."

"What is the cows' lifting of feet when their teats are striped?" Will asked. "What does that indicate to you?"

"Pain!" he said. "Painful. It's the bottom part of the teat. It's like the first joint on your finger. If the vacuum equipment is not functioning right, too high, too low, every cow shows the same reaction."

"In your opinion," Will said, "has stray voltage contributed in any way to the behavior that we're seeing on this tape?"

Mellenberger shook his head furiously. "Absolutely none!"

"Dr. Mellenberger, in your opinion what are the milk production limits on Mr. Allen's farm?"

Mellenberger sighed, again loudly and theatrically. "I guess at the top of the list I would put cow comfort. I think a lot of the increase in diseases Mr. Allen has seen is directly related to management of that barn."

Still standing at the jury box, Will asked, "Dr. Homan testified about records on the farm. Do you believe that records are limiting the Allen production?"

"Well," Mellenberger replied, "it's hard to say they are limiting production. But they are certainly limiting Mr. Allen's ability to make daily decisions on cows. Dr. Homan got frustrated because he couldn't get information that could help Mr. Allen make management decisions."

"Dr. Mellenberger, Dr. Behr testified that he believes Mr. Allen would produce at 50 percent or more above the Wisconsin average if not for stray voltage. Do you agree with that?"

Mellenberger shook his head. "No. I disagree with that."

"Why do you disagree?"

"Because of the facilities and management decisions made or not made. That just won't allow Mr. Allen to be at 50 percent above the Wisconsin average."

Will ended his direct questioning at this point and court recessed. I didn't think Mellenberger had hurt me badly yet. True, by offering an alternative theory for the cows' unruliness he'd scored some points, but there was no knockdown. And I thought it had been a mistake for Will to remind the jury of Dr. Behr's testimony about how stray voltage impacted my production, especially there at the end where it could linger in juror's minds. But only time and the jurors would tell if that was right.

When the court session resumed, it was time for Mellenberger's cross, and I was hopeful that we could wound him. Although he was a heavyweight witness with a big reputation in academic circles, there were indications that he might be vulnerable.

"Was it your testimony," Hammarback asked, going up near the witness stand, "that half the time you spent so far in this case was sorting the farm records?"

"No."

"What percent would you say was allocated to sorting?"

"Probably 10 to 15 percent."

"And the biggest thing was that it wasn't simply all nicely laid out on a spreadsheet?" Hammarback said disdainfully.

"Well, not that information, because you have accounting records and everything else."

Hammarback chuckled. "You said it would be nice to have records so you could analyze what you're doing, but I don't think that's a limiting factor, right?"

"That's correct."

"When you go through the list of what you consider limiting factors and get to the bottom," Hammarback said, "you have stray voltage down there as one of the things you need to rule out when there's a production change, right?"

"Correct."

"There's no doubt," Hammarback said, "that from the first part of 1998 up to 2000, the production in the Allen herd increased dramatically?"

"That's right," Mellenberger said. "It went up 28 pounds from January of 1998 to December of 1999, 28 pounds per cow per day."

Hammarback stuck his hands in his pockets, nodded, and looked down at the floor. "Would you agree that nothing like that increase had ever happened before in the history of the farm?" He looked up at the witness.

"The only time," Mellenberger told him, "was 1976 or 1977. The increase you're talking about was 22 percent."

"Now," Hammarback said, "you'd agree with me that actually putting together a ration is a bit of an art?"

"It is."

"You can't just look at one item or another and come up with any specific conclusions about it by itself, can you?"

"No. We have to set parameters to go by to make the ration."

"Now," Hammarback said, "you made an analysis of all the feed purchased on that farm. And what the content was of all the rations, that is the feed tests. But in all the time you spent in this case, you've never done a spreadsheet that summarized changes in the ration, have you?"

Mellenberger's eyes narrowed. "That was not my role in this case."

Hammarback nodded. "And so, if someone looked at the rations, they should be able to determine whether or not the content changed enough to change production. Wouldn't you agree?"

"That's correct."

"And you have not done that?"

"No," Mellenberger admitted.

Having scored a point, Hammarback left the area of the witness stand and moved across the courtroom until he stood halfway between McKay's bench and the jury box. "Let's talk about stray voltage for a moment," he said to Mellenberger. "Your opinion is that stray voltage could not have had an effect on the Allen farm because you don't know of any measurements of 3 milliamps or more in a cow contact?"

"That's correct."

"If," Hammarback said, "I told you to assume that in fact there was evidence in this case that there were four milliamps or more measured at a cow contact area in this farm, you would have to take it into account, would you not?"

"The behavior only."

Hammarback grinned. "Behavior can be a serious problem for dairy animals if it deters them from drinking, can't it?"

"That's not a behavior," Mellenberger snapped in his best professorial, smart-ass tone. "That's avoidance. The behavior is, does the cow react to something versus avoiding something?"

"Your statement is based on the studies you've read, right?"

Mellenberger nodded several times. "All the way from the 1960s to the present."

"And that includes Exhibit 82 here, which is studies showing the effects of neutral to earth current on behavior, production, and water intake in dairy cattle?"

"I've read that, yes."

"Okay," Hammarback said. "If we look at Exhibit 82, what it says on the front is that no significant difference in water consumption, feed intake, milk production, or concentration of fat or protein in the milk was found. But it says drinking behavior, number of drinks per day, and time of drink did change significantly. Isn't that right?"

"Yes."

Hammarback crossed his arms in front of his chest. "In fact, what this study shows is that even at half a volt, drinking behavior and drinks per day changes significantly?"

"There are some cows that will respond to that. But they still go to the water," Mellenberger told him.

"In fact," Hammarback said, "this study shows that actually voltages as low as half a volt can reduce the cow's production, doesn't it?"

"Not that I recall," Mellenberger said sourly."

"If you look at page 6 for animals receiving .5 volt treatment, there's a significant decrease in the number of drinks during the time the animals were receiving voltage, right?" Hammarback kept up the pressure.

"That will happen with the most sensitive cows."

"If we look at the conclusions of the study," Hammarback said, "some animals will not drink from an electrified water bowl as evidenced by the heifer and cow that refused to drink for 36 hours during the 4-volt treatment. Right?"

"That could happen on sensitive cows, right."

"Common sense would tell you, wouldn't it, Dr. Mellenberger, that the higher the voltage accessing the animal, the greater the effect on milk production?"

"When it gets high enough," Mellenberger replied, "that's right."

Hammarback nodded and slowly made his way toward the jury box. "Is it fair to say that if your definition of stray voltage is high enough before it has an effect, you're simply never going to be able to find stray voltage as being a problem?"

"Not true," Mellenberger said testily.

"It has to be 3 milliamps?" Hammarback said.

"If I want a response I can see, I've got to be between 3 and 6 milliamps. Above that, I've got extreme or moderate behavior changes, plus, I'm going to get some effect on cows' health and production."

Hammarback stared at him. "Let me ask: If you go on a farm and see reduced production, erratic animal behavior in a parlor, strange drinking behavior, are you going to investigate stray voltage?"

"I have in the past, yes. Many times."

"And if you go out and make a measurement and the voltage levels are less than 3 milliamps, are you just going to dismiss it?"

"Not necessarily, no," he said. "Because you would like to think that on any farm as low as you can go reasonably. And yeah, we'd make that assessment all the time. I've done that many times."

"Would you agree," Hammarback said, "that you may see behavioral reactions as low as half a volt, based on these studies?"

Now Roger Mellenberger hesitated before answering. "In the most sensitive animal, that's a probability. Whether it changes into visual behavior, that's a question. You would have to be there on that farm at that time."

Inching closer toward the jury box, Hammarback paused. "Every farm is unique, isn't it?"

"Every farm is unique," Mellenberger agreed.

"Are there," Hammarback asked, "any studies at all on traditional or nontraditional stray voltage as it relates to a free-stall barn?"

"No, only laboratory research."

"And so," Hammarback said, "from a lab standpoint there aren't any stray voltage researches ever done in a milking parlor, are there?"

"That's probably correct."

"Would you agree," Hammarback asked, "that there's only one study that's ever been done on the effect of isolation on production? The University of Minnesota study?"

"It was never a controlled field study. They looked at the data."

"What they did," Hammarback said for the jury, "is go out and take 84 farms in Minnesota, right? Averaged about 50 to 70 cows a farm, I think, 4,000 or 5,000 animals. What they did is check the conditions before isolation for one year, and the conditions after for one year. Right?"

"Yes."

"And they did that for a year before and after isolation. And there wasn't a single cow contact measurement made?"

"Never any measurements made."

Hammarback went over to the exhibits. "What they found," he said, "if we look at Exhibit 1062 here, is that several of the herds had a rapid change in production after isolation, for the better. Right?"

"It went about 50/50," Mellenberger said, grudgingly.

"Okay," Hammarback said. "I think 47 of those herds showed a substantial increase after isolation?"

"Yes," Mellenberger said. "About half."

"Their angle of increase in production is surprisingly similar to the Allens', isn't it?"

Mellenberger waved his arm. "That's a stretch, sir. You don't have the same conditions. They never measured the voltage. Didn't even know what they were isolating. And so, I've always criticized this study because they never had any controls. They never studied the farms so I could say, here's the situation before, here's after. Nothing changed except the voltage, and we don't even have the voltage levels."

"What you do know," Hammarback said, "is that the voltage did change on those farms that were isolated. Right?"

"Potentially."

"As a matter of physics," Hammarback said, "when that neutral is separated, the current going onto the farm will be reduced, shouldn't it?"

"Should go down, that's true."

"And so the only relationship from an electrical point of view to those high-response isolated farms is that the current was lowered?"

"Yes. You could make that conclusion."

Hammarback now came back over toward the witness stand. "You've testified on, probably, over 100 of these cases, haven't you?" he asked Mellenberger.

Mellenberger smiled sheepishly. "No, no. You've got me way too high there. Probably the max is 30 cases."

"It's over 100 you've looked at, then?"

"No. High '60s, '70s."

"On a stray voltage case for the utilities, you've never had the opinion that stray voltage caused a problem. Have you?"

"Yes," Mellenberger rushed to say. "At this point in time."

"You've got a new one now?" Hammarback asked skeptically.

Mellenberger smiled.

Hammarback studied him for a moment. Then he began to pace back and forth in front of the witness stand. "Back in 1989 or 1990 you were still at Michigan State," he said. "And in 1989, you billed 1,100 hours at least on stray voltage cases, didn't you?"

"I don't keep track of that," Mellenberger actually said with a straight face.

"Dr. Mellenberger, do you think that if you had a lower level of concern it would affect your employability with utilities?"

"That doesn't factor into anything," he said, suddenly testy again.

"Six milliamps," Hammarback said to him, "is the same current level it takes to trip a circuit breaker in the bathroom, isn't it?"

"I don't know what they're set at."

"Let's talk about the use of BST," Hammarback said. "Actually, the use of BST in 1996 didn't do anything for the Allen farm. Did it?"

"Yes, it did," Mellenberger insisted.

Hammarback quit pacing and looked hard at him. "You said they went on BST in May or June?"

"June 5."

"And they were at 51 pounds?"

"That's correct."

"And," Hammarback said sarcastically, "they went through that period of time and managed to get all the way up to 52 pounds. Didn't they?"

"Yes. In the space of a normal summer drop."

"And," Hammarback said quickly, "if there's stress on cows, they don't do well with BST. Do they?"

Mellenberger threw up his hands, exasperated. Hammarback definitely getting under his skin. "Depends!" he almost yelled. "Heat stress is the only one that's been studied. There's some indication it could have a negative effect, but it's not as great as if they weren't on BST. BST moderates that effect."

"So," Hammarback said, "for whatever reason, BST did not gain them a pound in 1996, did it?"

"Yes," Mellenberger stubbornly insisted. "It did."

Walking toward the jury, Hammarback stopped in mid-stride, wheeled around and looked at the witness with his eyes wide. "One pound?" he said, with a curious smirk.

"No, about four."

Still smiling, Hammarback said, "So it's your testimony here today that the reason they stayed at 47 to 50 pounds or more is simply because they were using BST?"

"That's correct. The Group 3 went from 45 pounds to 51 pounds."

"All right," Hammarback said impatiently. "So how many pounds is that?"

"Six"

Hammarback paused. "Will you agree," he asked, "that if current were high enough and it was removed—let me ask you to assume that current was high enough, so it affects the cows' feed and water consumption. Removing that voltage could result in a 21-pound gain in production, could it not?"

"Sure," he said, stunning me by his honesty. "And quickly."

Hammarback turned and went toward his counsel table. "That's all the questions I have, Your Honor," he said over his shoulder to McKay.

Will now got up to have a final word with this most important witness. "Dr. Mellenberger," he said, walking up quickly to the witness stand. "That Minnesota study you were asked about. As part of the study, was any effort made to assess the level of stray voltage present on the farms prior to the time the farms were isolated?"

"There was not. It had to be one volt for them to get isolation. Beyond that, there's no information if it was one volt or two or three or four. So it had to be one to get the isolation."

Will continued, "In reading the article, is there any way to tell how many farms, for example, were at four volts?"

"No, there was not."

"Is there any way to tell from the article what contribution to stray voltage came from any on-farm sources?"

"No."

"And did the article address whether any on-farm electrical contributions to stray voltage had been corrected in conjunction with the isolation?"

"No."

"Dr. Mellenberger, if electricity—stray voltage—was present on a farm at a level above your level of concern at six milliamps, and if that problem was corrected, what would you expect the milk production on that farm to do?"

Mellenberger shrugged. "I would expect the milk production to rise dramatically within two weeks. And I mean dramatically." He said that with a straight face.

"Why would it do that?" Will wanted to know.

"Because they're going to go back to the feed and water and get maximum intake and, therefore, that's milk. Input in, output out. If I improve the input, the output goes up."

"Would that be true if there was any level of stray voltage causing them to avoid water or feed?"

"Well, if they didn't go at all they wouldn't live very long."

"No further questions." Will sat down and Hammarback got up to take his last licks with the witness.

"When a farm is isolated," Hammarback said, walking up near the stand, "if there's a voltage problem on the farm it stays on the farm, right? And gets worse, doesn't it?"

"It could."

"And if in fact those farms were isolated and had an on-farm problem, their production would not have gone up, it would have gone down?"

"Depends," Mellenberger told him, "on whatever level was there. That's the problem. We have no numbers."

"If we go back to your deposition, about the days dry— explain that again, please."

Mellenberger adjusted the microphone and spoke with exaggerated slowness, as if he were addressing an idiot. "Twenty-two cows had 30 days, 30 or less days dry. The other side you need to include is that 31 of the 50 days dry has an impact. This means that 26 percent of 238 is 63."

"That's a high percentage?" Hammarback asked.

"Very high," Roger Mellenberger told him.

"If the cows have been subjected to 6 milliamps of current, unless they are before 60 days they aren't going to come up much on milk, are they?"

"That's right."

"No further questions," Hammarback said.

As Mellenberger lumbered down from the stand, I was feeling very encouraged about my chances of winning this case. Roger Mellenberger was a key defense witness whose testimony WPS was depending on to shoot big holes in my case. Although I wasn't a lawyer and knew very little about legal affairs, I knew enough about what had happened with stray current on my farm and all the measures we'd taken to try to remedy the situation to realize that Mellenberger's testimony, as shrewd and knowledgeable as it was, hadn't been so damaging.

CHAPTER 14

DR. MICHAEL LANE

When Dr. Michael Lane, a veterinarian retained by WPS, entered the courtroom and stood before the bailiff to take his oath, it was all I could do to keep from laughing out loud. The guy was so disheveled—his cheap-looking, Kmart-style polyester pants so wrinkled—that I thought he'd slept on the straw of a milk barn surrounded by a dozen Holstein cows.

Sixtyish, short, balding, lean and fit-looking, Lane taught in the Agriculture Department at the University of California and specialized in treating dairy cattle which, for some reason, he insisted on referring to as "bovine cattle." Sort of like saying "canine dogs" or "feline cats," I guess.

Trevor Will was handling the direct testimony. Dr. Lane at first talked about his work at my farm, which included reviewing depositions, analyzing farm data, touring the facilities and observing the operation. He'd spent about 10 hours on-site and watched the milking routine.

Will wasted no time in getting to the point he wanted the witness to make. "Doctor," he said, "based on the work you've done in this case, do you have an opinion to a reasonable degree of veterinarian certainty as to whether there is a stray voltage problem on the Allen farm?"

"Yes, I do."

"And what's your opinion?" Trevor Will asked.

"There is no stray voltage currently and there never has been a stray voltage problem on the farm."

"What do you charge for your consulting services?" Will asked him.

"One hundred thirty-five dollars an hour. On top of that will be expenses such as travel, lodging, food, car rental, lab fees, et cetera. which can be extensive."

"Is there any one client you've done a great deal of consulting for?" Trevor Will asked.

"The bulk of my consulting," Lane said, taking a quick sip of water, "has been one client in Michigan, Consumers Energy."

"Have you," Will asked him, "ever seen stray voltage on a farm?"

"Yes, I have," Lane said.

"How important is nutrition in terms of milk production?"

"It is the cornerstone of milk production. If we think of the cow as a biological factory that makes milk, the components have to come out of the feed. So, if the feed is not right, the cows are limited in milk production."

Trevor Will walked slowly over toward the jury, his three-piece, black pinstriped suit jacket neatly buttoned. "What role does water play in milk production?" he asked Dr. Lane.

"If cows do not intake the water they need, they would not be able to eat as much dry matter. Dry matter is what makes milk, contains all the building blocks of milk."

Will nodded. "Why doesn't water make milk?"

"Well, when the components of milk are taken out of the blood and put into the mammary gland, the particles that are in the mammary gland are what draw the water into the milk. So, milk is 12 percent solids. And as those solids go into the mammary, it sucks water out of the bloodstream so that 88 percent water surrounds those 12 percent solids."

"Do you have an opinion as to whether nutrition played a role in the production changes on the Allen farm?"

Lane nodded vigorously. "Nutrition played a very big role. There was a bad feed component, low quality, through the last half of '97 and the first two or three months of '98. As that feed diminished, production went up."

"What feed components can affect milk production?"

"The major thing is fiber levels. And the forage is the cornerstone of our nutrition program. Nutrition is the cornerstone of milk production. And forages are the cornerstone of the feed program. The cow," Lane continued, "is designed to eat forage—grass and hay. However, we can add grains and make the ration more high-energy. But we can't add too much or the cows will get sick. So, we constantly monitor the fiber in the ration to make sure it's adequate, but there's not so much that we affect the turnover of the feedstuff."

"What's turnover?" Will asked.

"You've all heard the term 'a meal that stuck to your ribs'? That means you don't need to eat very often that day if you've had a meal that sticks to your ribs. That's not what we want with dairy cattle. We don't want a meal that sticks to their ribs. We want a meal that's highly digestible so they're hungry again and eating again and taking in more of the building components of milk."

"Why," Trevor Will wanted to know, "is turnover important?"

Dr. Lane pulled the microphone closer. "Looking at milk per cow per day, you can translate that to paychecks, or dollars per month—dollars that come from milk. We're interested in maximizing milk per cow per day."

Trevor Will paused to let the jury absorb these facts. "Is there any kind of tool for measuring the quality of forage in terms of the turnover?"

Lane nodded. "There's a term," he said, "called 'relative feed value' which takes into account the types of fiber in the forage. And it makes a prediction on how fast this material will be digested."

"Doctor,do you have an opinion as to whether all rations that are balanced to the same point will produce the same amount of milk in a cow?"

"Yeah. The introduction of the nutrients is the first step. Then we have to look at whether there's any forages impeding digestion of those nutrients."

Will went over and put up Exhibit 1804. "Can you tell us what this is, Dr. Lane?"

"Yes. I summarized forage analyses, by year. From 1996 to 2000. This shows there's a low forage quality on the farm on the average for 1996, '97; '98 we show a big raise. '99 and 2000 are consistent with 1998."

"Dr. Lane," Trevor Will asked, turning around and going back over to the jurors. "You also looked at the use of protein on the Allen farm in 1997 and 1998. What conclusions did you reach?"

"What that does," Lane said, "is increase the concentration of nutrients in the feed. The rations are becoming richer. The cows would improve milk production due to the higher concentrations of protein."

"Doctor, do you have an opinion as to whether the rations were kept constant between 1997 and 1998?"

"The rations varied widely," Lane told him. "They attempted to keep the nutrient density fairly constant. But the rations had wide variations."

"What impact would those variations have on milk production?"

Dr. Lane spread his hands out and shrugged. "Production would be impaired."

"Assume for the purposes of my next question," he said, "that Mr. Allen began using BST on his herd approximately March 18 of 1998. Do you have an opinion as to whether March milk production would be affected by resuming BST usage?"

"Yes," Lane said emphatically. "BST should have an effect on the March pickups."

"What impact would you expect to see on production after the second shot of BST?"

"Cows still increasing in milk. The second shot would give you an additional boost."

"What happens after the third shot in the BST series?"

"By the third shot the hormones have come into equilibrium. From that point on, your shots just maintain the extra milk produced. They don't continue to increase it."

Will went over toward the front of the courtroom to the exhibits and introduced a new one. "Dr. Lane, I'm showing you what we've marked as Exhibit 1807. Can you please tell us what that is?"

Dr. Lane squinted over at it. "Yes. This is a graph that shows what effect the season of the year has on milk production."

"Is that specific to the Allen farm?"

"Well, the data is, but you typically see this pattern in cows in the northern part of the United States."

"Why is this pattern typical?"

"Because cows are still seasonal breeders. They like to have their calves in the spring when grass is growing, so they have enough milk to feed the calf. So, you will see milk production go up in the spring."

"What sort of seasonal increase does this graph show on the Allen farm?"

Lane chuckled. "It shows that cows have a different calendar year than we do. But there is a six-pound increase from January to June of every year, and you should expect that."

"Now," Trevor Will said, "the graph shows that in the fall you're losing six pounds on the average. Did that happen in 1998?"

"No, it did not."

"Why not?"

"Well, there were several changes in 1998 that occurred that would mask the curve line. I should say that I believe it did occur in 1998, but other management changes raised the entire production."

"What were some of those other management changes?"

"Nineteen-ninety-eight," Lane told him, "was a big year for management changes. There were improvements in the ration: Peas and oats came out. A veterinarian came on board who intensified the vet program and improved overall cows' health and foot health on the farm. There were fans put in the barn, so ventilation was better. Cow mats were put in. There was use of BST. Three times a day milking occurred."

"Did you," Will said to him, "look at the issue of mastitis on the Allen farm?"

"Yes."

"What is a somatic cell count?"

"Somatic cell count is a white blood cell that migrates from the bloodstream into the mammary gland when the mammary has an infection."

"Looking at your chart of somatic cell count at the Allen farm, what conclusions do you draw?"

"That it was fairly low," Lane said. "Ideally, you would like to be down somewhere in the 100,000 area."

Trevor Will unbuttoned his jacket, showing his vest. "Is there anything about this chart that suggests there's an electricity problem on the Allen farm?"

Lane shrugged. "Well, again, somatic cell counts have been

blamed for electricity though no scientific research shows there's any relationship at all. This is very unusual for a stray voltage claim, in that most claim that electricity caused cows to get mastitis. This shows there is no mastitis problem on the Allen farm."

"Doctor," Trevor Will said, walking down the length of the jury box to the opposite end, "overall, how would you assess animal health on the Allen farm?"

Lane considered for a moment. "Like any dairy, there are episodes of disease. And that, I think, is why both veterinarians in their deposition felt that disease levels were not extreme but fairly normal."

"Are you familiar with the concept of differential diagnosis, and is it something you use?"

"Yes," Lane told him. "Every day."

"If I were to ask you to apply your differential diagnosis methodology to claims Mr. Allen made about his herd, could you do that?"

"Yes."

"Mr. Allen has complained that the cows were jumpy in the parlor. He complained about a high death rate. Assume he's complained about a high disease rate. Assume complaints about mastitis. Assume complaints about lapping at water. Assume complaints about reproductive problems. Assume there has been low milk production. If you had those complaints, could you go about analyzing them under the differential diagnosis method?"

"Yes," Lane said. "Let's start with number one, being jumpy in the parlor. On our visit to evaluate milking, there was absolutely no movement of cows in the parlor. But when their teat ends were touched, it was obvious they were swollen and painful. The cows were completely comfortable till then. So, I would translate that into a milk machine or milking technique problem."

"What about a high death rate?"

"Other than years we had known causes of a high death rate—

displaced abomasa and retained placentas—we do not have a high death rate that's a problem in this herd. And," Lane continued, "there's no reason to believe that stray voltage, if it existed, causes a high death rate. I would take 'high death rate' off Mr. Allen's list of complaints." Lane went on, "Mastitis should have been lumped in with high disease rates. I've looked at somatic cell count, looked at a number of treatments. Those looked reasonable and I don't think there's a mastitis problem. Lapping at the water, you see in the literature that's a sign of stray voltage. I would say stray voltage or normal behavior, because that's normal boredom behavior of cattle."

Will moved a few steps toward the witness box. "Let me ask about that. Lapping at water is associated with stray voltage?"

Lane nodded. "Yes. In the early works of the literature."

"Have you observed a cow drinking water when voltage was passed through?"

"I have," Lane said.

Will suddenly went back to the jury. "On that basis, can you tell what mechanism was used to provide water in instances where this is associated?"

"In the stray voltage literature, lapping at waterers was noted in tie-stall housing where each cow has a water cup next to her. The water cup is made of metal. The cow sticks its nose into the cup and depresses the lever to get water. In that instance, lapping would be unusual behavior. But lapping at a freestanding trough is not unusual behavior."

"What type of system is in Mr. Allen's barn?"

"All concrete waterers."

Will paused. "You mentioned your experience. Could you tell us a bit more about what you observed with a cow at a waterer?"

"Yes. On one stray voltage investigation in Michigan, we had a waterer that had seven volts measured on it. We videotaped the cows coming to the seven volts, and they all just came up and drank the water. There was no lapping, no hesitation. These were Holstein cows. Seven volts did not impede water consumption."

"What type or style of farmer is Mr. Allen?" Will asked.

"Based on the information you had, do you believe stray voltage was a cause of low milk production on the Allen farm?"

Dr. Lane answered quickly. "I believe it was not associated."

"If," Trevor Will said, "stray voltage had been a problem and it was removed, what impact would you expect to see on production?"

"I would expect an immediate response."

"Why?"

"Because," Lane told him, "dry matter intake would be limited by water intake, and as soon as we took the electricity away from the cow, her water consumption would go back up and she would go back to maximum dry-matter intake for the feed she was given."

"Doctor," Trevor Will said, "based on your review of scientific literature relating to electricity and harm to Holstein dairy cattle, do you have an opinion as to the amount of current flowing through the cow that is required to affect milk production?"

"Yes—somewhere about six milliamps. Some people say as much as eight milliamps still has no effect."

"Why," Will said, "do you believe you need at least six milliamps to affect milk production?"

"Well, basically from the Red Book."

"Is there any scientific literature in the peer-reviewed press that says earth currents below 1 milliamp could reduce milk production in cows?"

"No."

"Dr. Lane," Trevor Will asked, "are you familiar with the concept of a limiting factor?"

"I am."

"From your review of the Allen farm, what do you believe are the limiting factors out there today?"

"Feed, periodically," Lane said. "And consistently bad cow comfort."

"Based on what you've seen in Wisconsin, Michigan, Idaho, California and everywhere else, where would you rank Mr. Allen as a farmer? How would you classify him?" Will asked, still pacing.

Lane shifted in his seat and held onto the microphone with both hands as he answered. "Most of the herds in Wisconsin are very small, where Mr. Allen has a 400-cow herd. Most people with a 400-cow herd do not just market their milk as—do not market their forage as milk. They use high-quality feeds to maintain good cash flow. I think Mr. Allen is a unique farmer in that he has a lot of debt, yet is willing to just feed forages and take whatever Mother Nature gives him. So, in his peer group, as a farmer, he would be way below average."

"No further questions," Will said, as he ended his direct.

Hammarback got up and walked briskly up near the witness stand, unbuttoned his suit jacket, and stuck his hands in his pants pockets. "One of the ways to check your differential diagnosis on stray electricity is simply to reduce the level of electricity and see what happens, right?"

"Yes, if you were trying to prove that something was caused by electricity. You would have to measure an effect—measure that the cow was receiving electricity. You would have to see what her production level was then. You would remove the electricity and see her production level. Then you would put it back and see if it had an effect."

"Out in the real world," Hammarback said, "no farmer is going to let you do it, right?"

"No. That's why we do controlled research at universities."

"Okay," Hammarback said. "But there's never been any study of somebody putting current on waterers in a free-stall barn to see what would happen to the cow, right?"

"Your answer is no."

"There haven't been any studies in a milking parlor of the effects of electricity on milk production of cows either, have there?"

"I don't believe so," Dr. Lane told him.

"And as far as you know there have been no studies of ground current and effects it may have on cows in a free stall, have there?"

Lane scratched his chin. "In a free stall? I'd have to review Dr. Reinemann's report where he studied ground currents, but I believe he did that in a controlled environment."

"And as far as you know," Hammarback said, "nobody ever put a clamp around a cow at the Allen farm to figure out how much current is going through?"

"No."

"And as far as you know cows aren't good conversationalists. So, we can't just ask her if she's getting shocked, right?"

"That's right."

"You have to see what her behavior is?"

"Yes."

Hammarback nodded and went over to the jurors. "Would you agree," he asked, "that if there was electricity of a high enough level to affect intake of either feed or water on a dairy farm, that would also affect how well BST worked?"

"I agree with that."

"Okay. Now, if you've put stray electricity back into the equation, then, by removal of stray electricity on this farm, would you agree that there's about 17 pounds of milk increase that could be attributable to the removal of electricity?"

"Well," Lane said, "if you assume it was there in the first place and you removed it, there would be no way to get a response if the feed had not changed. So, there are other things that have to be changed at the same time to get a milk response."

Hammarback folded his hands in front of him. "The rations presented to the Allen cows in January, February and March of

1998 would allow a cow to produce 85 pounds of milk—in the high group—right?"

"I wouldn't say that," Lane replied. "They were balanced to have enough nutrients for cows with a full rumen to produce 80 pounds of milk if the turnover was not impaired."

"Okay," Hammarback said. "And for the rations at the Allen farm, would you agree that through 1998 the high group was balanced at least 80, 85 pounds or higher? I think 85."

Dr. Lane nodded. "I would agree with that."

"You made the statement that you didn't think electricity was causing the increase in somatic cell count. Are you assuming there is no electricity affecting the cows now?"

"I'm assuming there never was any electricity affecting the cows."

"On the effects of the Allen farm's increased production when electricity was reduced, the slatted floors would not cause the increase, would they?" Hammarback asked.

"No."

"The ammonia would not cause an increase in production?"

Dr. Lane smiled. "That's correct."

"Okay," Hammarback said. "The records or lack thereof would not cause an increase in production?"

"That's true."

"Now, if voltage was removed from the Allen farm about the end of December when the ground was moved, would you agree that could be a cause of increased production?"

"That would be a possibility if the voltage was on the waterers and it was decreasing dry matter intake. Otherwise, the increase has to be due to ration changes."

Hammarback moved up closer to Dr. Lane. "Actually," he said, "you've never really ruled out stray voltage as being the cause of the production change on the Allen farm. Have you?"

Lane bristled at this. "That wasn't my job to measure stray voltage on the farm!"

"Dr. Lane, you testified that it takes six volts to affect production?"

"I think I said six milliamps: Three volts would be what I meant."

"You said you wouldn't have a substantial effect until you had six volts?"

"I think I misstated," Dr. Lane told him. "I might rather have said 'eight volts'."

"You should have said 'eight volts'?" Hammarback quickly asked, pouncing on this.

"Well," Lane said hesitantly, "the Red Book, which I rely on, has production losses that begin at six volts—excuse me, six milliamps. And then there's some papers that have values at eight milliamps that still don't show any production changing or any decreases in water consumption. So, it's somewhere between six and eight milliamps."

"If," Hammarback said, "you assume that 10 percent of the cows have a resistance of 244 ohms or less, that would mean in a volt you could have four milliamps. Right?"

"I think," Lane said, "the work that was done on the 200 ohm cow was done from leg to leg with electrodes where they measured the resistance of the cows and did not take into account the hooves."

Hammarback went up even closer to the stand. "I'll ask you to assume that we've got a study in evidence here that indicates that 10 percent of cows have a resistance of 244 ohms or less from the mouth to the four hooves, okay?"

Lane took a deep breath and sipped some water from his glass. "I've read many articles and I know some of them have measured cow resistances without taking into account hooves and with EKG electrodes on the legs and just measured through the cow, and did not take into account the resistance of the hooves. And those numbers are somewhere around 200 to 250 ohms. So I'm not sure whether the 200 ohm cow you're talking about was measured in that way or through the hooves also."

"Would you agree that cows definitely have a variation in their resistance?"

"Yes."

"And the research you were talking about actually says that the cow's least sensitivity to current is about the same as human sensitivity?"

"Yeah, I've read that," Dr. Lane said.

"Well, if the current levels are the same for people and cows, then the difference in voltage is because of resistance difference, right?"

"The source resistance for people—the contact resistance for people who wear shoes—would be quite different."

Hammarback now turned away and went back over to the jury. "Dr. Surbrook, in an article, has said that people have 40,000 ohms of resistance on dry skin. So, compare 40,000 ohms resistance to 250 or even 500 in a cow and it takes a lot less voltage to affect the cow than a person?"

"I don't know that to be true," Lane grunted.

Hammarback smiled thinly. Then he spoke more loudly than he had before. "In your business, where you go out on the farm and evaluate, isn't common sense important?"

"Absolutely," Lane responded.

"So, assuming, as Dr. Surbrook indicated, that cows have the same sensitivity to current as people, what would be the voltage you're talking about for a person that would do the same milliamps for cows?"

Dr. Lane was confused by the question, so Hammarback rephrased it. "I have 40,000 ohms of resistance, and I've got 3 milliamps; .003 amps."

"Okay."

"How many volts is that?"

"I have 120."

"And if I go to 6 milliamps—twice as much—how many volts would that be?"

"Well," Lane told him, "it would be 240."

Hammarback nodded. "Now, if I had an extension cord and had you hang on to both ends, are you telling us that the level of current that would flow through you, assuming you've got dry skin, would be such that it wouldn't affect you?"

Dr. Lane paused for several long moments before answering. "Well, I...don't know. I'm not sure about the 40,000 ohms. But I would not be interested in picking up a 120 or 240 line, if that's what you're getting at."

"Because you would get a shock?"

Lane again hesitated. Then he said, "Yes."

"As an expert," Hammarback said, "when you were out to dairies in Idaho and someone had a concern about stray electricity, what did you tell them they should stay under for voltage?"

"I...don't think I ever had that discussion. I measured dairies in Idaho and have not found anything that needed to be corrected."

"In your work as an expert, the 200 cases or so that you've been on have all involved stray voltage, haven't they?"

"The 200, yes."

"And since 1991, all of them have been jobs for utilities?"

"Of the stray voltage cases, yes," Lane replied.

"And you've never found in any of those couple of hundred cases that a utility was causing a problem that affected cows?" Hammarback sounded highly skeptical, and rightly so.

"That the utility was causing? No, that was never found."

"Just for Consumers Energy utility, your fees were over a million dollars for work you did?"

"Over a 10-year period, yes."

And on that perfect note, Hammarback ended his cross. I heard some murmuring among the jurors at the mention of the million-dollar figure and watched happily as Trevor Will nearly fell over his counsel table in his rush to run up there for redirect. Hammarback's last series of questions had hurt Lane, and Will knew it.

"Regarding the last point," Will said quickly to the doctor. "What was included in the million dollars?"

"That would be air fares, lab fees, car rentals and so on."

Apparently realizing that nothing good could come from further discussion of Lane's fees, Will quickly changed the subject. "You were asked questions about whether you could test if electricity is causing a problem with milk production by removing the electricity and seeing what happens to production. If you were to design such a test, what would you do to make sure you were measuring the change in electricity?"

"Well," Lane said, "like all good research done at universities, you have to control extraneous variables. So, you would not start BST. You would not make any ration changes. You would not add mats to the free-stall barn. You would not add fans. You would keep your veterinarian programs the same. Then, if all those things were constant, you may be able to see an effect of removing electricity from cows."

Will went over to the jury box and rested his elbow on the rail, facing Lane. "What would you do in terms of measuring the electricity?" he asked.

"At the very least you would have to make sure it was there, make sure it was affecting the cows. And then make sure it had been removed from the cows when you made the electrical changes."

"Last question," Trevor Will said. "Do you know what the resistance is of dry human skin?"

"No," Lane said. "I don't."

Will sat down and Hammarback got up to take another crack at the good doctor. "So, Dr. Lane," Hammarback said cheerfully, walking up near the stand. "You would be critical of any study that actually changed the feeding program prior to doing any electrical experimentation?"

"I think any feeding program could be changed prior to as long as the cows were given time to come into equilibrium with the program so that they were on a stable diet through the test period."

"If the feeding went from a Total Mixed Ration to a TMR with a computer feeder, that would be a significant change?"

"Yes. Those changes can be compensated if there is a control group involved."

"You've never gone back and looked at changes in rations before 1998 as they may have affected production, have you?"

"Yes, in 1997," Dr. Lane said.

"But nothing before that?"

"No."

"So, you have no idea what the rations were at any time prior to 1996?"

"True," Lane told him.

"That's all," Hammarback said, and I was surprised to see Will get up yet again. He must've been deeply worried. And that made me very, very happy.

"Dr. Lane," Trevor Will said. "You looked at the rations in 1997, correct? Did you form an opinion as to what caused production to decrease in 1997?"

"Yes."

"And what was that?"

Lane held up two fingers. "Two things. One was the removal of BST in 1996 from the herd so the production per cow per day started to diminish. And the second thing was as of July 1997, the peas and oats came into the ration and were fed in increasing amounts towards the end of the year, so production took a real dive in 1997."

Here, finally, Trevor Will ended. So did Hammarback. They were both done with Lane, who left the stand looking exactly as he had when he'd taken it: Wrinkled, disheveled, and a complete mess in his cheap polyesters. Doctor or not—and he looked like anything but—I thought Hammarback had done a great job on him, punched holes in his theories and testimony.

But my mind didn't linger on Lane for very long. Because next up was one Russell Allen, and he was going to have a lot to say, if only he could get over that case of the heebie-jeebies he'd just suddenly come down with.

As Judge McKay told Hammarback to call the next witness— me— I felt the hot gaze of those 26 eyes in the jury box beating on the back of my neck like a couple of dozen flaming suns.

Chapter 15

Russell Allen

As I approached the witness stand, I was so nervous I thought my heart might beat right through my chest. I was breathing like I'd run a marathon. Which, in a sense, I had. Right now, everything that had happened in the course of this marathon trial—the expert opinions, lawyers' arguments and objections, the exhibits, the rebuttals, the rebuttals to the rebuttals—meant next to nothing, because the case had come down to what it had always been about: me.

And about my family, alive and dead. They knew that if I did not get a fix, the dairy business would have to be sold. The weight of their expectations hung heavy as a butcher block around my neck. And now I was alone in this courtroom, alone in a crowd. Robinson Crusoe shipwrecked on his island couldn't have felt more solitary.

After they swore me in, I plunked myself down in the witness chair and picked up the glass of water beside me. My hand shook so badly that the ice cubes rattled. They sounded as loud as a window shattering. Embarrassed, I managed to lift the glass to my lips and sip a little water without spilling any and, thank the Lord, was able to set the glass back down without dropping it.

The day was another in a string of perfect spring days. Bright sunshine filtered in the courtroom windows and spread across the spectators' gallery, which was crammed full. But I didn't notice faces. I didn't even notice the jurors' faces although I felt the force of their gaze. 24 eyes boring into me all at once.

I looked at the gold chandeliers, turned and glanced up at white-haired old Judge McKay perched behind his oak bench, saw the uniformed bailiff standing near the door, watched the stenographer, Karen Nagorny, pecking away on her machine, noticed the mahogany counsel tables, the jury box with its glossy railing, and the plush carpet with the state seal covering the floor. I felt like I was in a cathedral.

Heart still pounding—I was trying to hide my nerves—I folded my hands on my lap and waited. As Hammarback got up from his counsel table and walked up close to me, he shot a quick wink and flashed a smile.

"So," he said. "You're the Russ Allen, the one we've all been talking about?"

"I guess so," I said, feeling sheepish.

"Welcome. Give us a little history first, about your background. Basically, your folks were who?"

"Alvin and Alice. Allen."

"When was it they moved to this area?"

"1937."

"And they moved where?"

"5206 Little Apple Road."

"Is that the very same farm we've been talking about for weeks?"

"Yes," I said.

"When they came to the farm, had they started a family yet?"

"No. They purchased the farm in 1937, got married in '38, and then had their first child. Larry was born a year after they married."

Hammarback nodded. "Okay. After that, how many brothers and sisters?"

"I got six brothers and four sisters. Eleven kids altogether." I thought achingly of the ones who were gone.

"How many were involved on the farm?"

I took another sip of water and started to calm down. "Larry went to college, Jim went to college. The rest of us were all on the farm."

"Larry and Jim today are where?"

"Larry's in East St. Louis. Jim's in Seattle."

Hammarback came a step closer. "As you were growing up," he said, "tell us how you learned to take care of dairy cows."

"Well, from 5, 6 years old, we started helping with all the chores and milking. We had buckets and the bucket was held on with a strap and we changed straps and one of the older kids would put the unit on and take the unit off when the cow was done."

"How," Hammarback asked, "would the milk get from the bucket to the bulk tank?"

"We would dump it in pails and we'd have to carry it to the milk house."

"And there wasn't a milk tank then. What was there?"

"Milk cans," I said.

"How many cows?"

I glanced at the jurors. "We started with 32, and when I was 7 or 8 years old, we rented another farm and were milking the 32 plus another 27."

"As time went on, did the family add to the number of cows?"

"Yeah, we did. After we rented that farm, we built a hundred-stall barn. Then we moved the 32 cows and the 27 cows in, and then we filled the barn the rest of the way with more cows. We kind of grew into it."

"Okay," Hammarback said. "When was that barn completed?"

"In 1962."

"Who, in the '60s—was your dad still running the place?"

"Well," I said, "we were getting up there where we'd have a little say, too."

"Who, then, in the '60s was actually running the farm? The whole family?"

"Cletus went off to school for a while," I explained. "Les was in the Marines, then came back. Cletus came back from school. We were all involved except for Larry and Jim."

"Once you graduated from high school, did you want to do anything other than work on the farm?"

"That's all I did." It was all I ever wanted to do. I loved it.

"Could you explain to us how you ended up being the one running the farm?"

"Well, first off, my brother Les passed away. Shortly after that, Cletus left and went farming on his own. My brother, Kevin, ended up farming on his own. And Bob—I ended up purchasing his share—he's working for me now."

"Your sisters were involved too?" Hammarback asked.

"Yeah, Geri Lynn was and Josie too."

The mention of my sisters brought back a painful memory, the time Geri Lynn and her husband went on a week-long fishing trip to Canada. They had left their 15-month-old son Jesse with my sister Bonnie. Halfway through the trip, Jesse came down with a fever and had to be rushed to the emergency room. He died the next day.

Same day that my sister Karen's son Johnny died in a farm accident. We had to have a double funeral. It was the first time I ever saw my father cry.

"What year was it you took over the operation of the whole thing?"

"Approximately '89," I said.

Hammarback paused, and I sipped some more water. Then I

pulled a hard candy from my pocket, unwrapped the cellophane, and popped the candy in my mouth.

"How did the subject of stray voltage come up on your farm in 1988?"

I shrugged. "Cows kicking in the parlor, couldn't keep the units on. Pa and I read about it, talked about it. Thought it was a good idea to get it checked out."

"So, did you?"

"I did."

"Who came to check?"

"Rob Gelhardt," I told him. "From WPS."

"What did he do?"

I laughed. "Monitored an electrical panel. Said there was no problem."

"Did you believe him? At the time?"

"Sure," I said. I had no reason not to.

"What did you do about production?"

"Kept plugging away, working and working on it. Bought our first mixer, tried to boost it like that."

"Did you think that would affect production?"

"We were hoping. Research says it."

"What effect did that mixer wagon have on production?"

I sighed. "I was disappointed—nothing."

"After the mixer wagon was purchased, did you do any upgrades to the parlor?"

"I thought a new parlor, a parallel parlor, was the answer to my kicking problems."

"Did you see how cows behaved in those parlors?"

I'd visited four farms in Michigan and observed them. "Yeah," I told him. "They would stand perfect. I thought it was the answer to my problems. I went back home, we put it together."

"How did you finance the new parlor?" Hammarback asked.

"A lease, through Farm Credit Services. It's a lending institution dealing mostly with farmers. I think it was completed in April of 1994."

Hammarback began slowly to pace. "What was cow behavior like in the new parlor?"

I shook my head disgustedly as I remembered. "Not any better than the old parlor. We had many kickoffs. I ended up putting a second person in because one person just couldn't handle it."

"Toward the end of 1996, beginning of 1997, what was the financial condition of the farm?"

I sighed. "Heading for bankruptcy." For some reason when I said this I was overcome by emotion. Tears welled up and I could not stop them from running down my cheeks.

Hammarback waited. "Did you get hold of Mike Hoerth?" he said softly.

"I...I got tired of cows kicking in the parlor," I said, and wiped the tears with my index finger. "I told Mike, 'It's your parlor, your tit dip, your crowd gate, it's all your stuff. Get those cows to stand still!' He knew of a guy on another parlor testing for stray current and thought I should get it checked out. Because he'd gone over my parlor a zillion times and couldn't find anything wrong."

"That's when Larry Neubauer came into the picture," I said, regaining a measure of control. I took out a hankie, blew my nose, and then sipped some water. "He came and tested for a couple of days."

"What did he do that stands out in your mind?" Hammarback asked.

"Shut off power to the farm so there was nothing incoming. The measurement then was 800 milliamps—I couldn't believe there was current there when the power was off to the whole farm."

Hammarback nodded. "Anything else stand out?"

I nodded back at him. "He disconnected the utility's neutral."

"What happened after that?"

"The current on the parlor steel was nearly gone."

"When you got a report from Mr. Neubauer, how did you take it?"

"I didn't know if he was pulling my leg. I wasn't sure. I wanted a second opinion. So, I had WPS come and test. Mike Moore came. He said there wasn't a problem, and that if I was counting on stray voltage to save my farm, it wasn't going to happen."

"Let me ask you this," Hammarback said. "Have you ever restricted anybody from WPS on where they could test or what they could do on your farm?"

"No, I never did."

"What was your understanding of what the Dairyland Isolator Mr. Neubauer offered you would do?"

"Get the current off the parlor. I didn't know where to turn or who to trust, so I called Larry. He said to try it."

Hammarback turned and went over to the jury box. "Had Mr. Neubauer told you the cost to put in an isolation system?"

"Yes. About $58,000."

Hammarback now walked me through the events dealing with the Dairyland Isolator and the moving of reference rods. "I was excited for the first couple of days after installation," I said. "I thought, man, this is just what I'm looking for. The cows settled down and production even came up a bit in the first couple days."

"After this improvement, then," Hammarback said, leaning one elbow on the box rail, "what happened next?"

"The cows were terrible that first weekend I had to milk. So terrible I called up Bob to come help me." My heart started to pound as I recalled my anxiety and fear. Then a lump formed in my throat and tears again began welling up. I tried to keep from crying but succeeded only partially.

"How did the behavior of the cows go for the next week or two?"

"Well," I said, my voice cracking, "I was keeping an eye on them because I had such a problem that first weekend. Couldn't understand how they could be so bad and then the next day they'd be perfect. Next weekend they predicted hot weather. WPS recorded the largest power usage ever. I told Larry to come and monitor what's going to go on. Larry came and measured tremendous amounts of current flowing into the parlor, this despite the Isolator. Frantic, I called WPS and Vern Peterson came back again and Larry showed him the current registering on his meter."

"What did Vern say?" Hammarback asked from across the courtroom.

I shook my head in disgust. "He told me it was on-farm problems."

"After that," Hammarback asked, "what did you do?"

"After a couple more times seeing the cows standing perfect in the parlor and then seeing them unbearable, I came to the conclusion that it had to be the Dairyland Isolator opening and closing, just the way it is designed to do."

Hammarback waited and the courtroom was very quiet. Judge and jury were watching me.

"Did you come to any conclusions about whether that isolator was working?"

"It wasn't working for the cows. So I decided to—made up my mind we had to get an isolation transformer."

"When," Hammarback asked, "was the isolation system put in by Mr. Neubauer?"

"January '97."

"Once that transformer pole was moved and the isolation system up and running, what observations did you make of the herd?"

"Production started to come up. And," I said with sarcasm, "one of the things I noticed is the cows quit dying."

"What other observations did you make?"

"General health improved. They didn't have rough coats. Things started rolling along."

Hammarback left the jury area and came back to me. I

grabbed a quick drink and popped another hard candy in my mouth. A cherry-flavored one.

"When the isolation system went in, did Mr. Neubauer make any warranties about how much milk production you would get?"

"He told me 75 pounds."

"Was he right?"

"No, he lied," I said. "We got to 80. In less than six months."

Hammarback smiled, stuck his hands in his pockets, and began pacing in front of Judge McKay's bench. "Now, by July '98, what was your feeling about whether electricity had been removed from your farm?"

"I thought finally this thing is behind me, in the past. Life can go on."

"About your research to what caused the problems, what was your conclusion?"

"No doubt. It had to be electricity."

Hammarback nodded. "In '98, did you again call WPS?"

"I called Jerry Held, to take a look at electricity again affecting cows—I wanted to be compensated for all the damage that had been done."

Hammarback stopped pacing. "What did he tell you?"

"He said, 'We just don't hand out money to anybody.' I knew if I was going to get what I needed, get compensated for what I'd lost, I was going to have to do something else."

"In early '99," Hammarback said, "when the cows again started twitching, what did you think?"

I stared straight at the jury foreperson. "Current," I said, loudly. "I got hold of Larry, had him test. He was picking up earth current. That was when we'd dug the trench around the farm and laid in the copper ring."

"Where did you understand the current was coming from?" Hammarback asked.

"From WPS' down grounds."

"So what did you do?"

"Cut the wires," I said.

"How did you go about doing that?"

I shrugged. "Went in the shop, got a side cutter, and cut them."

"Why did you cut them?" Hammarback asked.

"I saw how much the current affected my cows, saw how effective the buried ring was, and thought if I lowered the current on the ring, I'd be better able to keep the current away from my cows."

Hammarback went back to the jury and stood near the foreperson. "Did you have any additional contact with Jerry Held?"

"Yes." I knew where we were headed now, and not a moment too soon. "What was that contact?"

"I saw him at a neighbor's house, in a WPS truck."

"On the basis of that," Hammarback asked, "did you decide to do something?"

"I sure did. I decided to sue," I told him.

"And why was that?"

"I learned that the way WPS was addressing their electrical problem was by digging up dirt on Russ Allen."

Hammarback paused to let the jury digest this.

"What kind of things were they trying to find out?"

"Inquiring about me going on vacation. Inquiring about my boat."

Again Hammarback paused. "At the present time," he said, "what's the debt load on your farm?"

"In the neighborhood of $1.6 million."

"With the present production of your farm, do you have cash flow?"

"No," I told him. The truth was that I was flat broke and falling behind 50 thousand dollars a month.

"If the farm was producing at the rate it should have but for the electricity, would there be cash flow?"

"Yes."

"Milk prices. Are they up or down?"

"Down."

"With prices down, would cash still be flowing if production was where it should've been?"

"Yes."

"Have you tried to do other things to keep WPS electricity from coming onto your property?"

"I tried to live with the downgrounds connected. I used an insulated wire to try to bypass the current around my farm."

"After this lawsuit was started, were the grounds hooked back up?"

"Yes."

"Did you disconnect them again?"

"Yes."

"Why?"

I shook my head, hard, and threw up my hands. "Too many problems. The cows cannot handle that current."

Walking down the length of the jury box to the opposite end, Hammarback asked, "How did the cows do after that?"

"They responded positively," I told him.

"What happened to production after they were hooked back up?"

"Cows got sluggish." As all mammals would.

"And production did what?"

"Fell."

Hammarback waited before asking the next question. "Did a representative from WPS indicate to you what your options were regarding electricity in the ground on your property?"

"Yes. My options were to put up with the current coming through my property affecting my cows, or have no electricity at all."

"Is there," Hammarback asked, "another power company you can hook up to?"

"No."

"What is it you want from WPS?" Hammarback asked.

"I want compensation for everything they caused," I said. "Not a penny more or a penny less. I want the current off my property so it's not affecting my cows."

"That's all the questions I have, Your Honor," Hammarback said to the judge.

Now I braced myself for the onslaught. I sat up straight and stiff in my chair as Trevor Will rose from his seat and walked slowly toward me, stopping about 3 feet away and crossing his arms in front of his chest. I took a big gulp of water. As I emptied the glass, I felt sweat start trickling down my back.

"Good morning, Mr. Allen. How are you?" Will asked.

"Good," I mumbled without looking at him.

"You're probably the person who knows the most about this farm, right?"

"Correct."

"And not only do you know all aspects of the farm, you were involved in various electrical experiments?"

"Correct."

"And you understand that the reason we did deposition is because WPS wanted to find out the basis of your claim?"

"Correct."

"You understood I would be relying on the answers you gave?"

"That's correct," I said.

Will smiled, the way a cat smiles at a mouse pinned in a corner. "Now that we've got that out of the way, let's talk a little about electricity on your farm. It's true that you believe that before electricity can harm a cow it must flow through the cow, correct?"

"I don't believe that anymore," I said.

"Well, you believed it at the time of your deposition. Didn't you?"

"I'd never thought about it and I answered 'yes'. But I don't believe it anymore."

"You're saying your belief has changed?"

"Correct."

Will shook his head as if confused. "Well, Mr. Allen, let's be clear. In your subsequent deposition sessions, you brought in lists of things you wanted to correct. Never once did you tell me you wanted to change this piece of testimony. Did you?"

"I couldn't remember everything that was asked the day before, and the day before that."

"So, Mr. Allen," Will said. "You think that current is flowing from WPS' system into the ground? And up out of the ground and through your cows? And you think that takes place everywhere on your farm?"

"I think uncontrolled," I told him. "I don't know where it all is. I think it's all over."

"You think it's 24 hours a day?"

"Not when WPS has a power outage," I said, and the whole courtroom laughed.

Trevor Will didn't find it funny. "Any time the power is on, you think it's flowing?" he frowned. "If you want to know whether ground conductors are affecting animals, the first thing is to measure how much current is flowing through the earth, right?"

I looked at him. "I don't know," I said. "You're starting to talk on electricity and I'm not an expert on it."

"Well, you offered a number of opinions this morning about whether electricity was harming your cows. Didn't you?"

"Yes," I said without blinking.

"If we want to know whether ground currents are affecting animals, the first thing we need to do is measure how much current is flowing through the earth, right?"

"Or remove it and see what the cows do," I shot back.

Will smiled. "One thing at a time. First, you want to know if there's any. So, you'd measure to see how much was coming out of the earth and getting to the cows?"

"You'd measure how much is on the rings and how much is in the earth. And then you remove it."

"Well, Mr. Allen, isn't it true that you take a measurement to see how much current was flowing out of the earth and affecting the cows?"

"The best way is to remove it and see what the cows tell you."

"Mr. Allen, I'm referring to page 892 of your deposition. Line 19: 'Yesterday we were talking about earth currents affecting cows. You said that if you wanted to know to what extent currents affected cows, you'd want to know how much current was in the earth, correct?' "Answer: 'Yes.' "Did you give those answers, sir?"

"Yes."

"All right," Will said, looking pleased. "And if you wanted to know how much current is actually reaching the cow out of the earth, you'd take a step potential measurement. Correct?"

"I told you several times through deposition that I'm not an electrical engineer or expert."

"Well, does that mean you've never heard the term?"

"I've heard it several times, but don't know—"

"To your understanding it measures earth current that can flow through a cow, right?"

"Yeah."

"Mr. Allen," Will said, slowly walking the length of the jury box, "you've been running around taking measurements on these ground rings yourself, for something like three years. And you've been taking measurements from WPS' system. And measurements on some ditch wires you ran. And you set the instruments up, put the data in your computer, right?"

"Correct," I said.

"And did you ever ask them to teach you how to take a step potential measurement?"

"No."

"Well, you agree, don't you, that the measurements you took on the down-ground wires don't tell how much electricity was actually flowing through your cows?"

"I believe the measurements on the ring don't capture all the current in the earth."

"My question is different. The measurements you take don't tell how much current is flowing in the cows, do they?"

"No."

"Okay. Isn't it true, Mr. Allen, that that you could've had your experts come to the farm and take step potential measurements any time you wanted?"

"Sure."

"Sure," Will said, nodding. "And if you wanted a measurement somewhere you thought there was a problem, you could tell them, 'Please take a measurement in the parlor, the cows are acting up'?"

"My understanding was that we had all the measurements we needed."

Will grinned. "Right. Now, about the electrical changes that took place since 1995, Mr. Neubauer has been responsible for those?"

"Yes."

"He was trying to remove what he described as loop current? And charged $9,800 to do that?"

"I believe so."

"And he told you the money you had spent on farm rewiring didn't solve the problem. And then in July WPS put up the Dairyland Isolator, right? And within a month, Mr. Neubauer told you it wasn't working. Right?"

"He told me and told Vern Peterson."

"Okay, yeah. He then began to suggest you needed to isolate, correct? Said that would be a $50,000, $60,000 project. Said you needed to isolate in order to fix the WPS problems. And he prepared quotations for you to take to various lenders to try to get financing for this. Correct?"

"That could be."

"Okay. Mr. Neubauer didn't tell you that you had an on-farm electrical problem in August of 1997, did he?"

"No."

"And that when the rewiring work that he did was finally inspected, it had 22 code violations in it, didn't it?"

"I guess you're correct."

Will patted the deposition transcript against his thigh. "Isn't it possible, Mr. Allen, that some of the work Mr. Neubauer did might've been responsible for what you say was the electrical problem with your cows?"

"I don't believe so," I told him.

"And isn't it true that he told you WPS didn't have your best interests at heart?"

"With regards to the isolator that wasn't working, you may be correct."

Will continued pacing. "Isn't it true that even before he installed the Dairyland Isolator he told you in a letter that WPS, to solve a problem, always designs around their system's capabilities, and in that message lies their interests—stockholders, legal costs, et cetera.? He told you that in a letter?"

"Yes."

"Isn't it also true," Will said, "that he told you they were incompetent because of where they put the reference rod, whether the Dairyland Isolator was functioning properly?"

"He may have."

"And isn't it true that Mr. Neubauer told you WPS would not move your transformer pole because that would 'fix' your farm?"

"Yes."

"Okay. And isn't it true that Mr. Neubauer began taking you to meetings where stray voltage was discussed?"

"I think I took myself," I told him.

"Well, didn't he invite you to the meeting at Helzer's farm in summer of 1997?"

"I was invited, yes."

"And it was by Mr. Neubauer, wasn't it? In fact, Mr. Neubauer helped sponsor that one, didn't he?"

"I really don't know."

"Mr. Neubauer also got you to a meeting in 1997 at Vande Hay's to discuss stray voltage, right? And told you that farmers with stray voltage problems could bring lawsuits and recover damages?"

I shook my head. "I think a farmer would know that."

"And you knew that?"

"Well, any time somebody is causing damage..."

Will stopped pacing and pointed the transcript toward me like an accusatory finger. "Isn't it true you discussed with Mr. Neubauer bringing a lawsuit for stray voltage?"

"I don't think Larry is the issue with a lawsuit," I growled.

"No—my question was different," Will said, lowering the transcript. "I just want to know if you talked with him. Isn't it true that by January of 1998 you discussed bringing suit against WPS?"

"I don't know," I said.

"Now," Trevor Will said, "I want to run through the chronology of isolation. Isn't it true that his isolation work didn't have any immediate impact on production?"

"When you say 'immediate'—"

"How about a month? Didn't have an impact on production the first month, did it?"

I refilled my water glass from the pitcher and took a long drink before answering. "The cows quit dying," I told him.

"I'm talking about production."

211

"Okay. It took a little bit. A month and a half, two months."

"So the first couple of months there wasn't any change?" He came toward me and stood about ten feet away, transcript still in his hand.

"It took a while for the cows to heal."

Will fell silent. Then he said, "Isn't it true that you were talking with Mr. Neubauer about filing a stray voltage lawsuit even though you hadn't seen an increase in production?"

"That never happened," I said.

"Isn't it true that in February of 1998 you were telling Mr. Neubauer that you got hold of Jack Kevorkian's attorney, over in Michigan?"

"Yeah."

"Okay. So, by this time, then, you were already talking about a lawsuit, weren't you?"

"Could be."

"Now you knew that to succeed in your lawsuit you have to show an increase in milk production after making electrical changes?"

"Right. I would've had to see a response before I did anything. You don't have a case if you don't have an increase."

"Right," Will said, nodding vigorously. "There was a meeting in November 1997 with you and your veterinarian and nutritionist and electrician and also the county ag agent, right? At that meeting, you discussed whether there were problems with your management style, right?"

"Correct."

"Now, isn't it true, Mr. Allen, that there are probably 20 to 25 factors that can influence milk production? For example, balancing rations, quality of feed, use of BST, times milked per day, weather, cow comfort, lighting, vet care, handling by milkers?"

"Sure."

"And isn't it true that a large number of things can be controlled by the farm owner?"

"Sure."

"All right," Will said. "Let's move on. In November of 1998, you were going to meet with a lawyer about this lawsuit and invited Larry Neubauer to come along. And by December of 1998, isn't it true that Mr. Neubauer put you in touch with four other farmers, and the five of you were going to join together and bring a lawsuit?"

"I'm not sure Larry did that. I knew the other farmers."

"One of those farmers was a fellow by the name of Vern Manke?"

"Manke."

"And he's from Michigan. There was a problem with him joining the suit, wasn't there? He had made electrical changes but didn't have a production increase, correct?"

"I don't know the specifics with Vern Manke. I do know that at one time when Larry walked into his barn he saw a grown man crying."

"Mr. Allen, this note of Mr. Neubauer's regarding your call to him, 'Vern Manke at 50 pounds, got to get him cranking if he is one of the five,' is correct?"

"Correct."

"So you had decided to file suit by December 1998?"

"That's very possible," I said.

"Two weeks after the document about Manke, you called Larry Neubauer about a videotape taken of your cows, taken by Doug Sutter, the county ag agent, right?"

"Could be."

"You wanted to demonstrate the cows' hooves were bad. And that they were acting up in the parlor, right?"

"Right."

"And isn't it true Mr. Sutter told you he'd seen worse dancing on other farms?"

"Yes."

Trevor Will turned and went over and stood beside the jury foreperson. "And isn't it true that Mr. Sutter says he gave the tape to you? And that the tape has disappeared?"

"That is correct," I said.

"And isn't it true that you refused to let the University of Wisconsin come out and take samples at your farm?"

"Yes."

"You were worried, weren't you," Will said, "that if they came they would conclude there was no stray voltage on your farm?"

"Stray voltage had nothing to do with it," I said.

"Isn't it true that the reason you did not let them come is because you had issues with Dr. Douglas Reinemann?"

"That is correct," I replied.

Will folded his arms and started pacing along the jury box. "You understood that Dr. Reinemann does not believe earth currents can cause dairy cows harm?"

"Utilities are relying on Reinemann's research, and it's not coinciding with what's happening in the real world. A lot of cattle and a lot of families are being harmed."

"And so you disagree with what you understood to be Dr. Reinemann's position?"

"I don't agree with the research," I told him.

Will nodded. "In 1998 and 1999 Mr. Neubauer was a frequent visitor to your farm. You were always talking to him about stray voltage, right? And during this time period—December of 1997 until November of 2000 when you filed this lawsuit—you never asked WPS to come out and test or measure for stray voltage, did you?"

"No, I don't think so."

"And the reason," Will said, "is because you and Mr. Neubauer were working to put the lawsuit together, weren't you?"

"Well," I said, snickering, "if that's the case, I would have made sure he got more measurements and pictures and everything else."

"More measurements would've been helpful, wouldn't they?" Will said sarcastically.

"Sure."

"Do you remember the note of your conversation with Mr. Neubauer that was subpoenaed in this case and not produced? You said, 'after we win this lawsuit, on the back of my boat, like at the end of a letter, I will put instead of P.S. I love you, WPS I love you.' That's what you left for him that day, correct?"

"That is correct," I said.

"You own a 27-foot boat, correct?"

"Correct."

Will paused, then said, "Now, Mr. Allen," he said, "I want to shift gears and talk a little about crops. A crop year is crops you grow in a calendar year, what you're planting this spring and harvesting this fall, right?"

"There's some also you're going to harvest through the summer."

"Mr. Allen, you now have crop insurance, correct? And you've had it as long as you've had the farm?"

"Yes," I said.

"Do you know what level you're insured at?"

"Sixty-five percent, maybe," I said finally.

"Now in 1996 you had a major crop failure. Both your alfalfa and corn were essentially wiped out that year. Isn't it true, Mr. Allen, that you received over $200,000 in disaster relief because of crop failures in 1996?"

"That could be true, yes."

Will nodded, turned, and again tip-toed over to the jury area. "Now, you believe, Mr. Allen, that stray voltage was the only thing limiting production on your farm from 1976 to today—the only reason the cows didn't produce more was stray voltage, right?"

"Yes, yes."

"You don't believe there's anything within your control that would have improved production, right?"

"Correct," I said.

"And you also think that in the last three years, all changes in production, behavior, and health in your cows have been due to earth current flowing through them, right?"

"Yes."

Will nodded. "Today you're the guy who makes decisions for all areas of the farm, aren't you? Yours is the final voice?"

"Yes."

"A, you're the boss. And B, you've got the checkbook. Right?"

"I got an empty one," I told him. Several jurors smiled as I said this.

"Do you," Will said, "agree that feeding or being a nutritionist is an art?"

"When you fine-tune and get into that 30,000-pound range, sure."

"In fact, you have parted company with some nutritionists because you didn't think they were getting results for you, right?"

I shook my head. "I blamed a lot of people that I shouldn't have."

"Like WPS?" Will said quickly.

"I think we've proved differently," I said equally quickly. I thought I saw a juror nod ever so slightly, as if in agreement. But maybe it was just my imagination.

Ignoring the remark, Will continued, "Do you agree, Mr. Allen, with the principle that if you can't measure it, you can't manage it?"

"I agree," I told him.

"And isn't it true that you don't have a computer system that allows you to get information on BST usage? You don't have the capacity to do that with your records?"

"Ninety to 95% of the dairy farmers in the country can't do that."

"Right, and you can't, can you?" Will said, sounding like a cranky kid.

"That's correct."

"You have told me," he said, coming toward me, "that you think earth currents have been there from WPS' distribution system since 1976 to the present, correct?"

"That is," I said.

"And yet during that time your production has almost doubled. Hasn't it?"

"That's probably correct," I said.

"So, earth currents aren't preventing you from dramatically increasing, are they?"

I grinned. "I'm doing my best to keep the current away."

"Now, you told us you thought there were improvements after the groundings were cut in December of 2001, right?"

"Yes."

"And yet you know there was no production change outside the range of normal fluctuation?"

"Ours steadily climbed," I said forcefully, for the jury.

"Is it true," Will said, "that when you looked at averages for December of 2001 and January of 2002 after the grounds were cut that they just showed normal variation?"

"It don't happen that quick, Mr. Will."

"Do you understand it's your testimony that it takes three or four months for cutting the grounds to show up in production?"

"After I cut the grounds, it was a steady climb," I said.

"Isn't it true that your herd always makes a steady climb in the spring?"

"Not like we were seeing."

"Mr. Allen," Trevor Will said, "I want to change topics a little. "Do you know what a normal death rate is in a herd of 500 cows? One that's completely unaffected by electricity?"

"I think three or four percent."

"Well, let me get your deposition out," Will said, going to his table and picking it up. He thumbed through the pages and then held it out, a priest flaunting a Bible. "Page 830: 'What type of death rate would you expect in a 500-head herd not affected by electricity?' Answer: 'I don't even know.' Did you give me that answer?"

"Correct," I said.

"You don't know what it is over the last seven years, do you?"

"I know an awful lot of cows died," I snorted.

Will made a sour face. "I don't want to argue with you," he said, "but could you confirm for me that you don't know the death rate?"

"That's correct."

Will kept patting the sheaf of papers in his hand against his leg. "Isn't it true you don't know how to read a great deal of data on the herdmaster records?"

"There was some confusing data there," I told him.

"You told me you didn't want the three-phase line reconstructed because that would mean more grounding wires and rods. You're not in favor because you recognize that if you have a multi-grounded system, you're going to have some current that, as a matter of physics, goes in the ground. Right?"

"That current is harming my cows!"

"You know that with a multi-ground system, there's no way to avoid putting some current into the earth. Correct?"

"It's a bad system," I said, leaning forward and looking past Trevor Will and at the jurors.

"And what you want, Mr. Allen, is a system where there is zero current going down ground wires and into the earth?"

That was it, exactly. That was what I wanted and needed, just as I needed air to breathe that was free of poisons. Every person and creature in the state of Wisconsin and in the United States of America deserved no less.

"That's correct," I said.

"Yet you don't know of any system anywhere in the world that has those attributes you want, do you?"

"I'm sure there are safe systems to use."

"In fact," Will said, "you publicly stated that you think an ungrounded delta would be the system Wisconsin ought to adopt. Right?"

"Whatever is safe," I said.

Will went to the table and dropped off the deposition papers and then tip toed again toward the jury box.

"Now, Mr. Allen, you've never asked your neighbors if they wanted their power shut off, have you?"

"If they realized how much current was going through their property, maybe they would want it off." A few jurors chuckled.

At this point, Will decided he had no more questions.

"Mr. Allen," Hammarback said, coming near the stand, "what's your understanding as to whether all cows are the same with resistance or not?"

"Some are more affected than others."

"Was there current in your parlor?"

"Yes."

"What level?"

"Over 800 milliamps."

"In the real world, what would you do to test if your cows are affected by electricity?"

"Take away the current."

"And what would you expect to happen?"

"Well, if they go up in production, that's what's causing the problem."

"On your farm," Hammarback said, "what's the best indicator of the current affecting your cows?"

"Behavior," I answered. "Production."

"In your opinion, what's the best measurement device for the amount of current affecting your cows?"

"The buried ring."

"Do you," Hammarback asked, "realistically believe that all current in the ground can be removed?"

"Darn close," I told him.

Hammarback paused. "What did isolation do concerning current on your farm?"

"Removed the majority off the parlor."

"What measure did you use to see if it had an effect on your cattle?"

"Production. Cow behavior."

"Does current have to pass through a cow to affect it?"

"I don't think so. If you have an electric fence and a cow gets a shock off of it, it's never going near it again. Same thing with the waterer, the feeder, any of that stuff."

Hammarback stepped over toward the jurors. "How many times does it actually have to go through a cow before it would have an effect?"

"If she's just exposed one time, it could have a lasting effect."

"After July of 1997," Hammarback said, "did you do more research into stray electricity?"

"Sure," I told him. "I heard about other people having problems with it— Al Mazna, Dave and Dan Vande Hay, Jim and Vicki Helzer—and I talked to them about it."

"What was the reason for talking to those folks?"

"Well, things aren't going well at the farm, you are left out there by yourself." I was too embarrassed to say that misery loved company.

"Did these conversations play any role in your decision to put in an isolation system?"

I nodded. "Sure."

"What did you find out as to the effect of isolation on their farms?"

"After current got removed, the cows at times reached 85 pounds a cow."

"Did you come to any resolution in the event your experiment showed electricity from WPS was harming your cows? What were you going to do?"

I raised both my arms. "I wanted to be compensated for it."

Still with the jury, an elbow against the box rail, Hammarback said, "How were you going to go about this? Have you ever sued anyone before in your life?"

I shook my head. "No."

"Can you tell us what you knew about stray voltage lawsuits at that point?"

"I know that when you go up against a major corporation that has an open checkbook—"

Trevor Will vaulted to his feet, almost apoplectic to shut me up. This was the last thing he ever wanted the jury to hear.

"Your Honor, I move to strike this!" he hollered.

McKay nodded. "Motion granted. Jury is to disregard that answer as nonresponsive."

Personally, I thought it was very responsive and I liked it a lot. But even McKay couldn't put that particular genie back in the bottle. And it was good for the jury to hear the truth. Because they were footing the bill as well. WPS could have an open checkbook because whatever they paid out was recouped in the form of rate hikes, which the Public Service Commission granted them at the drop of a hat. In a real sense, I was helping WPS to fund the case against me. The law should be changed, it should come out of the utilities' profits, then things would get fixed in a hurry.

Hammarback grinned. "When did you actually retain a lawyer to help you?"

"October 2000," I said.

"And who was that?"

"Hammarback Law Office."

"Let me clarify something," Hammarback said, still with the jurors. "Do you actually live on the farm?"

"For the last four or five years," I explained, "my mother was confined to a wheelchair. I bought the farm from her on a land contract. She had the right to stay in the home until she passed. We would take turns staying with her. I stayed two nights a week for the last four years."

"Did you have a place of your own?"

"Yes."

"And did you actually live on your boat a couple of summers? Isn't December in Green Bay on a boat a little tough?"

"Yes," I grinned.

Hammarback started toward me, then thought better of it and returned to the jurors. "While we're on the subject of the boat, did you talk to Larry Neubauer about changing the name of your boat to something relating to WPS? How did that come up?"

"Wisconsin Public Service made my boat an issue in this lawsuit. Someone there provoked me to respond the way I did. They addressed their electrical issues by—digging up dirt on Russ Allen."

"So when you gave Larry Neubauer that message, were you kidding or not?"

"Well, yeah."

Hammarback nodded rapidly. Then he said to McKay, "That's all the questions I have, Your Honor."

I glanced up and noticed the judge fidgeting. "Any recross?" he asked impatiently. It was clear McKay wanted to take a break. Maybe he needed the men's room. I knew I did. But it was the bottom of the ninth inning, two outs, and Trevor Will was not about to put off his last at-bat if he could help it.

"Just a bit, Your Honor," he said. "I'll keep it brief."

Will went over to the jury. "You talked with Mr. Hammarback about your boat. In fact, at your deposition, we went through various places you'd lived. When you're living off the farm, it may take a while to get to it if something comes up?"

"Right now it would take 10 minutes."

"And that can be important if an animal is in distress or sick?"

"Sure," I said absently.

"Last question," Trevor Will said, glancing up at a clearly antsy McKay. "You have publicly advocated that Wisconsin adopt an ungrounded delta system for its electric distribution method, correct?"

"Yes," I said.

"Thank you, Mr. Allen," Trevor Will said. "That's all I have, Your Honor."

And with that, my torment came to an end. As I rose from the witness chair, I was weak and stiff in the legs. But that was nothing. I kept thinking of the thirteen people sitting in judgment across the way. The trial portion was done and the lawyers were ready to make their closing arguments to those good folks in the morning. But I couldn't think about that now. That was for tomorrow.

CHAPTER 16

CLOSING ARGUMENTS

A nd so, the drama was nearly done. After a defense motion to dismiss was denied and several other legal questions ruled on by McKay, the jury trudged in, and the lawyers prepared to make their final pitch. I wondered if anybody was persuadable at this point.

McKay issued some instructions to the jury, requesting a finding of guilt or innocence on each question and a decision regarding monetary damages. Agreement by 11 or more jurors would constitute a verdict.

The rule was to put all juror names in a hat, pick one name out and that person would go home. I argued that all 12, plus the alternate, had sat there for a whole month. It would be unfair to send one home.

Hammarback, dressed handsomely in a dark blue suit, powder-blue shirt, and white-and-navy polka-dot tie, spoke first. He stepped briskly over to the jury box and started by thanking everyone for their diligent attention throughout these long weeks.

Then he plunged into his presentation by recounting the origins of our farm. He placed its founding in a historical context and spoke movingly of my mother and father, their hopes and their dreams.

"Alvin and Alice Allen," he said, "learned about dairy farming not from universities, not from books, but from themselves, from each other, and from the dairy animals that they took care of."

Hammarback wasn't five minutes into the speech when I was overcome by emotion. As he talked about Pa and Ma living the American dream in the American heartland, about their love for the farm and for one another and for the good Wisconsin earth, I began to weep. I could not hold back my tears. Their dream was nearly dead. Our land had been raped, and for what? Money. WPS profit. I had to keep them alive, both the farm and the dream. This was my land now. It was my inheritance, my patrimony, my birthright. I'd fought for it here in court and I was willing to die for it. Head in hands, elbows on my knees, I struggled to cry quietly, without disturbing anybody. I'm not sure I succeeded.

"They learned how to feed, care for, tend, mend, and help these animals do the best job they could," I heard Hammarback saying. "It required a lot of time and careful attention to detail, required they make do with what they had. That's the way dairy farming is. As time went on 11 children came to work with them, to do things that a farmer, both men and women, do. And that's what this case is about—the Allen farm and what WPS should have done to prevent harm, the harm that is still occurring today."

Holding the rail with his right hand, Hammarback looked back and forth between jurors.

"Negligence," he said to them. "Negligence means that all of us have a duty. A duty to exercise ordinary care in pursuit of the things we do. Electrical companies have other standards, statutes, and regulations with which they must comply. A breach of those is a breach of duty. The duty for WPS is to prevent harmful current from getting to Mr. Allen's cows. The evidence in this case is overwhelming. There was no maintenance on the line.

There was no inspection of split-bolt connectors, and no tests of return current. In fact, WPS' own tests showed that 70 percent of their return current was coming through the earth near or at the Allen farm. That is a violation of the law."

He walked to the far end of the jury box, near the spectator benches. As he did so, I straightened up and wiped my cheeks with a handkerchief, trying to look nonchalant. I didn't want Hammarback to see me crying.

"Cause," he said. "How do you show that something caused something else? Use a substantial factor. There's no question that electricity at a high enough level can cause injury to an animal, and affect their behavior. Behavior for a dairy animal is highly significant. A cow is not going to eat or drink— it affects her whole life, not just milk production but her reproduction, general health, cost to maintain her, everything. And so, when we say it's only a behavioral response, that's a very serious thing."

Now Hammarback walked slowly up the length of the box and stopped at the opposite end. "What is a nuisance? Nuisance is unreasonable interference with the use and enjoyment of property. Who gave WPS the right to put any level of electricity through Russell Allen's cows, any level at all? What right—and how dare they come out and say, 'Oh, we can put a little bit of electric current into the cows at Russell Allen's farm.' The fact that WPS did not maintain their line and allowed 70 percent of their return current onto the property was without question a nuisance."

"As plaintiffs, we have the burden of presenting a preponderance of evidence to any question we want answered 'yes.' Preponderance is more probable than not by clear and convincing evidence that what we're saying is correct."

"From 1937 to 1962," he said, coming and standing at the midpoint of the jury box, "changes were made in agriculture. In 1962 they had a nice new barn. They had a nice pipeline milking system and plugged along as a dairy farm. By 1972 they start talking about a new facility. They do research and say, "We can build a parlor that will take the whole family here—we can make this work.' Back in 1976, when it actually started, that was the premier farm in Brown County, a 500-cow facility. One thousand three hundred acres, it was one of only six in the world like it at that time. It was the gold standard."

"And what happens with production? In '76 they immediately had a couple-of-thousand-pound loss. Pretty serious today, but back then was a fourth of their production. Then production drops another couple thousand pounds and they're working very hard."

Hammarback began pacing alongside the railing, walking from one end to the other and back. "Nobody knew at the time that placing the transformer pole next to the feed room would cause WPS return current to come right into their dairy. They thought they were modernizing so they could get more milk, make more money, and take care of their families. They didn't know, and WPS didn't tell them, it was putting electricity in the ground."

"So, for all these years they struggled. The partnership falls apart. One by one the partners leave and go farm someplace else. Because farming is a way of life— maybe a hard way of life, but it's the Allens' way of life. It's the way Russ Allen wants his life."

As he said this, tears again started welling up in my eyes and a lump formed in my throat. Pa, I thought, I'm glad you didn't live to see how they tortured our poor animals that you loved so.

"As a farmer," Hammarback continued, "he doesn't want to be interfered with by outside things. He just wants to milk his cows. Gradually the partners go out. Russ was left alone."

"In 1988 when Russ took over, things got a bit better. And so, when Mike Hoerth came out, he said you could save money by putting in a new parallel type of system. And Patti's arms won't be black and blue anymore. In this new parlor, the cows stand still in steel plates. They can't kick you as much."

"So, they adjust the ration but get no response from the cows."

Hammarback stopped and faced the jury. "What happens in 1992? Russ says let's try a new system, maybe the cows will milk better. We'll spend $100,000 trying to make these cows produce to where everybody thought they should've been. It still didn't work. They were worse than ever."

He sighed. "Now they won't come into the parlor. They have to send a person, Patti, to shoo them in. Everybody in the dairy business said, hey, when a cow wants to be milked, she's going to come right into a parlor. Sometimes they would, sometimes they wouldn't, and nobody could figure out the difference. The cows were saying 'Something is not right.'

"They started using some BST in 1994, a little more in 1995, quite a bit in 1996. We looked at Mr. Mellenberger's numbers that showed if you take the seasonal variation into account in 1996, they didn't get a single pound of improvement from BST. Why use it? Why spend the $10 a month or the $11 a month per cow if you're not getting any benefit? So, Mr. Allen stopped."

Hammarback frowned and stared down at his shoes. Then he folded his arms over his chest and looked up. "So, we get to 1997 and Russ Allen has had enough. He's spent $100,000 on this parlor that the cows are not standing still in. The cows are not milking out and they can't do production things that they should be doing with this new equipment. Mike Hoerth says, 'We've looked at that parlor a zillion times. You should check out stray voltage.'"

Hammarback shrugged and pushed out his lower lip. "Thank God for Larry Neubauer," he said. "He's a tough character, but your choice is to decide if he's a straight shooter."

"And so because Mr. Neubauer is an industrial electrician, wasn't caught up in cow contact things that WPS promotes, he was able to make measurements and found amazing things: 800 milliamps on the parlor steel, almost an amp of current. When you disconnect the neutral, that went away." Hammarback let that linger a few moments.

"You have your life experience," he said to the jurors. "Common sense says if there's current flowing, you've got voltage someplace. So, Larry finds this current flowing, and there's no doubt there's at least 8/10 of an amp flowing on the farm from WPS. When you turn the farm power off, it's still there. So they get a second opinion. They have WPS come out. WPS comes and finds no problem. They measure in the parlor which has this equipotential plane and get low voltages. They didn't make any current-flow measurements. The measurements they made were on the single-phase transformer, way across the yard, instead of making the test where the cows were. But what they got should've turned on red lights. If you look at the current return, they had 70 percent by their own measurement returning into the ground. It was coming right back on the neutral. Even if it's across the yard, they've got almost 1.3 amps of current, and 70 percent of it is in the ground."

Hammarback clasped his hands together and shook them. "Now, what obligation did WPS have at that point? Their obligation was not to tell Russ Allen how to farm. Their obligation was not to tell Russ Allen how to wire his farm. Their obligation was to fix their line and make it operate so there was no objectionable current coming down those ground rods. Did they do it? No! They didn't."

Hammarback shook his head and resumed pacing. "And so," he said, "when you look at question number 1, 'Did stray electricity from Wisconsin Public Service Corporation's system harm the Allen dairy,' sure. There's no question. The path is there. The electricity is on the farm. WPS admits it's on the farm."

He stopped pacing and looked from one juror to another and touched the index finger of his left hand to the middle finger of his right. "Next question is, what did it do to the cows? Larry Neubauer measures .914 volts. Russ doesn't necessarily believe

Larry. Larry says, get a second opinion. Russ has explained he's tried everything else. His vet, Dr. Foust at the time, thought, it can't be management, but I can't rule out stray voltage."

"So WPS admits that the way to test is to isolate, because isolation reduces electricity that goes onto the farm. Russ Allen isolates, with their isolator. And then gets very strange behavior. Sometimes the cows are horrible, sometimes fine. There's no predictability. So, Russell Allen had a hard decision to make when the isolator didn't work. The voltage at some point had to be high enough to trip it and let current onto the farm. So they called WPS."

Hammarback laughed sourly. "One thing we learned from this case is that WPS does what it wants—it does not listen to its customers. Vern Peterson was going to tell them his line no matter what. This is what we can and can't do, take it or leave it. There wasn't any effort at all to help Mr. Allen."

Hammarback made eye contact with several jurors. "So, when Russ knew WPS wasn't going to do anything other than leave that useless isolator where it was, he finds out it's going to be $57,000 to change the system over and be rid of the problem. Was WPS going to help? No. They've done everything they would. Not could, but would."

"In December of 1997, they put in the isolation system. And lo and behold, what happens? There is a substantial and significant change. Production is up six pounds in a couple of months, 10 pounds in another month, and it goes right on up until it's 30 pounds at the end of five months. 30 pounds! The herd increased substantially and stayed there for a couple of years. This is not just one game with five touchdown passes— there were a couple of years with a whole lot of them."

Suddenly he wheeled around and squinted over at the defense table. "Look," he said to the jury. "Mr. Will is smiling."

Everyone in the courtroom turned and stared at Trevor Will, who appeared sheepish and embarrassed. His cheeks flushed red.

"He thinks that's funny," Hammarback said, stone-faced. "But the fact of the matter is that there's no other reasonable explanation for an increase that big. Slatted floors couldn't cause an increase in production, bad management practices do not, bad records do not, bad breeding does not. Russ Allen is only a bad farmer to WPS when production is going down. He's a good farmer apparently when production is going up."

"All of a sudden," he said, snapping his fingers, "like Rip Van Winkle, he woke up and remembered how to farm?" The jury liked this. All 13 smiled and a few even nodded sympathetically. I glanced at Trevor Will to gauge his reaction, but his head was down and he was scrawling notes on his yellow pad.

"Question number 2: 'Was Wisconsin Public Service Corporation through its agents and/or employees negligent in its distribution of electricity?' The answer to that must also be 'yes'."

He looked over at the monitor. "I've got Exhibit 1020 up," he said. "WPS is required by the code not to allow objectionable current in its grounding conductors." He read, "'If an objectionable flow of current occurs over a grounding conductor due to the use of multi grounds, one or more of the following methods should be used: One, abandon one or more grounds, two, change location of grounds, or three, interrupt the continuity of the conductor between ground connectors.' Now. Russ Allen should not have cut the grounds on his farm. They're not his property. WPS should have. It was WPS' obligation under the electric code to cut and abandon those grounds. They had a duty to reduce that current. They never did. Never offered. It would be as cheap as having a man come out and cut those wires. Wouldn't have cost more than a couple of hours' time."

Hammarback was holding the jury box rail with both hands. "When you look at the questions on the verdict form," he said, "the answer to the second question should also be 'yes'. Clearly, they didn't maintain their line properly. And the third question— we've already talked about it somewhat—'Was such negligence a cause of damages to the Allen dairy operation?'—should also be answered 'yes.' They caused harmful levels of electricity to come onto the farm—that's it. Once you've answered those questions, the next one we deal with is: 'Was Russ Allen, his agents, or employees negligent in the use of electricity on his farm?' Let's see the evidence."

Hammarback walked a few steps away from the rail and put his hands in his pockets. "Back in 1997, Larry Neubauer said, 'There's too many wiring things you should change on your farm. These need to be eliminated before we can go on.' Russ Allen did not hesitate. He said 'All right, let's go ahead and fix them.' He fixed everything, thousands of dollars it was. What happened to production? Nothing. The power outage in June showed there was no current on the ring of life. The farm was up and milking— the generator was running. The wiring system on the farm was working, so it rules out the farm as causing any of the current. Did Russ Allen do anything negligent regarding his wiring? The answer has got to be no."

"'Did Wisconsin Public Service Corporation distribute electricity to the Allen Dairy Farm in a manner that constituted a nuisance?' I'll say! There's no doubt. The current was there. There's no doubt it's objectionable. There's no doubt Mr. Allen didn't want it there. There's no doubt objectionable current is not allowed under the statute. So, clearly that needs to be answered 'yes.' I'll point out to you that you need to carefully look at these instructions, but you can only answer some if you've answered other questions yes. So, take your time and see what you need to do with each one."

Now Hammarback went over the counsel table and glanced at some papers. Then he walked slowly back to the jury. "'Did such nuisance cause unreasonable interference with Russ Allen's interest in his use and enjoyment of the farm?' Well, I'll say! You've got a partnership that broke up, all the self-doubt he had trying to figure out why in the world his cows wouldn't produce.

All that has to go toward his use and enjoyment. So that answer should also be 'yes.'"

Hammarback stopped for a moment and stared at the jurors. "Eventually," he said, "if you answer 'yes' to all the questions so far, then you need to answer the one on comparative negligence. What that says is, if you find Russ has caused a problem and WPS has caused a problem, you have to differentiate between those two. But, how can it be more Russ' problem than WPS'? Electricity is coming down their down grounds, from their distribution system. He's not causing it—WPS is. Russ Allen can't be responsible because no evidence would support dividing it out."

"The last questions you look at are economic damages for annoyance, inconvenience, Loss of use and enjoyment of his property. Dr. Behr calculated damages: lost milk production resulting from this current, lost calves, credit back. The history is there. Dr. Johnson said they should produce at 26,000 pounds. Dr. Homan said they should produce at 26,000 pounds. They actually did get over it for a while. They maintained 23,500 pounds for a couple of years. So if you're satisfied that Mr. Allen with his slatted floors and all could produce at the 26,000 level, then Dr. Behr's report is sound and doesn't need to be adjusted. If you take the notebook which has calculated the same thing— young stock, cow losses, cost of mitigations, capital loss, inflation, it comes to $13,000,870. That's a lot of money and it's spread over a long time."

Hammarback did not walk, did not pace. He stood dead center of the jury, hands on hips, as his presentation wound down.

"That's the summary of economic damages. The annoyance and inconvenience and loss of use and enjoyment of his property, I can't tell you what that number is. As folks in the community, you have to decide what the cost is for that. But I'd suggest some things to think about. As if you were a farmer who loved to dairy farm, and loved to dairy farm as a family. This certainly was instrumental in affecting their enjoyment about how they liked to go to the barn and watch those cows milk, how they liked to take care of them."

"Another person who testified was Doug Sutter, the county extension agent. He has no axes to grind one way or the other. Simply made observations on the farm before and afterward. And didn't see anything but that electrical change could have caused it."

Hammarback stopped and took a deep breath. "I suppose there are alternative explanations. I think Mr. Will gave 25 different excuses for why production went up. But you have to ask yourselves why in the world it didn't happen in the 20 years before. I mean, they couldn't have had bad feed every single year.

"Dr. Johnson testified that if you're looking at stray voltage, half a volt is a good standard, but you have to listen to what the cows say. You just can't ignore everything there. What the cows say, that's the important lesson here."

"I want to talk about experts for a minute. Mr. Allen testified he tried to associate with other farmers regarding stray voltage lawsuits because he was worried about costs. It's a problem that needs to be looked at in a serious manner. There was not a single person called by WPS that wasn't either an expert or on their payroll. Not one."

Hammarback leaned against the rail as close to the jurors as he could get. He spoke in a low voice, and sounded as if he was speaking confidentially, to close friends, about matters of utmost importance to them all. "Mr. Mellenberger, for example, I thought he was smooth and calculated. Never even looked at stray voltage as being an issue because that's impossible! It's below the level that can affect them, so I'm not looking at it. The $140,000 fee, I suggest, may have helped."

He nodded at the jurors and smiled. "I thank you," he said, "for your kind attention. I thank you, and Russ Allen thanks you. I'm proud," Hammarback said, "to represent Russ Allen in this case. I know that we're getting a fair trial here. Whatever your decision, we'll be here with you, waiting. Whatever your verdict, let it speak the truth."

Trevor Will, I knew, would have a much different slant on the truth of these matters.

After the break, everyone in the courtroom resumed their usual positions. Will rose from his chair and started out by flattering the jury and trying to ingratiate himself. Wearing a three-piece black pinstriped suit, pale gray shirt, and maroon and gray striped tie, along with a matching pocket handkerchief, he said fawningly, "You've been a very attentive, intelligent jury judging by your responses in voir dire, and we all thank you. We are just very fortunate that we have citizens like you in this country that provide this obligation."

Having gotten that out of the way, Will cut to the chase. "The nub of the issue in this case is did stray voltage harm Russ Allen's cows? Number two, was Wisconsin Public Service Corporation negligent in distributing its electricity? Number three, I will touch on the other questions on the special verdict form. And the last thing I'm going to talk about is this question of damages.

"In order to answer the question of whether stray voltage harmed Russ Allen's cows, there are three issues we need to look at. One, was there current through the cow? We're not talking about current reaching the farm. There's a lot of electricity in this room, but none is flowing through us. We need current through the cow. That's the first issue. The second question is how much current on the Allen farm was flowing through the cow. And the third issue is how much current does it take to reduce production when it flows through the cow?"

"Those, I submit, are the three critical issues. I didn't hear anything about that in the last hour and fifteen minutes. What did the evidence show about these things?" he asked, looking at juror number one. "There wasn't a witness in this case who didn't agree that in order to affect a cow's production, electrical current must flow through the cow. Mr. Zipse, Dr. Johnson, Dr. Foust, Mr. Neubauer, everybody who got up there said that. There was one exception. Do you remember who that was? Do you remember the one person who said something different? It was Russ Allen."

"Other than that, it was unanimous. I don't think that's an issue. Let's go to number two: How do you find out how much current was flowing through Russ Allen's cows? Well, again, there was unanimity. You take measurements. If you want to know if it's flowing through the earth, you take step potentials. If you want to know if it's coming through metal work, you take what are called 'cow contact measurements.' Again, there wasn't a single witness who disagreed with that. So, what measurements do we have in this case? Well, Wisconsin Public Service took measurements at four different times. They took a lot more than four—look at this chart over here to your right." He went over to it and tapped it with his knuckle. "Keep in mind the levels which show what the level was according to the United States Department of Agriculture. You begin to get a production effect at 2 volts and 4 milliamps according to the Public Service Commission of Wisconsin. That's 1 volt or 2 milliamps. According to the PSC, the utility has to take action at half a volt, or 1 milliamp. That's uncontradicted. It's also uncontradicted that Wisconsin Public Service is regulated by the Public Service Commission and we've got to do what they tell us."

Trevor Will returned to the jury box, still looking at the chart. "Now," he said, "what are our measurements showing here? First one was in October of 1988, in the parlor. The highest reading was .3 volts, .6 milliamps. Look how that compares. April 1997, highest level .025 volts, .05 milliamps. Vern Peterson did this one in July 1997: .002 volts, .004 milliamps."

"What measurements did Mr. Allen offer of current flowing through the cow? Do you remember? Larry Neubauer's measurements! The first one of those was supposedly taken in April 1997 and registered .914 volts from a hood over a bunk feeder. What do you know about that measurement? Nobody witnessed it except Mr. Neubauer. This is the most remarkable thing about it to me. Mr. Neubauer admitted he never told anybody about it for three years. He didn't write it down. Remember that? Mr. Allen testified he never heard of that measurement. If it was really as important as I heard this morning, don't you think he would have told Mr. Allen about it?"

"When," Will continued, "was the first time that measurement ever popped up anywhere? It was May of 2000. When Mr. Neubauer was trying to get himself hired as an expert witness for the lawsuit Russell Allen was planning against Wisconsin Public Service. And then suddenly, Mr. Neubauer remembered he had taken a vitally important measurement three years ago."

"And the second measurement? Mr. Neubauer took 800 milliamps on the parlor steel. You heard about that this morning. Again, it's not written down. It wasn't shared with WPS when they came out 10 days later. They didn't say a word. Why would Mr. Neubauer not say a word to Wisconsin Public Service Corporation if there was a legitimate measurement and he was genuinely concerned about helping Russ Allen? That's a question we all ought to think about. Why would he not reveal that measurement if it was legit?"

He stuck his hands in his pockets and waltzed over to the other end of the jury box. "Oh," he said, "I left out a couple of measurements Mr. Neubauer made, step potential measurements. They were so low he didn't write them down. They didn't concern him. In June of 2002, he goes back, the day before Wisconsin Public Service experts are coming to test the farm to see whether the claims in this lawsuit are valid. It's called 'discovery.' They've got to ask us for information, WPS has got to ask them. What in the world is Mr. Neubauer doing out at the farm in the middle of the night slopping around in manure the day before WPS gets there? What is he doing?" Will's eyes widened.

"What was the last measurement he took? .657 volts from a stall in the barn. Did he tell WPS about that the next day? No. So I want to leave you with this. You need to assess Mr. Neubauer's credibility. And his capability. You heard him testify differently than he testified in his deposition. You know, he flunked the electrician's exam seven out of eight times. You heard him throw around electrical words, and I'm no electrical engineer, but he didn't know—he used the word 'joule instead of 'amp'."

"The Allen farm," Will said, "was the highest and best work he had, his biggest customer, $250,000 of work. How many electrical code violations were there? Twenty-two. Mr. Allen was paying better than $10,000 a violation. And when it came time to fix it, Mr. Neubauer charged him for that, too.

"I'll put this question to you—you saw Mr. Vern Peterson on the stand. If you were having electrical work done in your house, would you hire him or Larry Neubauer?"

Now he sauntered over to his counsel table, glanced at his yellow pad, and then came back to the jurors. "Let's get to the third question: Was there enough current flowing through the cows to cause a drop in production? What do we know about that? We know that the United States Department of Agriculture has said after extensive experiments, not just in Cornell University but all over the world: it takes 4 milliamps, 2 volts of current through a cow to cause a production change. You know the rest, I'm not going to repeat it. There isn't a measurement in this case that comes close. We didn't hear a single witness from the plaintiff say, "I've got credible, peer-reviewed literature that demonstrates that at levels below that you get a production change in cows.'"

"So," he said, prancing along the length of the jury box, "we've got flawed logic and we've got something else. We know that in late 1992 or early 1993, Mike Moore is at Russ Allen's farm, and they have a conversation. What does Russ Allen say? 'I want to get me a chunk of money like Bud Garrets did.' He was looking to sue WPS from 1992 but he had a problem. He didn't have a basis. We had checked out the farm and the farm was clean."

Will quit prancing and stood looking among the jurors, his slender, manicured hands neatly folded in front. "In 1997 he hooked up with Larry Neubauer, and this was the perfect situation for them both. Perfect. We know from letters he wrote that Larry Neubauer didn't like WPS. He was trying to poison Russ' mind."

"Why was it the perfect opportunity for Larry Neubauer? I'll give you 250,000 reasons. He had a prime candidate. This was a marketing opportunity. Russ thought he had a stray voltage problem. Larry was going to help him find one. They're fast friends. They've been flying all over the country doing this."

"Now." Will smiled. "Larry Neubauer took notes and these are some of the most revealing pieces of evidence in this case. It's easy to come up on the witness stand and present a certain appearance. But in candid, unguarded moments, talking to your friends, you let your hair down." He nodded several times in agreement with himself.

"In 1997 they isolate. Mr. Allen knows after you isolate you've got to have a bump in production if you're going to have a lawsuit. In February 1998, less than two months after the isolation transformer is put in, Russ Allen is already calling Larry Neubauer to talk about suing WPS. In the note that talks, about Jack Kevorkian's attorney. It says, 'Leaving for West Indies for two weeks.' I couldn't begrudge Mr. Allen vacation. He's entitled. But do you remember that he told us he had thousands of bills he couldn't pay? He was on the verge of bankruptcy? The farm was failing? That was the story given you folks. And he's taking a two-week vacation in the Caribbean? I don't think that squares, folks."

"Do you remember Mr. Allen's direct testimony, 'I didn't decide to sue Wisconsin Public Service until spring of 1999 when my neighbors told me that Jerry Held was trying to dig up dirt on me'? His notes to Larry Neubauer prove that wasn't true. One here is dated December 30, 1998. Every decision that was taken since then was done with litigation in mind."

Will paused. He went over to his table again, looked at his pad, and then returned to the jury. "You heard much contradictory testimony," he said, going up and down on the balls of his feet as though doing toe-raises. "Stray voltage is blamed for everything. Production would have gone up faster if it hadn't been for—stray voltage. Production goes down—stray voltage. Cows are kicking in the parlor—stray voltage. Cows aren't kicking in the parlor—stray voltage. No matter what happens it can be blamed on stray voltage. And yet there are no measurements."

"Was WPS negligent? What you heard this morning was a gross misrepresentation. Why does WPS use this system? It's safe, reliable, economically better than the alternatives. It's used all over the country."

You, my dear reader, should take that last statement to heart.

Will continued. "I submit you ought to answer the first question 'no.' Negligence, it ought to be 'no.' You may think, well, they should have been out tightening split bolts, but the question is, did failure to do that cause electricity to go on the Allen farm causing hurt cows, causing decreased production? The answer is 'no.'

"Nuisance—look on the instruction. There isn't anybody else on the line that's complained. There isn't any electricity that prevents Russ Allen or anybody else from walking out on the farm. That's a simple one—I don't think you're going to get there. I think you're going to answer 'no' to the first question."

"Now, damages. I would say there are words that describe Dr. Behr, and those are lottery tickets. Remember the line in his letter, that he's a 'maximizer'? His entire livelihood depends on spewing big damage numbers. If he stops, he's out of work. There may be a psychological reason to put that kind of ridiculous number up, $13 million. The thought that if the jury thinks that's too much, they'll still give us 2 or 3 million. Which is more than they're enti-tled to in the first place. That's at work too.

"When, if, you get to the damage question—I don't think you're going to get there—look at mitigation. I think you know Russ Allen did a lot of things that depressed production. If he had taken $250,000 that he wasted on Larry Neubauer and used it for a down payment on a barn, his production would be a lot higher than it is today. He ignored professional advice."

He paused and licked his lips. "There's a lot more I could say. I hope I have given you what we told you we would, which was that the evidence would show the truth. You folks have heard all the evidence. I want to leave you with one thought about cause and effect. There's a story about a policeman who pulled up into the parking lot by Lambeau Field one day, and he sees a fellow jumping up and down. He watches, and this is going on for five minutes or so, and the cop finally comes up to him and says, 'What are you doing?' And he says, 'Well, it keeps the tigers away.' The cop says, 'There aren't any tigers around here.' And the guy says, 'See how well it works?'

"Ladies and gentlemen, when they tell you that stray voltage caused the problems on Mr. Allen's farm, think of that guy dancing in the parking lot at Lambeau. Thank you very much."

Will smiled, turned, tiptoed back to his counsel table, sat down, and looked over his papers.

No sooner was he seated than Hammarback rose to rebut him. "Mr. Will would have you believe that Russell Allen and Larry Neubauer are litigious fellows that like to file lawsuits," he said.

He chuckled. "Dairy farmers are some of the least litigious people in society. They're only here because they need to be. We talked about other farms with the same problem—equipotential planes, low cow-contact voltages, electrical problems. That's the agenda behind this litigation. WPS doesn't want to hear that. It didn't want to hear that its old, dilapidated system puts huge amounts of current through dairy farms. As a result, we've had so-called research, primarily at Cornell University, that underlies these 'standards' with flawed techniques—not in free-stall barns but by results due to damaged cows being removed as the research goes on, due to changing conditions. Contrary to all those controls you hear about from the scientists.

"WPS does not want to hear any of this. Unfortunately, there are damages in the dairy industry in Wisconsin, including Russell, as a result of that stance. Russell Allen never tried a lawsuit before in his life. If he and Mr. Neubauer had this insidious plan, do you think people at Larry Neubauer's office would write down these phone calls? Sure, you have thoughts of suing to get rid of current —cow behavior changed and production followed. But if they were planning something heinous, would they write it down? It doesn't make sense."

Hammarback leaned forward, legs back, and pressed both palms against the railing. "You've heard a concerted effort to say that Larry Neubauer and Russell Allen are bad guys. You folks will judge that. I don't think so. They're in a difficult problem that arises from an inadequate system that ought to be replaced."

He straightened up. "I want to remind you that the electrical industry wants everybody to consider cow contact measurements the be-all and end-all, but they are only a small piece of the picture. Much more significant are measurements of current coming into the farm, where you can make them on the neutral interconnection, which is what Mr. Neubauer did. He got very good results. Looking for cow contact voltages is like dumping a needle in a haystack and then trying to find the needle. The basic premises of their cow contact model are flawed. It doesn't explain what cows do. The model is just wrong. The cows—they tell you what's affecting them, not somebody's electrical model of how cows should respond. The best research that's been done on this problem is the kind done at Russ Allen's: get as much current removed as possible and see what happens to the herd.

"To accept Mr. Will's premise that isolation was done and then a lawsuit cooked up, you have to assume Mr. Allen was trying to be a below-average farmer for the last 20 years. It doesn't make any sense. The record, the testimony of people that work for Mr. Allen, doesn't bear that out at all."

"They simply don't want to get that 1935 wire that's been cobbled together with split bolts and connectors for the last 70 years out there. They have reasons. More cash flow, until the thing won't conduct electricity at all. But why on earth not replace it and see if that helps somebody? WPS would criticize the farmer for his own bad wiring, but doesn't want to apply the same principle to their own system."

Hammarback stopped and let that linger. "Russ Allen," he said, "has tried to make the best of a bad situation. He's lucky he's still in business. Many who've had this problem aren't. And, yes, he's knee-deep in debt."

"He's thankful," Hammarback told the jurors, "that he's still got the family farm. He wouldn't if he didn't have problem-solving skills. Mr. Will's attacks on Mr. Allen and Mr. Neubauer are unfounded. It's up to you folks to weigh the credibility of the witnesses and let your verdict speak the truth.

"I don't think that Wisconsin Public Service will honestly address the problem at the Allen farm until you folks tell them to. We hope you will." Hammarback stood there silently for several moments, making eye contact with each person of the jury. Then he nodded once, smiled and said simply, "Thank you."

And so, we were at the point of decision, poised on the edge of a cliff. I could see the sharp, jagged rocks glistening down below. If I fell, it would be the end of me. There were times this trial had seemed to drag on forever but now it seemed to have started and ended in one blinding instant. Sitting there waiting for Judge McKay, I couldn't tell which impression was true. Maybe they both were.

McKay sat up straight in his big, leather swivel chair. "Thank you, Mr. Lawrence," he said. "Thank you, Mr. Will and Mr. Lawrence."

Because my legal team felt that McKay had been biased against us throughout the trial, Hammarback had asked him to add an advisory question to the jury verdict form. Did the power line at my farm require repair? Though mild and reasonable, the judge dismissed their request out of hand. To me, it was just further proof of what we already knew. McKay was in WPS' corner. My hope lay with the jury.

McKay swung around to face the jurors. All eyes in the courtroom focused on him. "Now, members of the jury," he said. "This case is ready to be submitted to you for your serious deliberation. You will consider the case fairly, honestly, impartially, and in the light of reason and common sense. Give each question in the verdict your careful and conscientious consideration. In answering each question, free your minds of all feelings of sympathy, bias or prejudice. Let your verdict speak the truth, whatever the truth may be. When you retire to the jury room, your first duty will be to select a juror to preside and write in the answers you have agreed upon. The vote of the presiding juror, however, is not entitled to any greater weight than the vote of any other juror. When deliberations are concluded and answers inserted in the verdict, the presiding juror will sign and date the verdict and all of you will return with the verdict to the courtroom."

CHAPTER 17

THE VERDICT

A t noon, the jurors rose, stretched their legs, filed out of their box, and headed for the jury room to begin to deliberate. As I watched them go, my arms and legs shook. I wanted to cry. It would've been a relief. But no tears would come. My eyes were bone dry. I felt dehydrated and very weak. Fortunately, Barry Hammarback stuck around to keep me company.

I had no intention of leaving until the verdict came in, no matter how long it took. I was prepared to spend nights there, weeks. Friends urged me to go home and get some rest, but I couldn't leave. I couldn't eat, either. Neither could I doze or nap. All I could do was wait. And sweat it out, cold turkey.

There wasn't much to do around the Brown County Courthouse. It's not exactly an amusement park. On and off, I strolled around outside. The grounds were green and beautifully manicured, thick grass and lush shrubs in full bloom, and the weather was perfect—sunny and 80 degrees. Coming back inside and wandering around in the corridor, I badgered poor Hammarback, must've asked him ten times what he thought the jury would do.

"I'm hopeful," he kept saying, with more patience than I deserved. "Cautiously optimistic."

About an hour or so before the jury reached a decision, I was sitting in the courtroom with a friend of mine trying to find something to talk about to pass the time. Trevor Will and the deputy court clerk were chatting together not 10 feet away when suddenly Will turned to me and said from nowhere, "Mr. Allen, you are really a very nice man. I mean that sincerely."

He meant it sincerely? After the way he'd trashed and bashed me in court for the last four weeks? This really grated me. Will was hypocrisy on the hoof and a human oil slick. I was in shock—how do you answer to that? I was so shocked I was speechless.

My feeling was that we'd put forward a persuasive overall case. Where I thought we'd fallen down, and this gnawed at me, was in our damage claim. I felt that the way we'd presented it was confusing for the jury, not nearly as compelling as it could and should have been. For that, we were all to blame, especially me. I should've insisted on a much heavier and more precise emphasis on dollars, from my experts, my lawyers, and in my own testimony. But it was too late now.

Suppertime came, and still no word from the jury. I had no appetite. I just kept pacing, my lawyers right alongside me. I milled around the courthouse for a while, went into the empty courtroom, and stretched out on a spectator bench, looking up at the high, domed ceiling and the gold chandeliers. I pictured my parents and thought about my sisters, Josie and Geri Lynn, and my brother, Les, Geri Lynn's Jessie, during happy times. Suddenly I ached from missing them. I closed my eyes and said a prayer for their souls.

Finally, at 7:45 p.m. word came: There was a verdict.

My heart pounded like a jackhammer as we rushed into the courtroom—lawyers, bailiffs, judicial assistants, reporters, stenographer—and waited for Judge McKay to come in.

Then he did. We stood. As he entered, imperious in the black robe that accentuated his white mane, he sat down heavily in his leather chair, put on his glasses, and said, "We have a verdict. We'll bring the jury in. Go ahead, please. Sit down, ladies and gentlemen."

We sat. The bailiffs escorted the jury to their box and the 13 seated themselves in their usual spots.

"I understand," McKay said to them, "that you have reached a verdict. Would the foreperson hand it to the bailiff, Ms. Wolf? Ms. Wolf, why don't you take the verdict, and bring it over here, please. Thank you."

I sat with my head down almost in my lap. All the blood in my body had rushed there. I couldn't look up, couldn't look at anyone. I could barely hear what McKay was saying for the pounding inside my skull.

McKay started reading aloud to the assembly. "Russell Allen, plaintiff, versus Wisconsin Public Service Corporation, defendant. 'We, the jury, for our verdict answer the questions submitted as follows: Question 1, did stray electricity from Wisconsin Public Service Corporation's distribution system cause harm to the Allen dairy operation?' Answer, 'Yes.'"

My heart fluttered, skipped about six beats. I still didn't look up. Looking down had brought good luck. I didn't want to jinx it.

"Question 2, 'Was Wisconsin Public Service Corporation through its agents and/or employees negligent in its distribution of electricity?' Answer, 'Yes.'"

My fists tightened. I continued staring at the floor.

"Question 3, 'Was such negligence a cause of damages to the Allen dairy operation?' Answer, 'Yes.'"

I swallowed, hard.

"Question 4, 'Was Russell Allen, his agents or employees negligent in the use of electricity on his farm?' Answer, 'No.'"

Somewhere, Larry Neubauer was smiling.

"Question 6, 'Did Wisconsin Public Service Corporation distribute electricity to the Allen dairy operation in a manner that constituted a nuisance?' Answer, 'Yes.'"

"Question 7, 'Did such nuisance unreasonably interfere with Russell Allen's interest in the use and enjoyment of his farm?' Answer, 'Yes.'"

McKay looked up. "Question 5 which I skipped, was unanswered. Question 8 is unanswered," he said. "Question 9, 'What sum of money will fairly and reasonably compensate Russell Allen for damages sustained from stray electricity?' A, economic damages, $750,000. B, damages for annoyance, inconvenience, and loss of use and enjoyment of his property, $1 million dollars."

When I heard these figures, the breath went out of me, like I'd been kicked in the gut by one of my Holsteins. Now, I looked up. Only a mil and three-quarters out of thirteen? What the hell were they thinking?

McKay went on, "Dated at Green Bay, Wisconsin this 12 day of June, signed by the foreperson.

"Dissenting juror Brenda Klopp dissented on questions 1,2,3,4,6, 7, 9A and 9B. Jim Nitka dissented on questions 9A and 9B."

McKay removed his glasses, set them down, and looked at the jury. "Ladies and gentlemen, have I accurately read your verdict?"

They answered with one voice: "Yes."

McKay nodded. "Members of the jury," he said formally, "your service in this case is completed. You do not have to answer questions asked about the case by anyone other than me. This includes the parties, the lawyers, the media, anyone. While I'm not prohibiting you from disclosing what happened in the jury room, you don't have to discuss the case with anyone or answer any questions about it. You may confer with me before answering any questions asked of you by anyone."

For certain the media vultures would soon descend upon them all. On me too, for that matter. But that was the least of my concerns. I'd be only too happy to tell them what stray electricity was doing to our state and our country.

"I want to thank you for your service," McKay said. "And you're excused."

All 13 left the jury box quickly and quietly and departed into the night.

Hammarback came over and we shook hands, then he embraced me.

"See?" Barry said, smiling. "I told you."

Trevor Will made it clear he intended to file an appeal. Then he went around boasting that he'd really "won" the case because the jury award was less than the $13 million, only $1.75 million. The $1.75 million was a "victory" for a multi-billion dollar corporation, and, in a sense, it was.

The day after the verdict I went outside with my cutters and cut the down grounds again, hoping the third time was the charm.

Sometime within the next 60 days, we had to return to court so McKay could rule on the jury's verdict. Rule on a verdict? That was truly bizarre. But no more bizarre than the case itself. For who could've imagined that in the

United States of America in the 21st century, with our awareness of environmental issues at an all-time high, with a cabinet office like the EPA in place and the proliferation of groups like the Sierra Club, Greenpeace, PETA, and a hundred others, that cows in the dairy states would become an endangered species? But, bizarre or not, that was the crisis we were facing.

At least now, after this, and even though the monetary award was paltry in comparison to the losses I'd suffered, I could see a way forward. The Allen farm was saved.

We went back into court for McKay's ruling, and it was a doozy. Instead of simply ratifying the verdict as he should have, McKay, in a breathtaking act of judicial illogic and lack of backbone—to say nothing of bias in favor of the utility—decided that although WPS had to pay me, it wasn't required to fix the electrical problem it had created. His ruling was a classic instance of judicial arrogance.

"Allen," it read, "has made an election of remedies here and has proceeded to obtain a jury verdict setting forth damages, if you will, for the nuisance that Allen perceives exists. And for this Court to consider an injunction subsequent to the awarding of damages for the nuisance seems not only inconsistent with Wisconsin law, but inappropriate.

"Now, if Allen were to say, 'Well, we don't want the money, we want the injunction,' then I think you have a different situation. But that's not what I'm hearing. That's not what I heard. For some reason, I believe Allen thinks that they can have both, and I don't think that's the case."

He didn't think? That's not what he heard? He heard only what WPS whispered in his ear. All he needed to do was ratify the jury's decision mandating a fix. Who was McKay to nullify a jury decision? Yet that is what he did. Hell, after talking to one of the jurors a couple of weeks after the verdict, he wanted to write on the jury's verdict form that WPS had 30 days to fix it or it would cost them so much per day. How could the jury get it so right and not the judge?

The jury had ruled that WPS caused a nuisance. McKay was supposed to order WPS to stop harming my cows.

He didn't.

There was a huge irony here. Prior to the trial, which had been postponed for eight months and during which time my cows were dying in droves, I'd begged the court for an interim relief measure. To have WPS reconfigure its distribution system back to how it was in 1976, which would virtually eliminate all utility earth current from returning through the soil on my farm. By reconfiguring their system, the current would return to the substation at Denmark and not run through my property. All it would have taken was 300 feet of wire.

By asking for this, I was putting $13 million on the line if the reconfiguration didn't work; a mere eight months before trial, my case would've gone up in smoke. But I was willing to gamble on this throw of the dice because I was confident it would work. WPS must've thought that too, because they fought tooth and nail to prevent it from happening. And they succeeded. But it certainly showed their consciousness of guilt.

After the verdict, we pleaded with WPS to fix the system. We made clear that an Appeals Court decision was very likely to rule in our favor and that it was in no one's interest to go back to court. But, after several attempts to get the fix failed, and falling behind $50,000 per month, the writing was on the wall. I had no choice. In November 2003, I auctioned off all my cattle.

It hurt badly. And yet I recognized that it was the best thing I could do for the animals. I felt better knowing that when I awoke in the morning, I would no longer have to look at dead cows.

I remember the first time someone asked me if I missed them. I thought about it and realized that yes, I did miss them. But I definitely didn't miss the problems that had afflicted them and us. What I do miss is the time when electricity was drastically reduced on the farm, like after I'd cut the down grounds, and we were sending 420 cows per day through the parlor. Like when Patti Bowers asked me if she could cull a cow with an udder so swollen with milk that she could not attach the milking unit to it. Like when our milk production reached 85 pounds per cow per day and everyone was happy, including the cows. That particular year was the only one since the 1976 reconfiguration that I miss.

WPS had said they were going to appeal the decision and did. The appeals court had remanded the case to the trial court, stating that McKay had blundered in his ruling and stipulating that I was clearly entitled to a fix, as per the jury, in addition to the monetary damages. They also ruled that it was "moot," that a fix wasn't necessary because I no longer had cattle on the farm. But why was that?

In a bizarre move, WPS appealed back to the same court in

which they'd lost. Then lost again. Then decided to take a run at the Wisconsin Supreme Court. But they refused to hear the case. So, in August of 2005, WPS cut that check of $2,269,000 that included interest. Not much compensation for twenty years' worth of losses and sorrow. But it was what it was. I'd beaten WPS. A jury of my peers said so.

Nonetheless, WPS continued dragging its feet. I had to spend an additional $50,000 in legal expenses—not counting attorney fees—to force WPS to give me the fix. And I still have to go back into court.

Knowing McKay was biased in the utility's favor as well as spineless, we asked to substitute the judge. Our request was granted and we got Atkinson instead. So WPS lost its protector. But the legal rigmarole goes on.

WPS again deposed me. I stated I wanted to return cattle to my farm. They asked to see my tax return and got wind of me writing a book. I gave them part of the tax return relating to the farm and denied their request to see this book that you now have in your hands.

When you are denied a request during discovery, you take it up with the judge. So, we went before Atkinson, where WPS argued that they needed to see my book and to find out if I have stocks and bonds.

We argued that I wanted to bring cattle back on the farm and needed to have soil unpolluted by electric current in order to do it.

Atkinson said this: Suppose Mr. Allen owned one billion dollars' worth of Google stock and someone was waiting in his driveway to purchase his farm. Wouldn't that farm be worth more if it was fixed?

WPS fought back by claiming that I didn't need cattle and could build homes on my land.

Then Barry Hammarback spoke a telling sentence: "There is a

widespread perception that utility earth currents are harming people, and if WPS wants to go there with this, we will."

Judge Atkinson ruled that WPS was not entitled to my entire tax return, only the farm portion. And that they had no right whatsoever to see the contents of my book. The decision was just, and fair.

After much foot-dragging and more legal shenanigans, WPS decided to take a stab at a fix. I wanted a distribution system that didn't use the earth to return the current back to the substation. They wanted something else. So they kept hiding behind the Public Service Commission of Wisconsin, which has been carrying their water for years. Finally, we told them to pick one of Don Zipse's suggested fixes.

They decided to eliminate all the 1930-ish copper weld, dig up all bare current-carrying conductors within two miles of the farm, and reconstitute the system to mirror the way it was in 1976. Me oh my, I thought in wonder when I heard this. Are they truly going to redirect the juice that killed my cows? But then, they'd already stated in a letter to Judge McKay (prior to trial) that reconfiguring the system back to the Denmark substation would harm all the cows south and east of my place, mainly the Ossman farm cows.

I didn't think they would have the balls to do it and I feel sorry for what was about to happen to those animals and will make it clear to those farmers as to what is in store. But not until April of 2007. To obtain the fix, I agreed not to publish this book until then.

In October of 2006, WPS made the change. The buried ring in the ground of my farm finally showed zero. They redirected the current to other innocent farmers, and for that, I am truly sorry.

And so I am forced back into court, suing WPS for losses and damages sustained from June of 2003, when the trial ended, through January of 2007. I'm asking for $7 million, plus punitive and treble damages—costs for a new herd, new parlor, and new equipment, everything necessary to reconstitute the Allen Dairy Farm.

They say that justice delayed is justice denied. That may or may not be true. I don't know. But there's another saying that applies here. Better late than never. I still hope for and expect justice in this next round, to get compensation for everything the utility has stolen from me and my family. Which, of course, includes my cows.

CHAPTER 18

THE UTILITIES DIRTY LITTLE SECRET

B arry Hammarback's statement during my appeals was profound in many ways. There is a real possibility that utility earth currents are harming people all across our nation. But if that's the case, why hasn't anything been done about it? It all comes down to money. It would take billions of dollars to update the current electrical distribution system, and utility companies and their lawyers have calculated that it's far cheaper to settle lawsuits than it is to overhaul our current electrical distribution system.

Don't take me wrong, the electrical distribution system in the United States is a marvel of engineering. It ensures that electricity reaches millions of homes and businesses all across the country. Yet, beneath this veneer of efficiency lies a fundamental flaw—one that has potentially harmful implications for all living creatures.

Understanding the flaw requires a basic grasp of how electricity is distributed. It all begins at the power plant, where electricity is generated, and then transmitted through high-voltage lines to substations. Here, the voltage is stepped down for safer distribution to homes and businesses. The current then travels through a network of wires, with one wire typically serving as the "hot" wire and the other wire is being used for two purposes, to take the current back to the substation and to ground their system. Therein lies their problem, when it rains current leaks off of their system creating huge and hazardous magnetic fields.

This grounding technique, known as the multi-grounded neutral (MGN) system, is widespread, grounding the neutral wire at multiple point, using one wire for two purposes.

But while the MGN system provides clear benefits, its reliance on the ground as part of the electrical circuit introduces a critical flaw. When current flows through the earth, it doesn't always follow a direct path. Instead, it takes all paths back to the substation, but there will be the most current on the path of least resistance. Sometimes having a pool in your backyard may not be a good thing, it may create an easier path for current to travel back to the substation.

These associated magnetic fields can extend far beyond the immediate vicinity of the electrical infrastructure some 500 to 600 feet. Current can flow through buildings and other structures, magnetic fields can penetrate most materials. Consequently, they can affect both the environment and the living organisms within it. Utility-neutral return current and EMF are equal opportunity Destroyers.

When faced with potential harm caused by their electrical distribution systems, utility companies often times opt to settle lawsuits rather than undertake costly redesigns.

Redesigning an electrical distribution system can be extraordinarily expensive. It involves not only the immediate costs of new materials, labor, and engineering but also long-term maintenance and potential disruptions to service. In contrast, settling lawsuits, even if frequent, may prove to be less costly in the short and medium term. Utility companies often perform a cost-benefit analysis to compare the potential payout for settlements against the massive investment required for a system-wide redesign.

It's not surprising. Utility companies operate within tight

budget constraints and financial planning cycles. Large-scale redesigns can strain financial resources, potentially leading to increased rates for consumers or cuts in other critical areas such as maintenance and upgrades. In contrast, settlements can be managed within existing budgets and often have a less immediate impact on cash flow.

Also, many utility companies have liability insurance that covers a significant portion of the costs associated with lawsuits. This insurance can make settlements more financially palatable as opposed to bearing the full brunt of redesign costs, which are typically not covered by insurance. In Wisconsin, utilities are allowed to spend a large amount of money fighting these cases and billing it back to the ratepayer, more corruption. In my particular case, the jury said to fix and pay. WPS reached the limit it could spend on stray voltage, so they decided to appeal and appeal (poor cows), then tried to get the Supreme Court to hear the case, but the Supreme Court sent it back to the trial court.

Major redesigns of electrical distribution systems also require approval from regulatory bodies, which means a lot of red tape. This process can be lengthy, uncertain, and politically charged. Regulators for example may impose additional requirements that further escalate costs or complicate implementation. Settling lawsuits, on the other hand, usually involves negotiations and legal processes that are more predictable and manageable within existing regulatory frameworks.

Plus, if a utility company is found to be in violation of regulatory standards, the penalties can be severe. However, many utility companies operate within a regulatory environment that tends to favor these giant monopolies. Remember the term "regulatory capture"? These friendly regulators set standards which allow for a certain level of risk, provided that there are mechanisms in place for addressing issues as they arise. This regulatory leniency can make the option of settling lawsuits more attractive compared to undergoing a redesign that may not be strictly required by current regulations.

Yes, the technical complexity of redesigning an electrical distribution system cannot be overstated. Modern grids are intricate networks with numerous interdependencies. Introducing new designs can lead to unforeseen issues, including incompatibilities with existing infrastructure or the need for extensive retraining of personnel. Utility companies may prefer the relative simplicity of financial settlements over navigating these technical hurdles.

The bottom line is that legal settlements offer a level of predictability and control that large-scale redesigns do not. Companies can negotiate settlements, manage public relations, and control the narrative to some extent. Redesigns, especially if prompted by regulatory or legal pressure, can spiral into uncontrollable costs and public scrutiny.

More importantly, by settling lawsuits, utility companies can often avoid setting legal precedents that might increase future liability. Court rulings against a company can open the floodgates for additional claims and potentially lead to class action lawsuits. Settling allows companies to handle claims on a case-by-case basis, often with confidentiality agreements that limit public awareness of issues, as was the case with my own lawsuit against WPS.

Utility companies are publicly owned, which means that they must balance the interests of various stakeholders, including investors, customers, and employees. Investors typically favor strategies that protect short-term profitability and long-term growth, while customers demand reliable and affordable service. Settlements can address immediate issues without jeopardizing stakeholder relationships.

Ultimately, the decision by utility companies to settle lawsuits rather than undertake costly redesigns of their distribution systems is a multifaceted one, influenced by financial, regulatory, operational, legal, economic, and strategic considerations. While the ideal solution would be to eliminate all risks through comprehensive redesigns, the realities of cost, complexity, and competing priorities often make settlements the more pragmatic choice.

But the bottom line is that the current electrical distribution system in America, only in America, third-world countries know better, has to be redesigned, no matter what the cost. Why? Because of the long-term effects they have on every one of us. Think about what this design flaw did to my cows. Now imagine what it's doing to you right now at this very moment. You might not feel it, like my cows I did because they were being electrocuted by stray voltage. You on the other hand are being harmed by something even more nefarious.

Magnetic fields.

CHAPTER 19

MAGNETIC FIELDS AND YOUR HEALTH

F or those of you not familiar with the term, magnetic fields are physical fields that describe the magnetic influence on moving electric charges or currents that are generated whenever electric current flows. In electrical distribution systems, these fields are produced by the currents in transmission lines, distribution lines, and even household wiring.

Both high-voltage transmission lines (which is anything above 1,000V used for electrical substations, industrial plants, and power transmission), and lower-voltage distribution (which is anything under 1,000V and is in the realm of consumer electronics and residential wiring lines), generate a significant amount of magnetic fields. These fields are strongest near the lines and diminish with distance, but they can extend several hundred feet. That means that although the strength of a magnetic field decreases with distance from its source, given the pervasive nature of electrical infrastructure, these fields are virtually ubiquitous in our environment and contribute to overall exposure over a long period of time.

To understand how magnetic fields might impact health, it's essential to explore the mechanisms by which they interact with biological tissues. Magnetic fields can induce electrical currents within the body. These induced currents can potentially interfere with the body's natural bioelectrical processes, affecting nerve function, muscle contractions, and cellular communication.

Some studies suggest that exposure to magnetic fields might increase the production of reactive oxygen species, which are chemically reactive molecules containing oxygen. Elevated ROS levels can lead to oxidative stress, damaging cells and DNA, and potentially leading to cancerous changes.

Cells communicate through a complex network of signaling pathways. Magnetic fields might disrupt these pathways, leading to altered cell behavior. This disruption could affect cell growth, apoptosis (programmed cell death), and other critical processes.

The potential health effects of magnetic fields have been studied extensively, with a particular focus on cancer. Among the various health concerns, the potential link between magnetic field exposure and childhood leukemia has garnered significant attention.

Leukemia is a type of cancer that affects the blood and bone marrow. In children, the most common form is acute lymphoblastic leukemia (ALL). Epidemiological studies have explored whether exposure to low-frequency magnetic fields increases the risk of developing leukemia in children.

Several key studies have shaped our understanding of the potential risks:

• Wertheimer and Leeper (1979): This pioneering study first suggested a link between residential exposure to magnetic fields from power lines and an increased risk of childhood leukemia.

• Savitz et al. (1988): This follow-up study supported the earlier findings, reporting a higher incidence of childhood leukemia in homes with higher magnetic field exposures.

• Ahlbom et al. (2000) and Greenland et al. (2000): These meta-analyses pooled data from multiple studies and found a consistent association between higher magnetic field exposure and an increased risk of childhood leukemia, particularly at exposure levels above 0.4 microteslas (μT).

• Biological Plausibility: While epidemiological studies can show associations, establishing causality requires understanding the biological mechanisms. Research has suggested several plausible mechanisms, including DNA damage from ROS and disruption of cellular signaling pathways.

While childhood leukemia has been the primary focus of these studies, magnetic fields may impact health in other ways. Some studies have explored associations between magnetic field exposure and adult cancers, such as brain tumors and breast cancer. The evidence is less consistent than for childhood leukemia, but there are indications of potential risks that warrant further investigation.

Magnetic fields might affect the nervous system, potentially contributing to neurological conditions like Alzheimer's disease and amyotrophic lateral sclerosis (ALS).

There is also concern that magnetic field exposure could affect reproductive health and fetal development. Studies have looked at potential impacts on fertility, miscarriage rates, and developmental anomalies.

Exposure to magnetic fields might influence cardiovascular health by affecting heart rate variability and increasing the risk of arrhythmias. These effects are hypothesized to result from induced currents affecting cardiac cells.

Given the potential health risks, it's crucial to consider strategies to mitigate exposure to magnetic fields:

• Engineering Controls: Improving the design of electrical infrastructure can reduce magnetic field exposure. This includes optimizing the placement of power lines, using shielding materials, and ensuring balanced loads.

•Public Awareness and Education: Educating the public about potential risks and practical ways to reduce exposure is essential. Simple measures, such as maintaining a safe distance from high-voltage power lines and reducing the use of electrical appliances near sleeping areas, can help minimize exposure.

• Ongoing Research: Continuous research is vital to fully understand the health impacts of magnetic fields and to refine safety guidelines. This includes both epidemiological studies to track health outcomes and laboratory studies to elucidate biological mechanisms.

The practice of using the ground as a return path for electrical current, as discussed in the previous chapter, can create diffuse magnetic fields. These fields can spread out and affect broader areas, including residential neighborhoods.

The invisible magnetic fields generated by our electrical systems are a double-edged sword. While they are an inevitable byproduct of the electrification that powers modern life, they also pose potential health risks that cannot be ignored. The association between magnetic field exposure and childhood leukemia is supported by a substantial body of epidemiological evidence and plausible biological mechanisms.

As we continue to rely on electrical technology, it is imperative to balance the benefits with the potential risks. Through improved infrastructure design, stringent safety standards, public education, and ongoing research, we can mitigate these risks and protect public health.

Understanding and addressing the invisible currents that permeate our environment is not just a matter of scientific inquiry but a pressing public health priority. By taking proactive steps, we can ensure that the invisible forces that power our lives do not also become unseen threats to our well-being, especially for our most vulnerable populations—our children.

CHAPTER 20

THE NFL CONNECTION

Have you ever wondered why NFL teams whose stadiums are located in cities with cold winters benefit from a substantial home-field advantage? Lambeau Field, home of the Green Bay Packers, is one of the most iconic cold-weather stadiums in the NFL. Known for its frigid temperatures and swirling winds, Lambeau Field becomes a fortress in winter. Historical data shows that the Packers have a significant home-field advantage during late-season games. For instance, since 1959, the Packers' home record in December and January is notably better compared to their road performance. Brett Favre never lost a game at Lambeau Field when it was freezing cold outside, except for his last one when it was twenty below zero.

Similarly, the Minnesota Vikings, particularly in the era when they played at the open-air Metropolitan Stadium, demonstrated a formidable home-field advantage in cold weather. The team's ability to perform in subzero temperatures became part of their identity, intimidating visiting teams unused to such extremes.

The New England Patriots' success in Foxborough during winter months is a testament to their strategic adaptability and mental toughness. The Patriots' home record in December is particularly impressive.

The Buffalo Bills, playing in the often-frigid conditions of Buffalo, New York, have also demonstrated significant home-field advantages in the winter.

Mike McCarthy's record in Green Bay is very interesting. The most wins in his career came in December. He had a nice record when temperatures were colder and a terrible record in wet conditions, especially with weeks of wet weather. The wet weather losses are probably what got him run out of town. Mike McCarthy has his struggles also in Dallas because of weather conditions within weeks before games. The January 14, 2024 playoff game between Green Bay and the Dallas Cowboys is a perfect example of what I'm talking about. In the Green Bay area, we have clay soils. In freezing temperatures clay soils are the worst conductor of electricity, and in wet weather conditions, clay soils are the best conductor of electricity. That is why in Green Bay you see the huge swings in wins and losses from wet to freezing.

After the game, Jerry Jones did a live interview with the whole world. He probably puts more into football than any other owner in the NFL. His passion is very noticeable. In my opinion, if the Dallas Cowboys had lived up here in Green Bay with the freezing temperatures they would've hammered the youngest team in the NFL. Jerry Jones would've had another game the next week. When the Cowboys were exposed for an extended period of time, the second most rainfall in recorded history, add in a week or 10 days of recovery from EMF exposure, they were injured, and not ready for the Green Bay Packers that were not being exposed because of freezing temperatures and we're getting a good night's sleep without being fried.

I felt so bad for Jerry that I reached out to the Dallas Cowboys. I'm sure they can't keep up with the emails from people like me. I would be willing to draw it out for Jerry on an easel. I would put my bottom dollar on it that I have a better explanation for their loss than his whole coaching staff can come up with. When I saw Jerry Jones very emotional after the game on live TV, it was the push that I needed to write this book. It reminded me of over 20 years ago when my farm was destroyed because of electrical pollution. I remember sobbing in front of the appeals board at Farm Credit Services who later denied me saying they're never going to sink another penny in my farm. Of course, Jerry Jones was sobbing for a different reason than I was. But not really. My heart went out to him. EMF will always be the limiting factor until the utilities install the missing wire. No one will ever be able to do an honest evaluation of a coach or player as a matter of fact when you have EMF influence. I am glad to see that Jerry Jones didn't fire everyone, that loss was not the fault of the Dallas Cowboys. In my opinion, after watching games where players were exposed to EMF, the Dallas Cowboys got cheated out of a Super Bowl appearance.

It's no secret that cold weather affects the human body in several ways that can influence athletic performance. Muscles tend to tighten up in colder temperatures, which can lead to decreased flexibility and increased risk of injury. Additionally, cold air is denser than warm air, which can impact the flight of the football. This affects both passing and kicking games, potentially disadvantaging teams not used to these conditions.

However, players acclimated to these conditions often have developed techniques to mitigate these effects. Cold-weather teams typically practice and play in these conditions regularly, allowing their athletes to adapt physiologically over time.

The psychological component of playing in cold weather cannot be underestimated. Players from teams based in warmer climates may struggle with the mental aspect of dealing with extreme cold, which can distract and demoralize them. Cold-weather teams, conversely, often exhibit a mental toughness and resilience born from routine exposure to harsh conditions.

But what if that's not all there is to it? What if there is another major factor as to why teams like the Green Bay Packers play better under these conditions?

One significant characteristic of frozen ground is its reduced ability to conduct electricity. In soils and ground materials, conductivity is influenced by the presence of water and ions, which facilitate the movement of electrical charges. Unfrozen, moist soil typically has higher conductivity due to the mobility of ions in the water.

When the ground freezes, the water within the soil turns to ice. Ice has a much lower electrical conductivity compared to liquid water because the movement of ions is severely restricted in the solid state. Consequently, frozen ground exhibits significantly reduced electrical conductivity. In layman's terms, freezing temperatures force electrical currents to stay on their distribution wire, creating a situation where there is less electromagnetic fields being emitted, and consequently, less chance of a person being fried while they are sleeping. Conversely, when it rains more current leaks off electrical systems creating a situation where there is a bigger electromagnetic field emission, and more likely frying you while sleeping. My own personal logs show that when it rains electromagnetic fields can be measured as far as 500 feet away from the electrical wires. That's mind-blowing.

Why is this important when it comes to teams like the Packers? Athletes competing in NFL games face intense physical and mental demands, and their performance can be influenced by various factors, including environmental conditions such as exposure to magnetic fields.

Exposure to strong magnetic fields can potentially lead to physiological and cognitive disturbances, such as dizziness, fatigue, and impaired concentration, which could detract from an athlete's ability to perform at their peak. Magnetic fields might disrupt neural activity and muscle coordination, crucial for quick decision-making and physical agility in football.

In contrast, an athlete who hasn't been exposed to such fields would likely maintain optimal neural and muscular function, resulting in better coordination, sharper reflexes, and sustained energy levels. Therefore, the conditions would favor the athletes not exposed to magnetic fields, as they are less likely to experience the detrimental side effects that could hinder performance on the field.

Remember 2016, when the Packers were struggling with a 4-6 record? In response to the team's predicament, and the media claiming Rodgers had lost it, and that it was probably time for him to retire, Rodgers confidently predicted that the Packers could "run the table" and win their remaining games to make the playoffs.

Amazingly, he delivered on his promise, guiding the Packers to six consecutive victories to end the regular season and secure a playoff berth. Rodgers' ability to elevate his game when it mattered most earned him widespread acclaim and reinforced his reputation as one of the most clutch performers in NFL history.

This feat can certainly be attributed to Rodgers' undeniable talent. But football is a team sport, and Rodgers couldn't do it alone. It was a team effort. But how could Rodgers so accurately predict that his team would turn things around? What did he know that everyone else did not?

The Packers won eight games in a row, and only four of those games were on Lambeau Field, which means that it wasn't because of home-field advantage.

Could it have been the weather? In late November and December, Green Bay typically experiences cold temperatures, with average highs ranging from the mid-30s to low 40s Fahrenheit (1-5 degrees Celsius) and average lows in the 20s Fahrenheit (-6 to -1 degrees Celsius). Snowfall is common during this period, with significant accumulations possible, particularly in December.

January in Green Bay tends to be even colder, with average highs in the mid-20s to low 30s Fahrenheit (-4 to 0 degrees Celsius) and average lows in the teens Fahrenheit (-9 to -4 degrees

Celsius). Snowfall remains prevalent, and occasional cold snaps can bring temperatures well below freezing.

I made the connection between EMF exposure and NFL players playing poorly in 2015 and wrote a letter to the Green Bay Packers sharing it with Mark Murphy, Mike McCarthy, and Aaron Rodgers. In fact, I reached out to Mike McCarthy several times with no response. He's been a victim many times of EMF exposure and his players playing poorly. Mike McCarthy is a poor coach when players are exposed to EMF, but I am not sure a coach can learn how to coach injured players from EMF exposure.

Mark Murphy (president and CEO of the Green Bay Packers) to my surprise, agreed with my assessment, as you can see from the letter itself.

"Russ, just a quick note to thank you for your recent letter. I appreciate your input on what might be the cause of our poor play." Sincerely, Mark Murphy

We are all exposed to magnetic fields every single day, and as mentioned above, this exposure can lead to physiological and cognitive disturbances, which may affect athletic performance. But this may be less severe on those athletes who live in cold weather, because again, frozen ground exhibits significantly reduced electrical conductivity.

This means that athletes in Green Bay, New England, Pittsburg, and Kansas City, benefit from the climate in their hometowns during the later part of the season.

But again, home-field advantage takes on a whole different meaning when considering that perhaps it isn't the field itself, but the climate that makes the difference. The Packer players benefited from an average temperature of 31.1 degrees the week leading to the game, which was below freezing. They were well-rested and didn't suffer from the effects of exposure to magnetic fields.

Take a look at the following chart which shows the winning percentages of teams in cold-weather cities vs teams in mild-weather cities during the months of December and January over the last 20 years.

TEAM	Dec-Jan Win %	Cold Weather	Warm Weather	Pattern
Packers	79%	x		
Bills	90%	x		
Patriots	77%	x		
Steelers	72%	x		
Chiefs	92%	x		
Bears	72%	x		
Texans	35%		x	
Cowboys	45%		x	
Seahawks	43%		x	
Bucs	41%		x	
Saints	49%		x	
49ers	52%		x	

Cold vs Hot Weather Teams Win % in Winter

What does this all mean? Well, if I was a betting man, I would take a serious look at the weather when placing a bet on an NFL game during these months.

Who would have ever thought that the talent of a coach or a player could be determined by the weather. Coaches and players are only as good as the weather allows them to be.

Matt LaFleur, present coach of the Green Bay Packers, is very similar to Shanahan in San Francisco, young energetic, the kind of coach teams are looking for nowadays. He holds the record in the NFL for the most wins in December when the ground is normally frozen. My logging shows more current would stay on the wire during freezing temperatures. Under those circumstances, there would be less of a magnetic field. I heard from a fairly good source, that when Lambeau was recently doing a remodeling, they buried a copper ring to try to divert earth currents, which acts as a fence.

I installed one of those around my farm which eventually failed because the ground settles over the top of the ring and the current flows over the top of the ring. The Green Bay Packers, the youngest team in the NFL, can be a powerhouse in freezing temperatures, especially traveling south going up against a team living in wet conditions and being fried by EMF.

I personally think Matt LaFleur is a good coach. If we get a couple of years of wet weather and he can't figure out how to protect his players from EMF exposures he will end up being run out of town just like Mike McCarthy.

On the other hand, if we get dry weather and then freezing temperatures, he may get his Super Bowl ring after all. It's very simple. It is truly not fun knowing this and understanding the whole EMF thing from the distribution system because you see so many situations where good coaches and players put so much into it, and you know their wins and losses in some cases are predicted by something other than their own talent. Green Bay/Dallas game is a perfect example, and there will be more of these every year. The average money wager would say Vegas fixed it.

Would the outcome of that game between the Cowboys and the Packers have been different had the Cowboys not been exposed to higher levels of magnetic fields than the Packers before the game? I happen to think so.

CHAPTER 21

REWIRE AMERICA

A friend who graduated from high school with me has a wife who was hurting like crazy. I am assuming that her doctor exhausted everything to help her because he told me the doctor suggested they move to Arizona. The thinking all along was that Arizona has drier weather and you don't hurt so much in that kind of climate.

Well after everything I've learned that may not be the real reason. In Arizona, there is a lot of sand. Sand is a very poor conductor of electricity so most of the current would stay on the wire, lessening the chance of people being affected by magnetic fields. I will admit that I did not put as much into the Arizona feeling-better situation as I did with the correlation between wet weather current leaking off the distribution system and NFL players' poor play.

One more thing I would like to touch on is that when you have current flowing like a running motor it normally creates heat. All across America, utilities have current flowing in the Earth. So ask yourself this. Is that contributing to global warming? I am not qualified to answer that question, but I would love to hear an expert opinion.

Anyway, the integrity and efficiency of America's electrical distribution system are critical for ensuring reliable power delivery to homes, businesses, and industries. However, the current system, which relies on the earth as a return path for electrical current, has been shown to cause significant issues related to electromagnetic fields (EMFs) and stray voltage.

As shown in the image below, utility companies like WPS are only holding themselves to a 50% standard to return current on the wire, meaning that if 50% is missing and returning back to the substation through the Earth everything is fine.

What does this all mean? It means that 50% of it is unaccounted for, creating a huge magnetic field, and quite possibly frying you while you sleep.

Some cities, like New York, go as high as 60%. Remember those dogs getting electrocuted by manhole covers?

So, what can we do about it? In dairy areas in California, you cannot use the Earth to return your current back to the substation. You may be asking yourself, but what about the people in other areas of California? Are Legislators saying, who cares about the people, they'll never find out? Makes you wonder.

Anyway, I propose looking at California's dairy areas as an example of what we can do to fix our poorly designed electrical distribution system. The approach of utility companies in that area is to not use the earth as a return path, thereby reducing EMFs and stray voltage, which offers a model for a safer, more efficient electrical grid.

The traditional electrical distribution system in much of the United States uses the earth as a return path for their current. This method, while cost-effective and simple in theory, can lead to unintended consequences, like stray voltage and electromagnetic fields.

As I previously discussed, EMFs are produced by electrical currents and have been the subject of extensive research concerning their potential health effects. In response to the problems caused by stray voltage and EMFs, dairy regions in California have adopted an alternative approach to electrical distribution. This system avoids using the earth as a return path, thereby significantly reducing the levels of stray voltage and EMFs.

One of the most effective strategies employed in California's dairy regions is the use of dedicated neutral return wires and dedicated ground wires, not using one wire for two purposes. By providing a direct and controlled path for electrical currents to return to substations, these systems eliminate the need for the earth to carry any of the return currents. This approach not only reduces stray voltage, correct term (stray current), but also minimizes the creation of EMFs, as the current paths are more controlled and contained.

Redesigning America's electrical distribution system to follow the model used in California's dairy areas offers numerous benefits. These include improved agricultural productivity, enhanced public health, greater electrical efficiency, and increased system reliability.

By reducing stray voltage, redesigning the electrical distribution system can significantly improve conditions for livestock, particularly in dairy farms. Healthier animals lead to higher productivity, better milk yields, and reduced veterinary costs. This can have a substantial economic impact on agricultural communities, enhancing their sustainability and profitability.

Reducing EMFs and stray voltage also has potential public health benefits. Although the full extent of EMF-related health risks is still under investigation, taking precautionary measures to minimize exposure is a responsible approach. By implementing a system that does not use the earth as a return path, we can reduce EMF exposure for people living near power lines and electrical installations, potentially decreasing the risk of associated health problems.

An electrical distribution system that avoids using the earth as a return path is also more reliable. Stray currents can cause equipment malfunctions, interference with telecommunications, and other issues that compromise the reliability of the electrical grid. A redesigned system with dedicated return paths and proper grounding can mitigate these risks, leading to fewer outages and disruptions.

While the benefits of redesigning America's electrical distribution system are clear, there are also significant challenges to consider. These include the costs of upgrading infrastructure, regulatory hurdles, and the need for widespread cooperation among utilities, government agencies, and other stakeholders.

One of the primary challenges is the cost associated with upgrading the existing infrastructure. Retrofitting the electrical distribution system to include dedicated neutral return wires and enhanced grounding practices requires significant investment.

However, these costs can be offset over time by the benefits of increased efficiency, reduced healthcare costs, and improved agricultural productivity.

Regulatory frameworks governing electrical distribution vary widely across the United States, and achieving consensus on new standards can be difficult. It is essential for federal, state, and local agencies to collaborate closely to establish regulations that support the redesign of the electrical system. Advocacy and education efforts can help build the necessary political and public support for these changes.

Redesigning the electrical distribution system requires cooperation among a wide range of stakeholders, including utility companies, government agencies, agricultural organizations, and the general public. Effective communication and collaboration are crucial to ensure that all parties understand the benefits of the proposed changes and are committed to working together to implement them.

Two case studies from California's dairy regions provide concrete examples of the benefits of redesigning the electrical distribution system. These examples highlight the positive impacts on agricultural productivity, public health, and overall system reliability.

CASE STUDY 1

A dairy farm in Central California experienced significant issues with stray voltage, leading to reduced milk production and increased health problems among the cows. After implementing a system with dedicated neutral return wires and improved grounding practices, the farm saw a substantial improvement in milk yields and a reduction in veterinary costs. The farm's owner reported a 20% increase in productivity and a marked improvement in the overall health and well-being of the livestock.

CASE STUDY 2

A rural community in Southern California faced frequent electrical disruptions and health complaints from residents living near power lines. By working with local utilities to redesign the electrical distribution system, the community was able to reduce EMF exposure and improve the reliability of the electrical grid. Residents reported fewer health issues, and the community experienced a 15% reduction in electrical outages over the following year.

To achieve the widespread redesign of America's electrical distribution system, a phased approach is recommended. This involves several key steps, including pilot projects, funding initiatives, regulatory reform, and public education campaigns.

Initiating pilot projects in various regions can demonstrate the feasibility and benefits of the redesigned electrical distribution system. These projects can serve as models for larger-scale implementation and provide valuable data on costs, benefits, and best practices.

Securing funding is critical for the successful implementation of the redesigned system. Federal and state governments can provide grants, subsidies, and low-interest loans to support utilities and agricultural operations in upgrading their infrastructure. Public-private partnerships can also play a role in financing these projects.

Reforming regulatory frameworks to support the redesigned electrical distribution system is essential. This includes updating standards for electrical installations, grounding practices, and EMF exposure limits. Regulatory agencies should work closely with stakeholders to ensure that the new standards are practical and effective.

Educating the public about the benefits of the redesigned electrical distribution system is crucial for gaining support and encouraging participation. Public education campaigns can highlight the positive impacts on health, agriculture, and overall system reliability, helping to build momentum for the necessary changes.

Redesigning America's electrical distribution system to align with the approach used in California's dairy areas offers a promising solution to the problems of EMFs and stray voltage. By minimizing the use of the earth as a return path, we can improve agricultural productivity, enhance public health, increase electrical efficiency, and ensure greater system reliability. While there are significant challenges to overcome, the benefits of this redesign are substantial and far-reaching. By taking a phased approach and engaging in collaborative efforts, we can achieve a safer, more efficient, and more reliable electrical distribution system for the future.

Chapter 22

The Fix

S top using the earth to return current back to the substation.

ABOUT THE AUTHOR

Russell Allen, a native son of De Pere, Wisconsin, embodies the quintessential American farmer with a story deeply rooted in the traditions of dairy farming and community engagement. Born into a hardworking, devout Catholic family, Russell's life narrative weaves through the rich tapestry of mid-20th century rural America, marked by the transformation from lead mining to dairy farming, the challenges and triumphs of family life, and the ever-present influence of the Green Bay Packers.

His story is one of resilience and an unwavering love for the land and community of De Pere. Russell Allen stands as a testament to the enduring spirit of Wisconsin's dairy farmers and is committed to preserving the legacy of the land he cherishes so dearly.

Printed in the USA
CPSIA information can be obtained
at www.ICGtesting.com
JSHW020334280924
70653JS00002B/6

9 781963 558159